Zen in Brazil

Topics in Contemporary Buddhism
GEORGE G. TANABE, JR., EDITOR

Establishing a Pure Land on Earth: The Foguang Buddhist Perspective on Modernization and Globalization
STUART CHANDLER

Buddhist Missionaries in the Era of Globalization
LINDA LEARMAN, EDITOR

Being Benevolence: The Social Ethics of Engaged Buddhism
SALLIE B. KING

Zen in Brazil: The Quest for Cosmopolitan Modernity
CRISTINA ROCHA

TOPICS IN
CONTEMPORARY
BUDDHISM

ZEN IN BRAZIL

The Quest for Cosmopolitan Modernity

CRISTINA ROCHA

University of Hawai'i Press
Honolulu

© 2006 University of Hawai'i Press
All rights reserved
Printed in the United States of America
11 10 09 08 07 06 6 5 4 3 2 1

**Library of Congress Cataloging-in-
Publication Data**
Library of Congress Cataloging-in-Publication Data
Rocha, Cristina.
Zen in Brazil : the quest for cosmopolitan modernity / Cristina Rocha.
p. cm.— (Topics in contemporary Buddhism)
Includes bibliographical references and index.
ISBN-13: 978-0-8248-2976-6 (hardcover : alk. paper)
ISBN-10: 0-8248-2976-X (hardcover : alk. paper)
1. Zen Buddhism—Brazil—History. 2. Japanese—Brazil—Religion.
3. Zen Buddhism—Japan—History. I. Title. II. Series.
BQ9262.9.B6R63 2006
294.3′9270981—dc22

2005027457

University of Hawai'i Press books are
printed on acid-free paper and meet the
guidelines for permanence and durability
of the Council on Library Resources.

Designed by Elsa Carl, Clarence Lee Design
Printed by The Maple-Vail Book Manufacturing Group

To my parents, Anna Maria and Hélio, who gave me a passion for learning.

Contents

Series Editor's Preface

The transformation of Buddhism into a Western religion has drawn the attention of many scholars, and the number of books on the subject has increased dramatically in recent years. The cultural focus of these studies has primarily centered on America, and American Buddhism is now a recognized feature of our religious landscape. What has not been recognized is the fact that Buddhism has found a home in South America as well. The South American story makes its debut with this volume.

Cristina Rocha gives us a fascinating account of Zen in Brazil through analytical lenses such as creolization and cannibalization in addition to the more familiar categories of indigenization, accommodation, modernization, and globalization. Beginning with the introduction of Sōtō Zen through Japanese immigrants, Rocha traces the growth of Zen in Brazil and its encounter with Catholicism and Afro-Brazilian religions. The strands in the web of adaptation are many, and Rocha argues that the Brazilian elites embraced Zen in good measure because of its international reputation. Zen was desired for its overseas social status as much as its spiritual message.

While many have noted that globalization takes place through localization, Rocha provides a unique counterpoint by showing that localization can also take place through globalization. Had Zen been available only in its Japanese immigrant form, it would not have appealed to non-Japanese Brazilians. Freed from its Japanese origins, Zen had become a sophisticated European and American religion, and that is why it also became Brazilian.

George J. Tanabe, Jr.
Series Editor

Acknowledgments

Over the years that it took me to complete this manuscript, many people and institutions assisted me and I am profoundly grateful to all of them. I would like to thank Judith Snodgrass and Mandy Thomas for their encouragement and inspiration and for continually challenging me to reflect on the entanglements of theory and the phenomena I was investigating. Without their support and intellectual stimulation, this project would most surely have been lost in blind alleys. My colleagues at the Centre for Cultural Research (CCR) were helpful sounding boards, critical readers, and good friends. I would particularly like to thank Francis Maravillas, who frequently engaged in theoretical discussions of my material, giving up precious time he needed for his own research. I am grateful to George Morgan for giving me insights on how to improve the manuscript and for his emotional support.

I am thankful to Michelle Spuler, who first showed me that my research was not a lone endeavor, but was part of the new field of Buddhism in the West. Many thanks to Martin Baumann, who gave valuable insights and worked meticulously with me to make my first paper on Zen in Brazil meaningful to an English-speaking audience. He continued over the years to assist me with comments and suggestions that helped greatly improve the manuscript. I am deeply indebted to Steven Heine and Ronan Pereira, whose generous invitations to speak at Florida International University and the University of California, Berkeley, gave me the opportunity to discuss my research with a larger audience. Steven has been with this project from the start and has given me much support throughout this journey. I am grateful to Harumi Befu for his encouragement and friendliness from the moment we met in Japan. He read my papers with interest and offered important suggestions for the research.

In Japan, Nakamaki Hirochika at the National Museum of Ethnology of Osaka provided the necessary support and means for the research. I am indebted to the Sōtōshū Shumuchō for allowing me to conduct interviews with its officer for Brazil, and to Matsunaga *rōshi* at Eiheiji, who shared his thoughts and memories of this time as a *kaikyōshi* in Brazil. Special thanks to Kuroda *rōshi* of Kirigayaji in Tokyo for his generosity in allowing me to stay at his temple and for the patience to answer my questions on temple life.

In Brazil, the director of the Museu Histórico da Imigração Japonesa no

Brasil, Célia Oi, and her staff were most helpful with the research. I am grateful to Moriyama *rōshi*, Coen *sensei*, Tokuda *sensei*, Myoshi *rōshi*, Eduardo Basto de Albuquerque, and Nelson Coelho for their time and interest in the project. Many thanks to the staff of Busshinji who graciously allowed me to research its archives and old photo albums.

Several institutions generously funded this project. In Brazil, my work was funded by a CNPq Doctoral Fellowship through the Department of Anthropology at the University of São Paulo. In Australia, the CCR at the University of Western Sydney supported my research through an International Postgraduate Research Award. My fieldwork in Japan was made possible by a Japan Foundation Doctoral Fellowship. A special mention to Jo Takahashi at the Japan Foundation in São Paulo who was always helpful throughout this project.

This research, however, would not have been possible without the support of people who were interviewed for the study; although they must remain anonymous, I would like to thank them all for their generous contribution.

This manuscript has benefited from comments and suggestions made by two anonymous readers who gave me important feedback on how to improve the manuscript. Many thanks to David Kelly, who offered to proofread the manuscript in a very short time, carrying it even through Christmas. I am grateful to Sarah Walls, who edited an early draft of this manuscript. The maps were generously drafted by Jemma Cummings. My friends in Australia, Japan, and Brazil gave me the emotional support and encouragement to keep threading this long path of academia. Finally, I am profoundly grateful to my parents, Hélio and Anna Maria Rocha, and sisters, Rosana and Ligia Rocha, for supporting me in my crazy endeavor to live in a distant land, too far away from their hugs and kisses.

Introduction

In February 2003, there was heated discussion on the Brazilian e-mail list Buddhismo-L over a widely watched, popular Sunday variety program on the TV Globo network.[1] The controversy arose when the program featured a woman who claimed to be a Buddhist but resorted to Afro-Brazilian and French-Brazilian Spiritist beliefs to prescribe a solution for personal problems. One of the first messages posted explained the issues at stake.

> Yesterday, by a samsaric[2] [sic] misfortune, I was watching the *Faustão* TV program. A woman, who claimed to be an astrologer, tarot reader, futurologist, Buddhist—obviously a deceiver—was there making predictions. Yes, shocking! At one point, while giving advice to the KLB singer, she said he was carrying the spirit (*encosto*) of someone he had dated who had later died. In order to be able to date his new girlfriend in peace, this woman advised him to go to a Buddhist center to make a symbolic cremation of this *encosto*. I immediately received 10 phone calls (including ones from my father, mother and wife). My mom asked me what I have been into in these past four years. My wife wanted details of what this cremation would be. A friend of mine, a convinced atheist, called me, as a joke of course, *macumbeiro* [a derogatory word for Afro-Brazilian religions, meaning witchcraft, sorcery]. There wasn't much I could say, but I believe that this notion of *encosto* does not exist in Buddhism, right? Anyway, I would like to clarify this point because I felt offended by that woman claiming to be a Buddhist. I felt humiliated, really. I believe that TV Globo has to apologize URGENTLY![3]

Reading this message, I realized how the theme of and interest in "Buddhism" has expanded over the years I have been pursuing my research. When I started it in 1997, the phenomenon of the rise of interest in Buddhism was still not plainly visible in Brazilian culture. Yet in the intervening years things have changed considerably. Mainstream magazine and newspaper stories feature Buddhism frequently (many times as cover stories), associating it with fashion, high culture, modernity, rationality, nonviolence, and tranquility, while profiling Brazilian and North American celebrities who practice it. Books by North American,

European, Japanese, Tibetan, Vietnamese, and Brazilian Buddhists have become increasingly popular among upper middle-class urban populations. In this context, Buddhism has become desirable symbolic capital to possess as it lends the prestige of cosmopolitanism and foreign trends to its followers. While reading the above message in 2003, I realized that for the first time Buddhism had become more than just an upper- and upper middle-class enclosed phenomenon. Unsurprisingly, it had reached disenfranchised classes through a very popular TV program, and not through the books, newspapers, magazines, and Internet sites written by and to educated classes.

Certainly, this e-mail message shows that in 2003, as in 1997, the meanings Buddhism has acquired in the encounter with Brazilian culture have not changed; they have just become intensified with time and extended in the sectors of society it was presented to. For instance, the writer's social location (upper- or upper middle-class sectors of society) and his feelings of humiliation and offense when his religious choice was confused with Afro-Brazilian religion (of mainly disenfranchised sectors of society) shows how Buddhism is employed as a marker of social distinction. The same point is exemplified by his friend calling him a *macumbeiro*, a term historically used to dismiss and condemn Afro-Brazilian religions as witchcraft. In addition, the easy creolization the woman makes among various religious traditions and the placing of the newly arrived Buddhism in this religious matrix shows how tradition creatively incorporates modernity and how plural and porous the Brazilian religious field is. Moreover, the message makes evident the role mass media plays in carrying global flows of Buddhism from metropolitan centers into Brazil—from Hollywood and, more recently, Tibetan and Indian Buddhist movies, books, newspapers, and magazine stories (consumed by the upper strata of society) to TV programs (mostly directed to the lower strata of society).

I have chosen this e-mail message as a point of departure because it evokes many of the themes that I myself found while conducting fieldwork. They include the aspiration toward modernity, the coexistence of modernity and tradition, the intense creolization of religious traditions, the role of global flows of media, people, technologies, and ideas in the construction of an imaginary of Zen, their entanglement with the local, and finally the desire for cultural capital and social prestige as a way of establishing visible markers of social distinction.

WHY ZEN IN BRAZIL?

My aim with this book is not only to expand our knowledge of Buddhism in the West and our understanding of the transplantation of religions across borders, but also, and more important, to deepen our insight into the interplay of the global and the local, the articulation of modernity vis-à-vis tradition, transformations in Brazilian society, the processes of creolization of beliefs, and the historical anthropology of modernity. Historical anthropology, in the words of Jean and John Comaroff,

> tries to dissolve the division between synchrony and diachrony, ethnography and historiography. . . . It focuses centrally on the interplay of the global and the local, treating as problematic the shifting line between them. It pays particular attention to the processes by which transnational signs and practices are welded into the diverse cultural configurations, into the contested realities and multiple subjectivities, of most late twentieth-century social scapes.[4]

Indeed, this book is fundamentally a study of how the discourse of modernity has historically influenced a sector of Brazilian society—namely, the intellectual elite until 1990 and the upper- and upper middle-class professionals from then onward—to adopt Zen as a sign of the "modern." Furthermore, this book addresses the changes or, as I call them, creolizations that have occurred in the religious field as a result of this influence. In other words, I am interested in *how* the global has been historically entangled in the local in Brazil, particularly in the domain of "high" culture among Brazilian cosmopolitan elites. Therefore, Zen is an especially relevant topic of research since it is the Buddhist school that has been carried into Brazil by powerful global flows and has worked as a stage for the encounter and negotiation of practices and beliefs among Japanese, Japanese Brazilians, and non-Japanese Brazilians. In addition, modern Zen was constructed as a response to the discourse of modernity in Japan and in the West.

By contrast, other Japanese Buddhist schools have until very recently been confined to the Japanese and Japanese-Brazilian communities, while other Buddhist traditions have not been as historically significant in urban Brazilian "high" culture. From this perspective, this research attempts to address Sahlins' injunction: "if the world is becoming a Culture of cultures, then what needs to be studied ethnographically is the indigenization of modernity—through time and in all its dialectical ups and downs, from the earliest develop-man [*sic*] to the latest invention of tradition."[5] Ambiguously situated as it is "on the borderlands of the Western world"[6] and constantly yearning for European and North American modernity, Brazil is a rewarding site to examine how global flows acquire local forms, and consequently how multiple modernities have emerged.

Whereas Buddhism in the West has become a new area of study in the United States and Europe in the past decade, Buddhism in Brazil has received little scholarly attention. This book in English is the first to illuminate the Buddhist boom that has been gathering momentum in Brazil since the mid-1990s. In this short period, Brazil has become the only country in Latin America where Buddhism has a growing adherence, resulting in a substantial expansion of the market for Buddhist books, media coverage, web sites and e-mail lists, organization of events, visits of the Dalai Lama, and so on. As a result, Brazil has become an important center of information on Buddhism for Latin America because of geographical proximity and for Portugal because of language similarity.

Flows of Buddhism into Brazil and their indigenization is an area that requires study—not because it is widespread there,[7] but because its adherents are part of a little-studied but important stratum of society: the white, upper middle-class intellectuals and professionals.[8] This sector is significant as it disseminates information and embodies cosmopolitan as well as local experiences. Clifford has observed that "studying up" (studying elite institutions) is becoming a more common practice among anthropologists, as it aids in the understanding of an increasingly interconnected world.[9] Gupta and Ferguson have highlighted the constraint that colonial geography—privileging fieldwork in Third World countries—still exerts over the choice of anthropological site.[10] According to them, even when anthropologists work in the United States, they are expected to research ethnic and racial minorities. The same is true for Brazil, where "First World" Brazilian anthropologists and sociologists—the educated descendants of European colonizers and immigrants—study mostly disenfranchised classes and ethnic minorities such as indigenous populations. Regarding religious traditions, most scholarly research has historically been on Catholicism and more recently on Pentecostalism, which has challenged the hegemony of Catholicism among disenfranchised sectors of society.[11] New research has been addressing alternative spiritualities, a phenomenon typical of the same sector of society that adheres to Zen.[12] Nonetheless, this new direction in anthropological studies is still a minor trend. By focusing on upper- and upper middle-class urban Brazilians, I aim to shed light on this little-studied group as well as employ their cosmopolitanism as a route to follow global flows of modernity and their creolization in Brazil.

TRACKING FLOWS IN AN INTERCONNECTED WORLD

From the outset I realized that establishing historical and transnational connections was central to an understanding of how and why Buddhism in general and

Zen in particular have found a place in the Brazilian religious field and urban culture. Undeniably, there are a number of historical factors that have a bearing on the story of present-day Zen in the country. Among them are the legacy of slavery, which established an indelible distinction between educated and uneducated classes; the postcolonial condition of Brazil as a peripheral country eagerly absorbing and recreating metropolitan cultural production (a case in point is the adoption of the European and North American Orientalist imaginary of Japan and Zen); the arrival of Japanese immigrants, which provided a counterpoint to this Orientalist imaginary; the presence of *kaikyōshi* missionaries of the Sōtō Zenshū (the only Japanese Zen Buddhist school represented in the country);[13] the advent of religious modernity with its trends of privatization of religious choice, pluralism, and turning to the self as source of meaning; and the impact of globalization. It was thus clear from the start that I should embrace fully the disciplines of history and anthropology and that if I wanted to encompass the transnational flows of Zen into Brazil, my field should be a multi-sited one.

In the past decade or so, several anthropologists have been reflecting on the implications of globalization and transnational communities for the ethnographic method.[14] From this perspective, traditional conceptions of the anthropological field as the territorially fixed, stable, localized, and bounded community have become inadequate. For instance, Marcus has called for "multi-sited ethnography" as a way of "examining the circulation of cultural meanings, objects, and identities in diffuse time-space."[15] For him, "multi-sited research is designed around chains, paths, threads, conjunctions, juxtapositions of locations in which the ethnographer establishes some form of literal, physical presence, with an explicit, posited logic of association or connection among sites that in fact defines the argument of the ethnography."[16] Even within single sites, Marcus sees the awareness of a much larger world system in the subjects' consciousness and actions as crucial. In the same vein, Clifford has observed that in such an increasingly interconnected world, "the ethnographer is no longer a (worldly) traveler visiting (local) natives";[17] rather, both are travelers as well as dwellers. According to Clifford, if one is to understand "local/global historical encounters, . . . dominations and resistances, one needs to focus on hybrid, cosmopolitan experiences as much as rooted, native ones."[18]

To this end, my own research addresses both experiences. Whereas I focus on the "local/global historical encounters" and the cosmopolitan experiences of my interviewees (as many of them were in fact cosmopolitans who traveled and were aware of developments of Zen in metropolitan centers), I also focused on *how* they engaged in their Zen practices in Brazil. Accordingly, I conceived this book as a multi-sited research in order to track the flows of Zen from Japan, Europe, and the United States into Brazil and as they made their way back into these countries as well as to Latin America.

I therefore decided to deploy Appadurai's global "scapes" to illuminate the creation of an imaginary of Zen in particular, and of Buddhism in general, in Brazil.[19] Among these are flows of people (Japanese immigrants into Brazil, Sōtōshū *kaikyōshi* traveling among overseas outposts, and non-Japanese Brazilians traveling to the United States, Europe, and Japan to learn about and/or practice Zen), flows of technology (by looking at who and what is discussed on Brazilian Buddhist e-mail lists and how these compare with the international Buddha-L), flows of media (looking at how media stories produced overseas influenced media production in the country and how they in turn influence Brazilian followers), and flows of ideas (contained in movies, in foreign books translated into Portuguese, and in Brazilian books). Importantly, such flows were never univocal, and these historically shaped disjunctures have been significant in the creation of a conflicting reception of Zen among Japanese, Japanese Brazilians and non-Japanese Brazilians in the country. Moreover, I regard the dynamic of these flows as a coursing through "rhizomes,"[20] that is, I view Brazil as one of the nodes, albeit less influential, in the web of the global flows of Zen.

Some last remarks on methodology. This is mainly an ethnographic account of Zen in Brazil. As such, I will be using a fieldwork writing style where "I," as the observer, am visible and situated. Following theoretical discussions in the field of anthropology in the 1980s, most researchers have agreed that an "invisible" writer masks the presence of choice in reporting what is observed. Self-reflexivity on the researcher's subjectivity assists the reader in understanding the selective perceptions and possible biases of the data analyzed. Indeed, the point of view of the researcher, his/her background, and personal characteristics should be made apparent to show the reader that this is but one of the possible interpretations of the facts analyzed.

Many readers will note the absence of Japanese references. Because my intent in this book was to investigate how "foreign" ideas, in this case Japanese Zen Buddhism, arrived and were indigenized in the country, I focused on what took place at the grass-roots level in Brazil. I felt that written documents would not clarify the deep ambiguity with which Sōtōshū dealt with the Brazilian case. Therefore, I decided that rather than analyzing Sōtōshū's institutional records, it would be more fruitful to give ample voice to Sōtōshū monks/nuns working in the country. Moreover, the time I was researching in Japan in 2000 coincided with the peak of the conflicts and the dismissal of Coen *sensei*[21] from Busshinji Temple in São

Paulo City. This reinforced my belief that interviews would give me a more updated picture of the current situation.

Contemporary scholarship usually refers to "Western Buddhism/Buddhism in the West" as undifferentiated categories, lumping together Buddhism in the United States and Europe. Moreover, Buddhism in Europe has itself internal distinctions that need to be addressed. The adoption of Buddhism in Catholic countries such as France and Italy should be differentiated from its adoption in Protestant nations. While here I use "Buddhism in the West" to refer to the new area of studies of indigenization of Buddhism in non-Asian countries, I would like to point out that I am aware of how problematic this category is.

Three practical aspects are important to mention here. First, whereas I have used pseudonyms for adherents and sympathizers, I have maintained names of missionaries, monks, and nuns who are key figures in developments of Zen in Brazil. I have done so with their consent. Second, I have used Japanese names for Japanese Brazilians and Japanese missionaries in Brazil in the Western style — first name followed by family name — as most of them have long adopted it and Japanese missionaries have followed them in this. Third, I decided to use "Japanese Brazilians" instead of *nikkei*, the more common term to describe Japanese descendents born in the Americas.[22] I chose the former term to evince the dynamics of living in both worlds, which overlap but never completely fuse into one.

WHERE IS THE FIELD?
RESEARCHING TRANSNATIONAL PHENOMENA

I started my fieldwork in Brazil in 1997, while I was still associated with the Department of Anthropology of the University of São Paulo. I conducted extensive fieldwork in Brazil from 1997 to mid-1999, when I moved to Australia. Since then, I have returned to Brazil twice, each time for a three-month period of research, in 2000 and 2002. In Brazil, my spatially nonlocalized sites were an international e-mail list (Buddha-L) as well as the Brazilian e-mail lists Buddhismo-L and Zen Chung-Tao,[23] which I monitored daily, books published on Zen by Brazilians and those translated into Portuguese, magazines and newsletters published by Brazilian Zen groups as well as by Sōtōshū, and media stories. Researching e-mail lists and the Internet, as well as using e-mail, was fundamental for me to be "in" the field, while I was spatially "out" of the field. Many times, when transcribing interviews in Australia, I realized I had doubts or follow-up questions. I solved this by e-mailing my "informants" in Brazil or Japan. In addition, the e-mail lists enabled me to be "in" the field on an everyday basis, whereas the Internet allowed me to read stories published in Brazilian magazines and newspapers on Zen and other Buddhist traditions on their web sites. In this way, the boundaries between "the field," as the place of collecting data, and "home," as the place of analyzing this data and writing up, became blurred, reflecting the interconnected condition of my subject of study.

My main localized site was Busshinji Temple, but I also conducted short-term fieldwork (usually a week) in the Zen centers managed by non-Japanese Brazilians in Rio de Janeiro City, Ouro Preto (in Minas Gerais State), Ibiraçú (in Espírito Santo State), and Porto Alegre (in Rio Grande do Sul State). Located in São Paulo City, Busshinji is the head temple of Sōtōshū for South America and a branch temple (*betsuin*) of the two Sōtōshū head temples—Eiheiji (Fukui Prefecture) and Sōjiji (Kanagawa Prefecture) in Japan. Busshinji is a unique and rich site in that it houses two disparate but entangled congregations composed of Japanese Brazilians and non-Japanese Brazilians. In all these sites my research comprised a combination of participant observation, in-depth interviews, a survey, and archival research. Throughout my entire fieldwork in Brazil, I conducted sixty in-depth interviews, each of about one to one and a half hours' duration. Of these, thirty-nine were with more recent followers, eight with people who have been historically associated with Zen, and thirteen with monks, nuns, and missionaries. When I returned to Brazil in 2000 and 2002, I conducted follow-up interviews in order to evaluate changes occurring in Brazilian Zen. In addition, I conducted an anonymous survey in all the above-mentioned Brazilian sites, to which I had eighty responses. My participant observation involved weekly visits to Busshinji in order to participate in daily activities such as dharma talks,[24] *zazen* (meditation), dharma study groups, retreats, funerals, memorials, calendrical Buddhist festivities, and elections. I tried as much as possible to be present in activities that catered to both Japanese Brazilians and non-Japanese Brazilians.

In 2000, I received a fellowship from the Japan Foundation to conduct a four-month period of fieldwork in Japan. I had previously lived in Japan for one year (1992–1993) while conducting fieldwork for my master's dissertation on tea ceremony and the identity of the Japanese in Japan and in Brazil. There, while I was affiliated with the National Museum of Ethnology of Osaka, I conducted in-depth interviews with two former Sōtōshū missionaries to Brazil, with the officer in charge of Brazil at the Sōtōshū Shūmuchō (the headquarters of Sōtōshū in Tokyo), and three non-Japanese Brazilians who had been training in the head temples of Sōtōshū in Japan (Eiheiji and Sōjiji). Furthermore, I conducted archival research at Sōtōshū Shūmuchō as well as undertook participant observation in a monastery (Bukkokuji) in Obama-shi and a temple (Kirigayaji) in Tokyo.

I decided to participate in a seven-day retreat at the monastery for two reasons. First, I wanted to understand the differences between retreats in Japan and Brazil and the adaptations that have occurred. Bukkokuji was a good site since its abbot, Harada Tangen *rōshi*,[25] subscribes to what many scholars have come to call "modern Buddhism,"[26] a strand of Buddhism present mainly among non-Japanese Brazilians in Brazil. Second, I wanted to acquire the embodied experience of a retreat in Japan. The complete silence, the lack of eye contact (neither ever quite achieved in Brazil), the choice of food, the intense sessions of sitting and walking meditation (from 4:00 A.M. to 9:00 P.M.), the stretching breaks in the cemetery adjacent to the monastery—all assisted in creating a bodily experience that gave me a different perspective with which to explore Zen in Brazil. In saying this, I am not suggesting that there is an authentic Zen practice in Japan as opposed to a less authentic one in Brazil. Bukkokuji is itself an exception in that it accepts foreigners and allows men and women to sit side by side, the latter unheard of in Japan. My main intent was to participate in a "practice" so often referred to as the "right" one by some missionaries in Brazil who subscribe to modern Buddhism.

In addition, I spent two weeks at Kirigayaji, a temple in Tokyo. I chose this temple because its head monk, Junyū Kuroda *rōshi,* is the brother of Maezumi *rōshi,* the founder of the Zen Center of Los Angeles. The connection with Brazil comes through Coen *sensei,* a non-Japanese Brazilian nun who first trained in Los Angeles under Maezumi *rōshi* and then went on to Kirigayaji for a period of adaptation until she started training at Aichi Senmon Nisōdō, a nunnery in Nagoya. Since then, she and her disciples have used Kirigayaji as a base in Tokyo. Because of its links with the United States, this temple works as a strong point of contact between North American Zen teachers and practitioners and Brazilian ones.

Living in a monastery and a temple, albeit for a short period of time, showed me how different these two environments are. While the former is a place of intense training for monks and nuns, the latter caters to the spiritual needs of the surrounding community. In Brazil, the lack of monasteries/nunneries made temples double as training places as well. Such a situation created conflict between those who wanted to use Busshinji for *zazen* practice (mainly non-Japanese Brazilians oblivious to the differences between temples and monasteries in Japan) and those who wanted to use the temple for funerals, memorials, and festivities (mainly Japanese and Japanese Brazilians). When I was in Japan, the conflict became heated and culminated with Coen *sensei*'s dismissal as head of Busshinji in January 2001. This meant that it became very difficult to secure interviews with the representative of Sōtōshū Shūmuchō and also with a former missionary who had held a high post at Eiheiji at the time. I believe both of them saw me as a non-Japanese Brazilian in Japan interested only in inquiring about the conflict. In order to get an interview, I constantly had to stress that I did not want to talk about the conflict, but instead wanted to know more about the history of Sōtōshū in Brazil, the level of their influence over the branch temple in Brazil, and the plans it had for Brazil's future. As it turned out, both men ended up talking about their view of the conflict, as if realizing that if things were going to be published, they might as well give their version of the story. I do address the conflicts in this book, but I do so in order to analyze the various understandings of Zen in the country.

Many Zen teachers who subscribe to modern Buddhism and cater to mainly non-Japanese Brazilians have added to the conflict by regarding "real" Buddhism, which for them was centered on meditation, as degenerated in Japan, since it had collapsed under the weight of cultural accretions (meaning devotional practices). My time in Japan showed me the opposite. For the entire fieldwork period I lived in a small six-tatami apartment in Kyoto whose window overlooked a cemetery. Arriving at *o-bon* season in August, a time when the dead come to visit their descendents, I saw an endless stream of families, including young children, washing their ancestors' headstones while a Buddhist priest chanted beside them. Soon afterward came *higan* (in September), another occasion for ancestor worship, and there they were chanting and washing headstones again. My window at the Kyoto apartment gave me a vantage point to see Buddhist activity not based on meditation, but meaningful nonetheless. The time I spent at Kirigayaji also made me realize how meaningful funerals and memorials are, and how grateful the families are toward the monks. I tried to recall how many times I had been to a cemetery to see my grandparents, and sadly I can say that I have never done so. I believe I am not an exception in Brazilian urban centers. This realization had a profound impact on how I started to view devotional acts.

To be sure, the Buddhism I experienced in Japan revolved more often than not around death, something for which Japanese Buddhism is often criticized. Yet I felt it created meaning for people as much as *zazen* may be meaningful for Westerners. Aware of my non-Japanese background, I tried as much as possible to be impartial in the face of both kinds of practices.

THE MODERN IN ME

When I was growing up in the 1960s in Brazil there was no Internet, the TV and newspapers were black-and-white, and telephones always black. Information from overseas was sparse and took longer to arrive than today. Indeed, communication and transportation had yet to take the huge leap they took in the 1990s; meanwhile, the country was closed for most imports in a bid to protect the national industry until 1990. Yet I had a deep sense of the "unknown out there," as friends and family traveled and brought long-sought items such as French perfume and North American blue jeans with them. Brought up in an upper middle-class home in the sprawling megalopolis of São Paulo, at an early age I realized that there was a fervent rush and anxiety to follow the latest fashions from the United States and Europe. From books, music, movies, theater, dance, clothes, fashion, and behavior, the good, interesting, and modern things all came from overseas. From the early 1980s onward, I began traveling extensively—studying in the United States, working on a British cruise ship, backpacking in Europe, doing fieldwork for my master's degree and Ph.D. in Japan, and traveling in Asia. Still, a sense of being truly modern always eluded me, as I was most often perceived as a woman from the "Third World." Very much like the villager in Africa who told Jean and John Comaroff that "things modern seem always to be in the next village,"[27] I realized that the quest for modernity was not one to be won, but to be given up.

However, every time I go back to Brazil I am reminded of the obsession with "the First World," "the developed world," the "modern other." That such an obsession has always been there is evident from our colonial past, but in the 1990s it was exacerbated by neoliberalist economic policies that further deepened the gap between the rich and the poor. Indeed, according to a 1995 World Bank study, "Brazil has the most unequal distribution of wealth of any country in the world; the richest twenty percent of the population earn twenty-six times as much as the poorest twenty percent of the nation (the comparative figure for India is five to one, and eleven to one in the United States)."[28] In addition, research in 1998 showed that while the top 10 percent of the Brazilian population accounted for nearly 50 percent of all individual income, the bottom 70 percent earned about 25 percent.[29] Significantly, this enormous gap in turn created more anxiety as to whether modernity was a possibility for the country. Newly coined expressions for Brazil such as "Belindia"—an amalgam of Belgium and India—indicate the level of tension over when, how, and whether Brazil will become truly modern.

From this perspective, it is not surprising that I chose to analyze the appropriation of Zen in Brazil through the lens of modernity. Possibly, a researcher who is neither Brazilian nor from the same social stratum of society might not have chosen the same path. Indeed, this immense "struggle" toward modernity that Brazil and other colonized societies have historically undergone has shaped the way we *imagine* the world. Appadurai has argued that the intensification of the global flows of media and migration has had a deep influence on the "*work of the imagination* as a constitutive feature of modern subjectivity."[30] For him, "the work of the imagination is a space . . . in which individuals and groups seek to annex the global into their own practices of the modern."[31] Significantly, the globalization of Buddhism in general and Zen in particular has taken place through Japanese migration into the country, as well as through mass-mediated images carried by the cultural industries.

MODERNITY AND TRADITION: A PAINFUL DEBATE

It became clear in the early stages of my research that the way Zen has been perceived and adopted at different times within Brazilian history is related to an aspiration for modernity. Since this is a theme that runs throughout this book, in this section I will briefly problematize the notions of modernity and tradition so that we may understand the complex ways in which both tropes are associated with Zen in Brazil. Hall argues that "the West" is neither a geographical territory nor a natural entity, but rather a historically produced category.[32] From this perspective, a society is considered Western not when it is located in a discrete, geographically uniform region such as the "Western Hemisphere," but when it is developed, industrialized, urbanized, capitalist, secular, and modern. For Hall, the binary opposition between "The West" and "The Rest" is a discursive formation that emerges as a result of a set of historical forces that were central to the formation of Europe's identity. These include the process of Reformation and Enlightenment as well as Europe's encounter with the "New World."

Both processes gave Europe a sense of itself, an identity against which other non-Western societies and cultures were measured. The idea of progress that emerged during the Enlightenment was defined in terms of a single linear model of development according to which societies and cultures were hierarchically ranked as more or less "civilized" or "developed" depending on either their temporal distance or proximity to modernity.[33] Such a view rests on a set of historicist assumptions according to which modernity is understood as "something that became global *over time*" and that certain cultures and societies can only ever experience a *belated* modernity, having been consigned to "an imaginary waiting room of history."[34]

As Sakai argues, the West-and-the-Rest opposition posits a hierarchical structure according to which the historical distinctions between "modern" and "premodern" are mapped onto a set of geopolitical divides between "the West" and the "non-West."[35] For Sakai, the category of the non-West (or the Rest) is implicated in the West, as they need each other to establish their own identity. Yet at the same time, while the distinction between the West and the Rest is being undermined by the accelerating processes of globalization, the idea of being a part of the West is still a persistent and alluring *fantasy* for countries like Brazil whose identity and culture have been historically entangled with the Western (European) project of modernity.

The linear model of historical development and progress derived from the Enlightenment has not only influenced the shape and direction of the European colonial project, but has also influenced the struggles and aspirations of anticolonial and nationalist intellectuals. While many Latin American countries have inherited the universalizing ideas of Enlightenment humanism such as citizenship, democracy, human rights, and social justice, they also had to contend with the historicist assumptions—"first in Europe, then elsewhere"—that underlie these categories of political modernity.[36] Indeed, Latin American countries have forever struggled with the belief that theirs was a "second-rate version of North Atlantic modernities which they 'failed' to follow."[37] Throughout much of Latin American, and particularly Brazilian, history, the theme of modernity has been the central pole around which the idea of national identity was woven.[38]

Although there was never any doubt about Brazil being part of the West (or "the Occident," as it is expressed in Portuguese), its colonial history, along with its sense of its geographical distance from Europe and North America, has given rise to a pervasive uncertainty regarding its status as a thoroughly modern nation. Modernity has always been viewed as something foreign, something that Brazil is perceived to have lacked and thus had had to import from "metropolitan" centers of power. At different historical times Brazilian elites oscillated between admiration and desire for European—and after World War II, North American—modernity on the one hand, and celebration of the specificity of Brazilian national culture on the other. Nevertheless, the anxiety around where Brazil stands in relation to the "advanced world" has endured.[39]

While this anxiety is centered on a clear-cut separation between what is national (regarded as "authentic" Brazil by some, or an obstacle to modernity by others) and what is foreign ("inauthentic" for some, or modern for others), this attempt to separate is flawed. As Hall argues, discourses that rely on the binary opposition between "tradition" and "modernity," "West" and "East" simplify the issue by essentializing the categories of both the West and the Rest, a homogenizing maneuver that erases internal distinctions within each category.[40]

Writing in relation to Latin America, García Canclini corroborates Hall's argument. In one of his works García Canclini makes the case that the modernization of these societies did not end traditional forms of production, beliefs, and goods, but created hybrid cultures that encompass a complex, multitemporal articulation of traditions and modernities.[41] Given the disparities between "deficient" political and socioeconomic modernization on the one hand and "exuberant" cultural modernity on the other, he asserts that while dominant classes have embraced the project of modernity, they have preserved a niche of privilege for themselves.[42] In this context, the forms of political and economic modernity such as democracy, citizenship, industrial modes of production, and high technology coexist with archaic power relations, paternalistic regimes, artisanal forms of production, and, I should add, de facto slavery.[43]

Since modernization in Brazil was a top-down process carried out by authoritarian regimes in the 1930s and 1960s/1970s, it preserved and recreated the social, economic, and cultural divisions between the elite (or educated classes) and the rest of society. The Brazilian literary critic Roberto Schwarz has rightly observed that this disjuncture does not mean that Brazil has experienced a belated modernity, but rather that this very contradiction is a dynamic element of national culture, one that encompasses a fascination with foreign models as well a desire to deploy them in their own culture.[44] We should keep such contradictions in mind when we look at Zen in Brazil since—except in relation to Japanese immigrants—it has historically been a practice of the cultural elite. Given the avant-garde status that the Zen boom has enjoyed in the United States and Europe, it is not surprising that members of these elites adopted the practice of Zen as a symbol of cosmopolitanism and modernity. Indeed, Brazilian intellectuals have played a key role in the dissemination of metropolitan ideas and models, traveling to these centers, translating books produced overseas, and publishing magazine and newspaper stories locally.

In a more recent work, García Canclini examines the influence of globalization on the debate on modernity in Latin America.[45] He points out that instead of effacing tradition, globalization intensifies the disjuncture between the traditional and the "hyper-modern," popular and elite cultures, and the local and the global that characterize these hybrid cultures. He concludes by saying,

> Historical and local differences persist not so much because globalizing powers are still insufficient, but because their way of reproducing and expanding themselves requires that the center not be everywhere, that there be differences between the global circulation of goods and the unequal distribution of the political capacity to use them.[46]

Indeed, while the advent of the cultural industries and mass media has enhanced the popular appeal of cosmopolitanism, the distances between the margins and the centers and the haves and have-nots have not been eliminated.

As a final note on the term "modernity," Habermas sees modernity as an unfinished project that has not been superseded.[47] From this perspective, the use of the term "postmodernity" for the transformations taking place since the last quarter of the twentieth century is not appropriate. Indeed, many scholars have shunned the use of "postmodernity" to encompass this new mode of interconnection between cultures and have instead employed "globalization," "advanced modernity," "late modernity," or "modernity at large." Here I have opted for "modernity" to argue that the Enlightenment and civilizing project are still current in these globalized times.

JAPAN AS A MODEL OF MODERNITY

Given the centrality of modernity to the construction of Brazilian national identity, I argue that the aspiration to be modern mediated not just Brazil's relationship with Europe and North America, but also its relationship with Japan and its cultural products. To this end, I identify a number of key moments in Brazilian history during which the debate between what was national/traditional and what was foreign/modern emerged clearly in relation to Japan, Japanese immigrants, Buddhism in general, and Zen Buddhism in particular.

I argue that the adoption of Zen in Brazil is part of the process of "cannibalizing" the modern other in order to become modern itself.[48] Throughout this book I show that the Zen adopted by national elites since the late 1950s, and by the media and popular culture in the 1990s, is an aspect of what Lopez, Bauman, and Sharf have called "modern Buddhism"—characterized as empirical, rational and in accord with modern science.[49] Moreover, I contend that the practice of Zen on the part of the Brazilian cultural and intellectual elites from the 1950s onward was driven by a desire to acquire and accumulate cultural capital as a marker of social distinction locally and overseas.[50] That is to say, the consumption of Zen by members of the elite expressed their desire to distinguish themselves from the tastes of popular classes while at the same time associating themselves with overseas cultural elites. Finally, I contend that Brazil occupies both a peripheral and (albeit small) central position of influence in relation to the practice and dissemination of Zen. Despite the well-known asymmetry of global cultural flows—that is, the fact that global flows of culture chiefly radiate from metropolitan centers toward peripheries—I argue that Brazil has managed to become a center for some metropolitan centers (France and the United States) as well as for countries that, unlike Brazil, did not undergo a Buddhist boom (Portugal and other Latin American countries). Indeed, Zen in Brazil was never isolated from the trends occurring overseas. The rotation of Sōtōshū missionaries amongst the diverse temples outside Japan, the missionaries who defected from Sōtōshū but continue to teach in Brazil and Europe, the arrival of Japanese immigrants, intellectuals traveling and translating books on Zen, the media, and more recently the Internet, and Brazilian e-mail lists linking Portuguese- and Spanish-speaking sympathizers and adherents have meant that Brazil has received inflows, but has also produced counterflows of Zen.

SYNCRETISM, HYBRIDITY, AND CREOLIZATION

Though the concept of syncretism has been historically used to analyze religious encounters, here I have decided not use it for three reasons. First, although syncretism has staged a comeback as it is redefined,[51] it has historically been associated with impurity as a pejorative term to denote a stage prior to Christian monotheism. In other words, the term was used to evaluate religious blending from the point of view of one of the religions involved. Second, syncretism conveys the image of two clear systems overlaid,[52] whereas I would like to complicate this image by addressing other intersecting influences and negotiations, which in turn created multiple, disjunctive beliefs and practices of Zen in Brazil. Indeed, Brazilian anthropologist Rita Segato has argued that

> Brazil has produced a model of multiple interpenetrations usually described as syncretic. I do not think it is enough to use the term syncretism to encompass the meetings and fusions typical of this system. What is significant about it is that plurality continues to be present, although through a particular multicultural mechanism that makes each culture in contact involve, embrace, invoke or simply mark its presence in a much bigger sector of the population than in a specific social group.[53]

Third, although this book is fundamentally an inquiry into how Zen has been indigenized in Brazil, its approach is a more inclusive one. It does not consider solely traditional religious fusions, but diverse intercultural mixtures. Following García Canclini,[54] I use the term "hybridity" to encompass the diversity of registers to be analyzed here: the globalization and localization of Zen in Brazil, the country's position as a meaning-producing center/exporter as well as a periphery that imports foreign forms of Zen, Zen in the media, popular culture, and high culture, and the relationship between Zen and modernity and tradition. In addition, I use the trope of creolization as a development of hybridity, as it gives us an insight on *how the process* of hybridity takes place. Here I shall first address the notions of creolization and then hybridization in order to show where they overlap and why creolization appears to be a more fertile trope in this study of Zen in Brazil.

The term "creolization" originates from the Spanish *criollo* and Portuguese *crioulo,* both deriving from the Latin verb *creare* (to breed or to create). Historically the term has been used in different ways by different societies. Thus, "in Peru the word was used to refer to people of Spanish descent who were born in the New World. In Brazil, the term was applied to Negro slaves born locally. In Louisiana, the term was applied to the white francophone populations, while in New Orleans it applied to mulattoes."[55]

Until recently, the concept of a "creole culture" was deeply connected to the encounter of African and European culture in the Caribbean. As a result, the term was extended to encompass the language spoken by these so-called creole people, which in turn was regarded as a simplification of European languages. Lately, however, linguists have regarded it positively as they have come to realize that such languages were the result of the superimposition of the dominant language's lexicon over the dominated language's own syntax, grammar, and morphology.[56] The resulting language revealed a twofold predicament: at the same time that it demonstrated that colonial peoples have yielded to and adopted the dominant language by using its lexicon, it showed also that they have clung to inner forms of their own language as a matrix for this lexicon, a sign of resistance.[57]

Many scholars of culture have detached the trope of creolization from its Caribbean and linguistic rootedness and applied the term more broadly to processes of cultural mixing. In the field of anthropology, Hannerz was one of the first to make a strong statement for the concept of creole culture as "our most promising root metaphor" to make sense of the way "two or more historical sources, originally widely different" get in contact, intermingle, and mix.[58] The itinerary that the terms "Creole" and "creolization" have followed is clearly marked by Stoddard and Cornwell.

> In Trinidad today there is a slippage between the notion of "Creole" as the African side of the population, the notion of "Creole" culture being the national culture of Trinidad and Tobago, and the notion of "creolizing" as the continuous process of intercultural mixing and creativity. It is the latter, extended sense of creolization and *créolité* that cultural theorists appropriate as a synonym for hybridity.[59]

It is this latter sense, inflected by its linguistic facet, that I wish to employ when analyzing Brazilian Zen. Nevertheless, I should mention a caveat before using the term in this way. The word "Creole" derives, as mentioned, from the Portuguese *crioulo*, which even today is a derogatory term for Afro-Brazilians. Its use here may lead some readers to think the history of Brazilian society is deeply connected with that of the Caribbean. Nothing could be further from the truth. Thus the use of the trope of creolization does not mean that this study involves Afro-Brazilians, nor am I implying that the phenomenon I am analyzing has any relation whatsoever to Caribbean colonial and postcolonial history.

However, before making use of creolization as a trope to understand the process of cultural mixing in Brazil, it is necessary first to examine where creolization and hybridity overlap and where both terms have their distinct uses. The concept of hybridity has increasingly gained currency in the past decades in cultural theory, postcolonial studies, and anthropology.[60] Papastergiadis has observed that hybridity acknowledges that "identity is constructed through negotiation of difference." Such identity is not a synthesis of the combined elements, but an "energy field of different forces."[61] In other words, identity is not a tidy product, but an ongoing construction through negotiation. Likewise, Bhabha has argued that a hybrid is not simply a mixture of the two previous identities, but a "third space," a place for "the negotiation of incommensurable differences, . . . where difference is neither One nor the Other but *something else besides,* in-between."[62]

Some cultural and postcolonial theorists have used creolization as a synonym for hybridity.[63] I contend that creolization does not necessarily "tend to fusion," but as Papastergiadis has argued for hybridity, it reveals "the presence of fissures, gaps and contradictions."[64] Similar to hybridity, I suggest that creolization underscores the notion that identity is not a seamless combination, a synthesis of two or more worlds, but a field of energy. An equally fitting metaphor is the one employed by Yuri Lotman, a Russian semiotician who defines culture as a dynamic rather than static entity—culture would be "more like a river with a number of currents moving in different rates and intensities." Culture in this case would be in a "state of constant creolization."[65] As much as culture is not a synthetic whole, creolization is not a product but a *process* of interaction and change.

Ultimately all terms are problematic, as they are historically entangled in colonizing processes, but I believe the trope of creolization has several advantages over the term "hybridity" in this study. Hybridity, as a metaphor for cultural contact, carries with it the predicament of its origins in biological science where it was juxtaposed to notions of racial purity and fear of mixing.[66] Hybridity also derives from horticulture and animal-breeding practices, which in turn juxtapose it with ideas of sterility and passivity, since hybrid plants and animals do not hybridize by themselves. Finally, "hybrids are, by definition, native to nowhere," while "Creole" means just the opposite, "to become indigenized, to create a home where one is not at home."[67] Notwithstanding the contemporary recuperation of hybridity as a subversive practice/agency within postcolonial and cultural theory, which has moved the concept away from biological and essentialist discourses of identity and authenticity, it still has to grapple with the dilemma of the discourse of race.

Creolization as an analytical trope, on the other hand, although having originated during colonial contact, carries notions of creativity, agency, and innovation on the part of the colonized. Furthermore, the concept of creolization, when inflected by its linguistic facet, highlights *how* the continuous contact and negotiation take place. In this respect, Noble and Tabar have rightly pointed out that the trope of hybridity has been for the most part theory driven, that is, there are very few empirical studies "exploring the dimensions by which hybrid elements are articulated."[68] By contrast, the notion of creolization has been shown to be a fertile analytical trope in many ethnographic studies in that it reveals the *process* of the construction of identity. Indeed, as Prothero notes, "by attention to two levels of interaction (grammar and lexicon), creolization theory allows for a richer and more sophisticated analysis."[69] In this light, I will be using creolization to unravel *how* this process takes place, while hybridity will be used more loosely, whenever I mention the meeting of two or more cultures, practices, and beliefs.

Likewise, many scholars have used the notion of creolization to analyze how postcolonial societies negotiate contact and change.[70] In Buddhist studies, Prothero deploys the notion of creolization to analyze the ways a white American man, Col. Henry Steel Olcott, creolized the Protestantism of his upbringing with Buddhism in his adulthood. Prothero notes that "while the lexicon of his [Olcott's] faith was almost entirely Buddhist, its grammar was largely Protestant."[71] From this perspective, I believe that in the context of an analysis of Zen Buddhism in Brazil, the trope of creolization is meaningful as it sheds light onto how Japanese immigrants and descendants have placed a Brazilian religious vocabulary over a Buddhist matrix, while non-Japanese Brazilians and Catholic Japanese Brazilians have been involved in the inverse process.

BOOK STRUCTURE

Keeping these three key arguments in mind—the aspiration for modernity, the desire for social distinction, and the peripheral/central position of Brazil—I will now give a brief overview of each chapter, pointing out how these key themes interlace with my findings. I structured this book as a historical itinerary, departing from the Japanese immigration and Orientalist ideas carried into Brazil in the nineteenth century and arriving in present-day Brazil. I should, however, warn the reader that each chapter is a glimpse of a particular path, among the many others existing, through which I choose to track the story of Zen in Brazil. This book, therefore, does not intend to be a "holistic road to another society,"[72] but a journey into the complex ways in which Brazil is entangled with the world at large.

In chapter 1, I address the theme of modernity in relation to Japan and Japanese immigrants into Brazil. I argue that in order to comprehend how Zen was accepted and creolized in Brazil, one has to appreciate how Japan and Japanese immigrants were regarded in the country. In the early twentieth century, when the nation was discussing the acceptance of Japanese immigrants, Brazilian elites constructed an admiring discourse of Japan's fast economic, military, and social developments as an example that Brazil should follow. In what Lesser called a process of "double assimilation" and that could also be called "cannibalization," Brazilian elites claimed that Brazil would become modern by taking up Japanese immigrants while the immigrants would assimilate into Brazilian culture.[73]

Following this discussion, I explore the lives of some Zen missionaries in Brazil. I argue that the discourse of modern Zen that emerged from the writings of D. T. Suzuki and the Kyoto school of philosophy not only influenced the West, but also flowed into Japan, informing some of the *kaikyōshi* who went to Brazil. I contend that the conflict between traditional and modern Zen was mirrored in the congregation, as Japanese Brazilians and non-Japanese Brazilians subscribed to each form of Zen respectively. In addition, through the lives of missionaries and their travels among the various foreign missions, I show that Zen in Brazil is deeply connected with developments in Japan and the United States.

In chapter 2 I track the flow of ideas into the country by addressing the role of intellectuals in importing modern Zen. I show that Orientalist European ideas of the "exotic east," rather than the local Japanese community, mediated the Brazilian elite's concepts of Japan, Buddhism in general, and Zen. Accordingly, Zen was disseminated in elite culture and not confined to the Sōtōshū temples in the country. In this context, I argue that Brazilian cosmopolitan intellectuals traveled to specific locales overseas to acquire the cultural capital that would distinguish them from other sectors of society. In their desire to cannibalize the latest "modern" vogue, to become modern themselves, they chose to travel to metropolitan centers. While in the late nineteenth century that meant going to France, after World War II the United States took its place. As the Brazilian anthropologist Ruben Oliven has observed, "modernity is also frequently confused with the idea of contemporaneity, in the sense that adopting everything that is in vogue in advanced countries is seen as being modern."[74]

In chapter 3 I discuss the current coexistence of modernity and tradition in religious terms by analyzing the Brazilian religious field and profiling Zen sympathizers and adherents. I ask how it was that Zen could have been adopted, and even become a common adjective in Portuguese, given the mainly Catholic, Afro-Brazilian, and Spiritist Brazilian arena. I argue that modern Buddhism constructed by Asian elites as compatible with science, and thus superior to Christianity, was adopted in Brazil as a strong shield against what was perceived as a hierarchical, authoritarian, dogmatic, superstitious, and hence "backward" Catholic Church. Since religious modernity is characterized by privatization of choice, pluralization of traditions, and a turning to the self as a source of meaning, it is hardly surprising that Buddhism packaged as a rational, logical, and individual practice and ultimately as a philosophy (not a religion) would be embraced as a path to modernity. Indeed, in their aspiration to modernity, Brazilian intellectuals traveled East so that they could go West. Most adherents I interviewed had a history of shunning Catholicism and some of being Marxist militants in the 1960s and 1970s. However, as discussed earlier, modernity does not efface tradition, and thus here I address the creole religious practices that emerged since Zen arrived in Brazil.

In chapter 4 I explore the role of the cultural industries, in the form of newspapers, magazines, the Internet, movies, and TV, in disseminating Buddhism in Brazil. In this context, I apply Appadurai's five "scapes" to examine how the flows of Zen into and out of Brazil occur in and through their disjunctures.[75] I argue that the North American "Tibetan chic" trend created a media frenzy in Brazil, which helped to create and popularize a Buddhist boom in the late 1990s. However, since globalization does not efface local differences, I contend that social distinction is still preserved since only certain sectors of society appropriate Buddhism, and they do it in different ways. Therefore, I discuss the roles of fashion, taste, and lifestyle in creating a habitus that maintains social distinction.

In the final chapter I approach the theme of modernity and tradition through actual Zen practices and beliefs in Brazil. I argue that tradition and modernity are not opposed but, in fact, enmeshed. Whereas one might suppose that the Japanese and Japanese-Brazilian Zen practices and beliefs are "traditional" and that non-Japanese-Brazilian ones are "modern," this is not the picture that emerges from my fieldwork. Both groups have creolized practices. Not only do Japanese Brazilians employ Catholicism to create a creolized Zen, but some are also interested in *zazen* and see Zen not as a religion, but as a philosophy. On the other hand, non-Japanese Brazilians have devotional as well as merit-making practices, deemed "traditional." In what I call "creolized Zen," each group superimposes a new vocabulary onto its own religious grammar. Therefore, in this chapter I discuss and challenge the binary oppositions between "ethnic" and "convert" Buddhism that North American and European scholars frequently use as a typology to profile adherents. To this end, I demonstrate that their location in the field as Westerners, and (many of them) as Buddhists, has greatly influenced the construction of this binary opposition.

Finally, in the conclusion I try to think beyond Zen in Brazil, pointing to the broader issues this book addresses. My fieldwork, multi-sited and decentered, reveals the complex ways in which modernity is articulated with tradition and how the discourse of modernity has shaped and still shapes the way Brazilians construct their world. Similarly, by tracking global flows into the country, I bring to light how the global is profoundly enmeshed in the local. Brazil is both a periphery and a center for global flows of Zen. It demonstrates that these flows do not only radiate from core Western nations to the periphery, but also in the opposite direction and between peripheries. Moreover, globalization does not homogenize the world. The analysis of hybridization and creolization of Zen in Brazil points to the way that the global is adopted in distinct ways by the local. As a last point, the Brazilian case contributes to a more nuanced picture of the often-described gap between "convert" and "ethnic" practices. My fieldwork shows an overlap between these two kinds of practices.

1 The Japanese-Brazilian Junction: Establishing Zen Missions

MARCH 2000, BUSSHINJI TEMPLE

The room is buzzing with excitement. Folding chairs are arranged in rows. Japanese men wearing suits and ties are sitting in the front and Japanese women are at the back, as is appropriate in Japanese culture, where men take precedence. In the middle are many T-shirted non-Japanese Brazilians, men and women mixed, as befits their culture. This is the Forty-Seventh General Assembly of the Comunidade Budista Sōtō Zenshū da América do Sul (Sōtō Zenshū Buddhist Community of South America), and, as usual, it is taking place in the basement of Busshinji Temple in São Paulo City. There are about 115 people present, most of them non-Japanese Brazilians and second-, third-, and fourth-generation descendants of Japanese immigrants; very few are part of the old, first-generation Japanese community.

This morning elections are taking place, and there is tension in the air. Two congregations are vying to run Busshinji's administration—one composed of the old, traditional, first-generation Japanese board, the other composed of Japanese Brazilians of second and third generations who align with the non-Japanese Brazilians. To aggravate things, after a five-year hiatus a new *sōkan* (superintendent for South America) has just arrived from Japan. In the interim, this position had been filled by the missionary in charge of Busshinji, a non-Japanese-Brazilian woman named Coen de Souza, who trained at the Zen Center of Los Angeles for three years and then in Japan for a further twelve years. Although Coen is a non-Japanese-Brazilian nun, she had slowly gained acceptance among the Japanese community because she worked hard to preserve the rituals the Japanese community expects to be performed. Speaking both Japanese and Portuguese fluently, she was a successful intermediary between the Japanese and Brazilian communities. Paradoxically, her success was also the source of tension. From 1995 (the year she was appointed) until 2001 (the year she lost her position in the temple), Coen increasingly attracted Brazilians of non-Japanese ancestry and began to conduct most of the temple's activities in Portuguese. On that very morning she had reluctantly consented to run for the presidency of the Japanese descendants' faction. Because of the growth in the number of non-Japanese-Brazilian adherents under Coen's missionary work, this congregation had succeeded in gaining control of the temple in 1998, when both groups disputed elections for the first time. Now, with the presence of an "authentic" Japanese missionary (the *sōkan*) to oversee the elections, would the coalition of non-Japanese Brazilian and young Japanese descendants still prevail?

The new *sōkan* starts his speech (in Japanese, using a translator), and his tone is conciliatory: "In the past five years, when there was no *sōkan* in South America, the number of adherents of the Sōtō Zenshū increased, thanks to Coen *sensei's* work. There are many Zen groups in the U.S., France, Spain, and they speak many languages other than Japanese. Therefore, it is only natural that conflicts arise. But these conflicts are not necessarily negative. Let's think of conflicts as an opportunity for growth."

Yet the general mood is not one of appeasement, and the old disputes for power are pervasive. For instance, halfway through the assembly, following a series of speeches by former members of the 1998–2000 administration, a Japanese man suddenly stands up and bursts into Japanese. He is obviously upset. Many non-Japanese Brazilians call out angrily that he should be speaking Portuguese, but he persists. One Japanese descendant aligned with the non-Japanese-Brazilian side shouts that they are in Brazil and should therefore speak Portuguese. Commotion takes over the room, only to be settled after some time when a translator offers his services. It turns out that the Japanese man was a member of the administration prior to 1998. He wanted to speak directly to the *sōkan* and to his fellow Japanese present so that his words would not be misinterpreted. His speech is cut short and he goes back to his seat. The assembly proceeds with only minor incidents, and in the end a new board composed of the Japanese descendants (aligned with the non-Japanese Brazilians) is elected. The morning is coming to a close, and everyone stands up to prepare the room for the big lunch that is ahead. *Feijoada* (a typical Brazilian dish purportedly originating from the food of slaves and consisting of black beans and meat, rice, oranges, and vegetables) is served alongside sushi and Japanese green tea. Forks, knives, and chopsticks rest on the table — an appropriate set of utensils for the ever-present contentions that Japanese, Japanese Brazilians, and non-Japanese Brazilians experience at Busshinji.

An occasion such as an election is a very telling situation. It is a time when sides are clearly taken and decisions are made about who will hold power and for what purpose. The negotiations and, more recently, acute open conflicts over whose Zen is to be practiced at Busshinji have been unrelenting since non-Japanese Brazilians started frequenting the temple. The issues at stake are ethnic resistance against the surrounding society and the religious identity of both groups. Just as *feijoada* and sushi can be served at the same meal and are enjoyed with gusto by all,

Zen in Brazil encompasses the disjunctures of practices and beliefs among Japanese, Japanese Brazilians, and non-Japanese Brazilians.

In this chapter I will examine the flows of Zen practices and beliefs carried by Japanese immigrants into Brazil. I contend that if one is to understand the acceptance of Japanese immigrants and Japanese Buddhism in Brazilian society at large and how this created a specific form of creolized Japanese-Brazilian Zen, one has to consider two factors. First, Japanese immigration to Brazil aimed to avoid the racist popular clamor that had occurred in the United States and thus help promote a better interaction with the Japanese in Brazilian society. Second, throughout the twentieth century Brazilian elites admired Japan due to its fast economic, military, and social developments both in the years following the Russo-Japanese War (1904–1905) and during her post–World War II recovery. This admiration derived from Brazil's position as a peripheral country desiring a stronger role in the world — a role Brazil perceived Japan was securing for itself.

After outlining the milieu in which Japanese immigration took place in Brazil, I will discuss the establishment of Sōtō Zenshū missions in the country. I argue that the experiences of *kaikyōshi* missionaries in Brazil have been shaped by what Reader has referred to as Sōtōshū's "dualistic attitude" toward *zazen* (meditation).[1] I also contend that the discourse on Zen that emerged from the writings of D. T. Suzuki and the Kyoto school to resist Western cultural hegemony not only fed the Zen boom in the West, but also has more recently had an impact on the Zen practice of some Japanese. In this chapter I will show that Japanese Sōtōshū missionaries who catered to the (mostly) non-Japanese-Brazilian community since 1968 embraced Suzuki's ideas on Zen wholeheartedly in Japan prior to their arrival in Brazil. Their ambivalent attitudes toward meditation and rituals created conflicts, which were mirrored in the congregation. Here I will present the missionaries' side of the conflicts as they evolved through the years to reveal the way the Japanese-Brazilian and non-Japanese communities negotiated their place in Busshinji Temple.

JAPANESE IMMIGRATION IN THE AMERICAS: SHIFTING FROM THE UNITED STATES TO BRAZIL

Official negotiations between the Brazilian and Japanese governments had started as early as 1895, with the signing of the first Brazil-Japan Friendship Treaty. Significantly, in negotiating Japanese immigration into Brazil, both governments — the Japanese in particular — made sure they learned from the mistakes made during the

Japanese immigration to North America and Hawai'i. At the end of the nineteenth century Japan was leaving a feudal system behind and embracing modernization through rapid urbanization and industrialization. The consequent drastic social changes and economic difficulties hit the rural population especially hard. High inflation combined with low rice prices and a new and rigorous land tax system resulted in widespread poverty in rural areas.[2] Consequently, the Meiji government (1868–1912) saw emigration as a safety valve to relieve pressure on the land, while creating colonies that would grow food for export back to Japan. The opportunity came from countries such as Hawai'i and the United States, which needed labor.

Here, I will use first Hawai'i then the United States as sites to compare emigration to Brazil for a number of reasons. As it took place at a similar time, Japanese immigration to these countries was generated by the same economic, social, and political difficulties in Japan. In addition, these countries received a large intake of Japanese immigrants. Finally, the United States is a particularly good locale of comparison because of the large body of scholarship on immigration and on Zen Buddhism. Peru, Bolivia, Argentina, Mexico, and other Latin American countries also received an inflow of Japanese immigrants, but their numbers were far smaller and there is very little scholarship on them. Furthermore, Peru is the one other country in South America to have a Sōtō mission, but its only temple (Jionji, in the town of Cañete near Lima) has been inactive since the head abbot passed away in 1992. Jionji is a branch temple of Busshinji Temple in São Paulo City, which, as mentioned earlier, is the *betsuin,* or the branch establishment that is the headquarters of Sōtōshū in South America.[3]

The first official wave of Japanese contract laborers settled in the sugar plantations of Hawai'i in 1885. Hawaiian authorities demanded that only one in four immigrants be female in order to maximize the number of workers for the plantations. An undesirable result of such a gender imbalance was that without family support there was a lot of violence, drinking, prostitution, and gambling in the plantations. The stark disparity in gender created a negative view of Japanese immigrants. One attempt to solve the problem was the institution of "picture brides." Japanese women were sent to Hawai'i and to America to marry immigrants. This measure had only limited success. Although the institution of *omiai* (arranged marriage) was a common practice in Japan, these "picture brides" were regarded as prostitutes in both recipient countries and the system seen as a refusal by the immigrants to assimilate into local society through intermarriage. Another attempt to alleviate the pressure in plantations was to send Buddhist *kaikyōshi* to cater to the needs of the expatriate community. Though this cultivated more of a sense of home, it also provided Hawaiians and North Americans with additional ammunition for racism as it further marked them as separate from mainstream society.[4] Buddhist priests arrived soon after the first immigrants settled in both countries: the first Jōdo Shinshū (True Pure Land) *kaikyōshi* arrived in Hawai'i in 1889 and in the United States (San Francisco) in 1898.[5] The growth of the community, too, caused problems. The anti-Asian campaigns, which previously targeted the Chinese and led to the Chinese Exclusion Act of 1882, were redirected toward the Japanese when they started arriving in large numbers. The Gentlemen's Agreement Act of 1907, which established a system of quotas, was only the first of a host of measures taken by the U.S. government to halt Japanese immigration altogether. This was successfully accomplished in 1924 with the National Origins Act.

In light of the North American experience, both causes of racism were tackled when immigration to Brazil was negotiated. On the one hand, the São Paulo government required that only family units receive subsidies to migrate. This secured stability and cohesion in the Japanese labor force. On the other, the Japanese Ministry of Foreign Affairs prohibited Japanese priests—with the exception of Japanese Catholics—from accompanying the immigrants to the new country because the Buddhist or Shintō presence could prove to be evidence of Japanese nonassimilation into the mainly Roman Catholic Brazilian culture.[6]

While Japan needed to find new recipients for her rural workers, Brazil was in dire need of plantation workers because of the boom in coffee production (1850s–1930) west of São Paulo State. This demand for a workforce was made even more acute because it took place at a time when slavery was being phased out (it was finally abolished in 1888). Brazil was not the only country sought out by the Japanese government as the intense anti-Japanese sentiment built up in the United States. Peru received the first group of contract laborers before Brazil, in 1899, but the high level of anti-Japanese sentiment there and the consequent violence associated with death by disease prompted officials to seek other ports.[7]

JAPANESE AS THE "WHITES OF ASIA": THE QUEST FOR DOUBLE ASSIMILATION

The first immigrants sought by planters and Brazilian authorities in the 1870s were of European background—Portuguese, Italians, Spanish and Germans—consistent with the bid to whiten Brazilian society.[8] However, they rebelled against the harsh conditions of work under farmers who had so recently been using slave labor. In 1902, the Italian government prohibited Italians from accepting subsidized transportation to Brazil because of complaints by unpaid workers. The short-

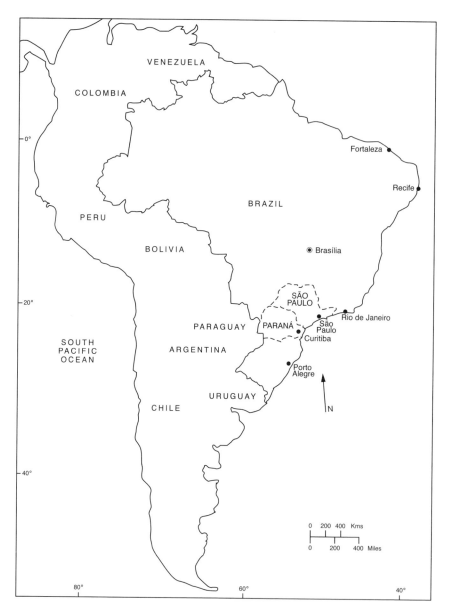

FIGURE 1

Map of Brazil with São Paulo and Paraná States highlighted. This is the area where the great majority of Japanese Brazilians live.

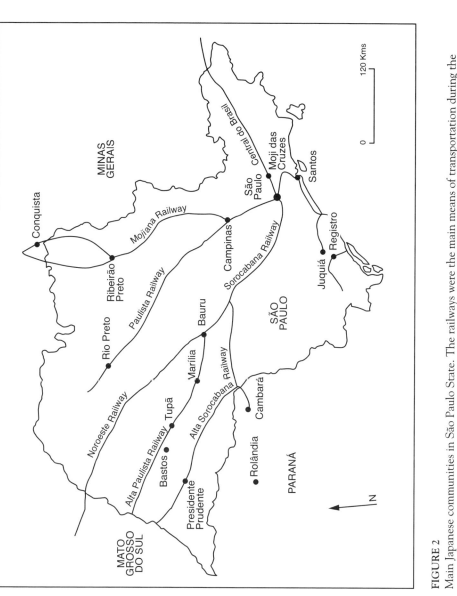

FIGURE 2

Main Japanese communities in São Paulo State. The railways were the main means of transportation during the expansion of coffee farming into the west at the beginning of the twentieth century. By the 1940s the Japanese immigrants had settled in the towns along them.

age of European immigrants, their high wages, and social activism made the Brazilian government realize that it would have to turn to other ethnic groups. In light of this situation the Meiji government acted on two fronts: internally, it demanded that emigration companies recruit only experienced farmers and ones who had no history of political activism; externally it promoted Japanese immigrants as hardworking, diligent, adaptable, quiet, and eager to assimilate.[9]

Lesser has argued that immigration played a central role in defining a Brazilian national identity and the nation's future from the 1850s onward, when the country's elites realized that slavery would be abolished in the near future.[10] The Brazilian elite, following a Lamarckian theory of eugenics that asserted the possibility of constituting a single "national race," established a hierarchy of desirable immigrants, placing Europeans at the top. For them, whitening was inextricably associated with progress and civilization. When these migrants proved to be either too expensive or a conduit for rebellions, other ethnic groups such as the Japanese, the Syrians, and the Lebanese were construed as white. In other words, although "white" continued to be a conspicuous category used to profile the Brazilian "race," what was considered white was constructed differently at diverse historical moments.[11] According to Lesser,

> Immigrants challenged the simplistic notions of race by adding a new element—ethnicity—to the mix. Of the 4.55 million immigrants who entered Brazil between 1872 and 1949 . . . it was the 400,000 Asians, Arabs and Jews, deemed both nonwhite and nonblack, who most challenged elite notions of national identity. Double assimilation was the key to creating a clear national identity: as colonists became Brazilian, Brazil would become European.[12]

Lesser's concept of "double assimilation" is crucial as it explains the complex ways in which the Japanese were regarded in Brazil. Mesmerized by the Japanese advances in medicine and science as well as by its military expansion during the Meiji period, Brazil constructed Japan as an example of a "nonwhite race," a race that had become modern (thus Western and white) overnight, a role also intensely desired for Brazil itself. Because of the prominent place Japan began to occupy in the world and because of the strong confluence of needs between Brazil and Japan—the high demand for labor in Brazil and the Japanese need to export workers—the Japanese were regarded either as non-Asians or as "the whites of Asia" and placed in a category comparable to Europeans.[13] For the Brazilian elite worried about the question of national identity, "double assimilation" meant that

the Japanese would assimilate into Brazilian culture while "leading Brazil to economic and military power by re-creating the homogeneous society believed to exist
in Japan."[14]

In this context, Japanese men were portrayed positively as industrious, intelligent, focused on the future—a far cry from the typical North American and
European discourse of the feminized, and thus easily dominated, Asian male. As a
result, while Europe and the United States regarded Asia as territories to be occupied, Brazilian elites saw Japan as a place to be emulated. In Lesser's words, "if Brazilian Orientalists sought to possess Japan, it was only so that Brazil could become
more like it."[15] This marks a major difference in the way the Japanese immigrants
were received and their presence negotiated in Brazil.

The ideology of whiteness was also strained by the reality of Japanese laborers
in Brazil. While the urban elite regarded them as an asset to the country, the rural
population did not find them as "white" as promised. Conflicts frequently emerged
in rural areas. Moreover, in the first half of the twentieth century there was also a
concerned discussion about the prospect of the "mongolization" of the "Brazilian
race." In the 1930s this fear was exacerbated by a concern that the immigrants were
still subjects of the emperor. Indeed, the fear of the "yellow peril" was so great in
Brazil during World War II that Japanese schools were closed, Japanese-language
newspapers were prohibited (there were four Japanese daily newspapers published
in São Paulo with a total circulation of around fifty thousand), and speaking Japanese in public and private (including houses of worship) was banned. The Japanese
did not prove to be as adaptable and submissive a group as marketed by the Japanese
government. They, too, protested against living conditions on the farms and left to
establish their own farms as soon as they could. Despite these difficulties, the U.S.
National Origins Act of 1924, in conjunction with the stagnating Japanese rural
economy, greatly increased Japanese immigration to Brazil. From 1908 to 1923,
Brazil received 33,266 Japanese immigrants; the next decade saw this number qua-
druple to 141,732. However, the advent of World War II sent numbers down to a
trickle.[16]

Nevertheless, the positive images produced in the first half of the twentieth
century—of Japanese people as hardworking, diligent, honest, and intelligent—
have endured in Brazilian society. It is noteworthy that in the 1980s and 1990s
Japan was constantly portrayed in the Brazilian media in the same way it had
been at the beginning of the century: the country that rose from the ashes of
World War II to become an economic superpower. Documentaries, TV commer-
cials, movies, magazine reports, and advertisements all saturated Brazil with positive images of Japan and the corollary connection between Japan and the Japanese

Brazilians. For instance, one TV commercial in the early 1990s for products made in Brazil by a Japanese company boasted, "Our Japanese are better than theirs." The commercial thus conveyed the idea that not only would the product be better than the ones made entirely in Japan, but the Japanese Brazilians who worked in the company would be superior to the Japanese, as they had acquired Brazilian traits of wit and creativity. As I will reveal in chapter 5, this resulted in the Japanese Brazilians themselves taking more pride in their ethnic background and non-Japanese Brazilians taking increasing interest in Japanese culture.[17]

TRANSNATIONAL RELIGIOUS PRACTICES

Although the Meiji government had decreed that no Buddhist or Shintō priest should travel to Brazil to proselytize, this injunction was not strictly observed. Indeed, the *Kasato Maru*—the first ship to dock in Brazil in 1908—carried a priest from the Honmon Butsuryū (a branch of the Nichiren school) who later established a temple near Lins, in São Paulo State, in 1937.[18] Scholars give slightly different dates for the arrival of Buddhist and Shintō missionaries and the establishment of temples and shrines in Brazil, but they agree that in the 1920s and 1930s Jōdo Shinshū (both the Higashi and Nishi Honganji branches), Shingon, Tenrikyō, Ōmoto, Seichō-no-Ie, and many other religious groups were established in Japanese *colônias* (communities) in rural Brazil. Official missions arrived only in the 1950s, when Japan's defeat had decreased the fears of the "yellow peril" considerably.[19]

There were other reasons for the fact that Buddhism was not actively practiced in Brazil before World War II. First, Buddhist family practice in Japan revolves mainly around funerals and ancestor worship. The eldest son traditionally inherited responsibility for taking care of the *ie* (household), worshipping ancestors, and maintaining a *butsudan* (Buddhist altar) at home, while it was the younger siblings who left the country to seek a better life elsewhere. Religious practice was not central to their lives because these immigrants were not charged with performing rituals for the ancestors. They went back to religion only at the death of family members in Brazil. Second, most of the immigrants planned to return to Japan as soon as they had amassed the necessary means. As a result, when an immigrant passed away (in most cases due to malaria) her/his soul was thought to fly back to join the *ie* in Japan.[20] As long as the Japanese immigrants thought of themselves as visitors and not permanent settlers, that is, until the Japanese defeat in World War II, the *ie* continued to be located in Japan.[21] At the time of *kyaku shi* (a visitor's death), funerals were improvised: a fellow immigrant who knew some chanting

FIGURE 3
The *Kasato Maru*, the first ship to arrive at the port of Santos in 1908 (courtesy Museu Histórico da Imigração Japonesa no Brasil).

(called then *bōzu gawari*, or priest substitutes) would be summoned and a coarse tablet would be made and placed on a table or shelf in the main bedroom, creating a makeshift *butsudan*.[22]

Another factor in the low profile of Buddhism among early immigrants was the proliferation of state Shintō at this time. The *Nippon gakkō* (Japanese schools established in rural areas) was not only a place for teaching Japanese language and culture (with material sent from Japan), but also a meeting place for the community, the headquarters of the agriculture cooperative organization, a ballroom for weddings, and a community shrine for the recitation of the Imperial Rescript on Education of 1890.[23]

A fourth factor is that conversion to Catholicism was common among Japanese immigrants in the new country. Some even converted to Catholicism in Kobe, before embarking for Brazil, in order to avoid prejudice upon arrival in the new country.[24] Most commonly, however, parents baptized their children after their arrival in Brazil. This was done so that they would not be bullied in school, as a way of associating them with influential Brazilian godparents (for instance, the farm

FIGURE 4
Celebrations at the *Nippon gakkō,* the Japanese schools in rural areas (courtesy Museu Histórico da Imigração Japonesa no Brasil).

owner) who would help them ascend socioeconomically, and finally to assimilate into Brazilian society. Kojima has pointed out in his discussion on Japanese Brazilians in Curitiba (Paraná State, southern Brazil) that all his interviewees asserted that children had to be Catholic in order to be accepted in Brazilian schools.[25] Wagley argued in 1963 that "to be Brazilian is to be a Catholic," thus converting to Catholicism strongly contributed to the "Brazilianization" of the immigrants.[26]

"BRAZILIANIZATION:" THE LAST HALF OF THE TWENTIETH CENTURY

After the Japanese defeat in World War II, conversion to Catholicism and "Brazilian ways" was emphasized since immigrants realized they could not return to their homeland. As a result, two kinds of *nisei* (second-generation Japanese Brazilians) were created. On the one hand, the eldest brother was in charge of inheriting the *ie* and family farm/business, was closely tied to Japanese values and the Japanese way of life, spoke Japanese, and accordingly followed a Japanese religion. On the other hand, the younger siblings not fluent in Japanese undertook the mission of socioeconomic ascent, as they went to university and converted to Roman Catholicism. According to a survey undertaken between 1987–1988 by the Centro de Estudos Nipo-Brasileiros (Center for Japanese-Brazilian Studies), 60 percent of the Japanese immigrants and their descendants were Roman Catholic, while only 25 percent followed Japanese religions. As for the *nisei*'s parents' religion, 3.6 percent of the first generation were Catholic while 77 percent were Buddhist. This picture changed considerably when *sansei* (third-generation Japanese Brazilians) were asked about their parents' religion: it was found that 56 percent were Catholic while only 15 percent were Buddhist.[27]

This determined effort at upward mobility through education is not without reason. Brazil's history of slavery associated manual labor with disenfranchised classes, while work demanding tertiary education was identified with the upper classes. In this context, this functional distinction among siblings paid off: by the end of the twentieth century the great majority of the Japanese were university educated and belonged to the middle classes. A survey of residents of São Paulo City in 1994 by Seade (State System Foundation for the Analysis of Data) showed that 53 percent of Japanese-Brazilian adults had a university education, against only 9 percent of São Paulo City's larger population.[28] In addition, Japanese Brazilians constituted 10 percent of all teaching staff at the elite University of São Paulo.

Regarding their middle-class status, a 1995 survey by the Datafolha organization found that 80 percent of Japanese-Brazilian families in São Paulo City (where the vast majority live) had monthly incomes ten times the legal minimum wage, which at the time was around one hundred dollars. By comparison, a 1994 Seade survey found that only 30 percent of all families living in the city had salaries that high.[29] Assimilation was also clear in the number of mixed marriages. The above-mentioned survey conducted in 1988 by the Centro de Estudos Nipo-Brasileiros found that while only 6 percent of the second generation were the offspring of mixed marriages, such was the case for 42 percent of the third generation and 61 percent of the fourth generation. It is important to underscore once more that this picture of intense assimilation must be attributed not only to immigrants' efforts, but also to the immigration policies adopted by both governments, as well as the immigrants' positive image as "white," hardworking, and modern.

Finally, the attitude of Japanese Brazilians toward Japanese religions changed in the second half of the twentieth century. Japan's defeat in World War II made most Japanese immigrants realize that they could not go back to the homeland after all. As they approached old age and became increasingly middle class and urbanized, their lifestyles entailed less hardship and secured more free time than life on the farms.[30] When the ban on Japanese religious clerics was lifted, several Buddhist and Shintoist traditions, Japanese new religions (*shin shūkyō*), and "new" new religions (*shin shinshūkyō*) sent official missionaries to Brazil to establish temples and shrines.[31]

ESTABLISHING THE SŌTŌ ZENSHŪ MISSION IN BRAZIL

In September 1955 Rōsen Takashina *zenji*, the head priest of both Eiheiji and Sōjiji, the two main Sōtōshū monasteries in Japan, traveled extensively in São Paulo and Paraná States (where most Japanese immigrants lived) for a period of three months to survey the possibility of establishing a mission. While in the country, Takashina *zenji* founded Zengenji, a temple located on a farm in Mogi das Cruzes, a town on the outskirts of São Paulo City inhabited by a large number of Japanese immigrants and descendants. Before departing he signed a document expressing his intention of setting up a *betsuin*, a temple that would be the official seat of the South American Sōtō Zenshū mission. In 1956, Ryōhan Shingū *sōkan* (superintendent-general) arrived, and Busshinji was established in São Paulo City. These two temples, along with a temple in Rolândia (in the state of Paraná) established in 1958, have catered to the Japanese-Brazilian Sōtōshū community ever since. In 1974, Hakuunzan Zenkoji, or, as it is known in Portuguese, Mosteiro Morro da Vargem, was established in Ibiraçu (Espírito Santo State), this time to cater to non-Japanese Brazilians. Contrasting with the numerous Zen centers around the country that do not belong to Sōtōshū, this temple is also considered part of the Sōtōshū mission because the abbot—Christiano Daiju Bitti, a non-Japanese Brazilian who trained in Japan—maintains close ties with the school.

Since most immigrants were originally from Hiroshima, Fukuoka, Kumamoto, and Okinawa, sites of strong Jōdo Shinshū (True Pure Land) and Jōdoshū (Pure Land) adherence, the Sōtōshū congregation was a small one, comprising six hundred families. Since the establishment of Sōtōshū in Brazil in 1955, it has dwindled to around three hundred because of the difficulties of keeping second, third, and fourth generations as members.[32] In contrast, Jōdo Shinshū (Higashi Honganji) had five thousand families in 1990.[33] In 2001, I was told by Nichirenshū that its congregation was composed of five thousand families, while Shingonshū set its number at seven hundred families.[34] The same disparity takes place in the number of temples: while Sōtōshū has only four temples in Brazil and one (not active) in Peru, Nishi Honganji has thirty-seven temples and twenty-two *asso-*

FIGURE 5
Busshinji Temple in São Paulo City.

ciações (associations are centers with no resident priest), Higashi Honganji has eighteen temples and eight *associações*, Honmon Butsuryushū has eleven temples, Nichirenshū and Shingonshū each have four temples, and finally Jōdoshū has three temples in Brazil.

Like Sōtōshū, these Buddhist traditions sent missionaries to Brazil in the early 1950s to seek families who were members of their denomination prior to their migration to the country. In 1958, as part of the celebrations of the fiftieth anniversary of Japanese immigration, these Buddhist schools were united in the Federação das Seitas Budistas do Brasil (Federation of the Buddhist Sects of Brazil). Since then the federation has been in charge of the celebrations of the arrival of the first immigrants, Buddhist festivities, as well as visiting nursing homes run by the Japanese community, and collecting food and clothes to be donated to the homeless. The most visible of these activities is *hanamatsuri* (Buddha's birthday), as it

FIGURE 6

Hanamatsuri celebrations in São Paulo City. Coen *sensei* to the left of the elephant, and Yomei Sasaki, the head of Jōdoshū in Brazil, to her left.

involves a procession of finely robed priests and Japanese children in the streets of Liberdade (Japan Town in São Paulo City). Indeed, in the last decade *hana-matsuri* has become a beacon for media coverage and for non-Japanese Brazilians interested in Japan and Buddhism.

From the time of his arrival, Ryōhan Shingū, the *sōkan* in charge of Busshinji Temple and the mission in South America from 1956–1986, did not work alone. He was assisted in São Paulo City as well as in Japanese communities west of the state by *shudōshi* (local monks), chosen from among the previously mentioned *bōzu gawari*, and retired immigrants who knew the community well and had free time to dedicate to religion. These immigrants would form a group (*shudōshi ko-shukai*) around the official Japanese missionaries (*kaikyōshi*) who were sent from Japan usually for periods of four years. It is noteworthy that these *kaikyōshi* rotated among the overseas missions so that either before or after their term in Brazil they were assigned to Hawai'i, Los Angeles, and San Francisco. Accordingly, the mission in Brazil was not isolated from international trends, for these *kaikyōshi* became "carriers" of ideas, techniques, and experiences of proselytization among overseas communities.

MODERN BUDDHISM: CONSTRUCTING THE WESTERN DISCOURSE ON ZEN

These continuous flows of Buddhist practices carried by *kaikyōshi* often contrasted with ideas non-Japanese Brazilians were receiving from the North American Zen boom of the late 1950s and 1960s. The appropriation and construction of Zen, which took place in many Western countries, had a similar departure point. D. T. Suzuki (1870–1966) and the Kyōto school scholars, particularly its founder and Suzuki's friend, Nishida Kitarō (1870–1945), were fundamental to the creation of a Zen discourse in Japan and in the West. Recently this discourse, its creators, and their association with Japanese nationalism have received strong critiques from Western scholars such as Bernard Faure, Donald Lopez, James Heisig, John Maraldo, and Robert Sharf.[35] A brief overview of this Zen discourse will give some pointers that will be useful in the analysis of the disjunction of practices and beliefs between, on the one hand, *kaikyōshi* catering to the Japanese-Brazilian community and, on the other hand, *kaikyōshi* catering to (mostly) non-Japanese Brazilians. The Western Zen discourse carried into Brazil by *kaikyōshi*, intellectuals, and lately the media has become pervasive.

Sharf has observed that Suzuki and the Kyōto-school scholars were "internationally minded intellectuals," fascinated with Western culture while at the same time anxious about its universalizing discourse.[36] Attempting to create a response to what Hall referred to as "the West and the Rest" discourse discussed in the introduction, these university-educated intellectuals "appropriated key concepts from the West, while at the same time appearing to challenge the cultural hegemony of Western modes of thought."[37] Furthermore, these purveyors of Zen were writing in the milieu of the so-called Shin Bukkyō (Nationalistic Buddhism), a movement also developed in response to the Western secular critique of religion. In order to secure Buddhism a meaningful place in Japanese modern society, Shin Bukkyō intellectuals deployed European ideas of anticlericalism and antiritualism of the Reformation and the rationalism and empiricism of the Enlightenment to reconstruct Buddhism as "'modern,' 'cosmopolitan,' 'humanistic,' 'socially responsible,' a 'world religion' [that was] empirical, rational and in full accord with modern science."[38]

Influenced by Shin Bukkyō and by the contemporary discourses of Japanese uniqueness, Suzuki and the Kyōto-school intellectuals recreated Zen as the very essence of Japanese national identity, which would denote the cultural superiority of Japan over the West. According to this discourse, because Zen was constructed not as a religion, with its rituals and doctrine, but as an individual spiritual experience, which would lead to "an uncompromisingly empirical, rational and scientific mode of inquiry into the nature of things," Zen was able to live through the enlightenment trends coming from the West.[39] By identifying this spiritual experience with a "timeless," "pure," and "invariable" Zen "essence," and differentiating it from its cultural expressions (regarded as degenerate, "impure" accretions), these Zen advocates were able to regard it as transcultural and universal. Zen would not be associated with any particular religion, philosophy, or metaphysics, but would be "the spirit of all religion and philosophy."[40] Given that Suzuki and other intellectuals who popularized Zen in the West were not part of institutional Zen sects and lacked formal transmission in a Zen lineage, it is not surprising that they advocated "authentic" Zen as an individual, lay experience that did not require an association with institutional tradition. Indeed, this discourse was so influential that two of the *kaikyōshi* whose lives will be presented here severed their association with Sōtōshū while pursuing "authentic" Zen.

Faure refers to this Zen discourse as "Orientalism 'by excess,' a 'secondary' Orientalism, [one] that offers an idealized, 'nativist' image of a Japanese culture deeply influenced by Zen."[41] One could also think of a "reverse Orientalism," where Japanese scholars created a discourse of resistance, appropriating categories that the West deployed to classify them and then inverting the trend. Indeed, not only did they use the same essentialized categories to refer to themselves (the Oriental vis-à-vis the Occidental), but they also asserted that the Oriental (meaning Japanese) traits were superior to Occidental ones. In sum, by making Zen rational and in accordance with modern science, and thus superior to superstitious Christianity, while at the same time fashioning Japanese culture as embedded in Zen, Japan would have a superior zeitgeist if compared to the West.

Lopez has taken a step forward in his critique by linking this Japanese Buddhist response with responses of other Asian Buddhist societies in the late nineteenth and throughout the twentieth centuries. For Lopez, the encounter of these traditional Asian Buddhist societies with modernity—mostly through a colonial situation—prompted the invention of a Buddhist tradition that would ensure its survival against the Western secular challenge. Lopez called this newly created pan-Asian and Western tradition "modern Buddhism," for "it shared many characteristics of other projects of modernity."[42] These characteristics were mentioned before, but he adds some new features worth alluding to, as they will help us better understand the kind of Buddhism preached by *kaikyōshi* working with non-

Japanese-Brazilian adherents. First, modern Buddhism regards the recent past and contemporary practices as a degeneration and seeks a return to the "authentic," "original" Buddhism of the Buddha, which is the Buddha's enlightenment experience, hence the central role played by meditation in modern Buddhism.[43] Second, Lopez argues that modern Buddhism is a sect, with its own doctrines, lineage, practices, and sacred scriptures. Unlike the traditional master-to-disciple personal transmission confined to a single school, this sect transcends cultural and national boundaries, since its leaders and followers are intellectual cosmopolitans who are in contact with other Buddhist traditions. They seek to create an international Buddhism whose essence would be identical once the "cultural accretions" are removed.[44] Third, the distinction between monks and laity is blurred, with lay followers taking up traditional monks' practices of study of scriptures and meditation.[45] Finally, the leaders of modern Buddhism were marginal figures in their own countries. As we will see in this chapter, *kaikyōshi* catering mostly to non-Japanese Brazilians embody all these traits. They regard *zazen* as a central Zen practice, whereas they are marginal in their own country, they are highly influential in Brazil, they are in contact with other Buddhist traditions in the country and overseas, they believe there is an identical essence in all Buddhist practices ("the only difference is the color of the robes," says Tokuda *sensei*), and finally their followers are neither completely laypeople nor monks.

In the following section I will briefly shift the focus to Sōtōshū's historical choices over the role played by *zazen*, family temples, and monasteries so that I can clearly portray the two kinds of *kaikyōshi* sent to Brazil. I contend that the negotiations and conflicts between traditional Zen *kaikyōshi* vis-à-vis modern Zen *kaikyōshi* mirrored those between Japanese-Brazilian and non-Japanese-Brazilian congregations.[46] In very broad lines, there have been two definitions of Zen Buddhism in Brazil, both sides claiming to practice "authentic" and "true" Zen Buddhism. While some *kaikyōshi* and the Japanese-Brazilian congregation have asserted that Zen comprises devotional practices, worship of ancestors, and funeral rituals, other *kaikyōshi* and non-Japanese-Brazilian practitioners influenced by modern Zen have claimed that Zen relies mainly on *zazen* in order to experience enlightenment.[47] Nevertheless, in chapter 5 I will show that this division is a superficial picture of Zen in Brazil. A more detailed approach reveals a blurred area where Japanese Brazilians, who have been Catholic for many generations, have become interested in Zen through *zazen*, while some non-Japanese Brazilians have developed a devotional attitude toward Zen. For my purposes here, however, I will keep the bigger picture of division so that I can illuminate Sōtōshū's and consequently the *kaikyōshi's* approach to Zen as well as the influence modern Zen had on some *kaikyōshi*, which in time generated bitter conflicts between the two congregations in Brazil. I argue that the experiences of the missionaries in Brazil and the sides they have taken in the conflicts have been profoundly shaped by these opposing attitudes toward *zazen*.

SŌTŌSHŪ'S HISTORICAL CHOICES

Much before conflicts erupted in Western countries between traditional under-standings of Zen (classically associated with the Japanese community) and modern ones (associated mostly with the non-Japanese community), Sōtōshū itself had a history of a dualistic attitude toward *zazen*. Reader has argued in his now classical works, "Transformations and Changes in the Teachings of the Sōtō Zen Buddhist Sect" and "Zazenless Zen? The Position of Zazen in Institutional Zen Buddhism," that while asserting that *zazen* is at the core and is the essence of the teachings of Dōgen (1200–1253), very few Sōtōshū priests actually practice it. According to Reader, the belief that *zazen* was a hindrance to the popularization of the sect has made patriarchs and the institution alike opt throughout the sect's history for a functional relationship with the congregation rather than an emphasis on monastic Zen practices. After Dōgen's death, his successors realized that in order to expand, the sect would have to incorporate more popular customs and practices such as funeral services and memorial rituals. This move has paid off: from the fourteenth and fifteenth centuries onward the Sōtō sect has expanded greatly and today is the largest Zen Buddhist denomination in Japan. Since 1872, Japanese priests have been allowed to marry, eat meat, and have free choice of tonsure. As a result, temples have become hereditary, with the firstborn son expected to succeed his father.[48] Current statistics show that the choice of the temple-household sys-tem over Dōgen's monasticism has prevailed greatly. In 1996, Bodiford pointed to more than 90 percent of Sōtōshū's priests being married and managing Zen temples as a hereditary family business, entailing the existence of over fifteen thousand family-run temples and only thirty-one monasteries in Japan.[49]

These statistics beg the question of whether this ambivalence toward *zazen* would be a predicament had Sōtōshū not expanded to the West. Participating in the Japanese religious arena as a supplier of funerary and memorial rites, like any other Japanese Buddhist school, made Sōtōshū the largest Zen sect in Japan, and no apparent dilemma ensued. However, once it confronted this modern Zen dis-course constructed for and in the West, Sōtōshū found itself in a predicament. Therefore, one has to keep in mind that it is this difference between Japanese practices and beliefs and Western expectations that creates the predicament I am discussing here.

ZAZEN OR NOT *ZAZEN?* THE PREDICAMENT OF SŌTŌSHŪ'S MISSIONARIES IN BRAZIL

Naturally, when Sōtōshū sent *kaikyōshi* overseas no open conflict was expected, since *kaikyōshi* were sent to continue the temple-household system and cater to the Japanese community. Nevertheless, upon arriving in Western countries these *kaikyōshi* encountered a demand for monastic Zen and *zazen* by non-Japanese followers, which grew stronger over the years. This generated acute conflict concerning the authenticity of Zen practices and evinced Sōtōshū's own dualistic discourse toward the authenticity and legitimacy of its practices. In an interview I conducted, a representative of Sōtōshū Shūmuchō (the headquarters of the Sōtō sect in Tokyo) expressed concern over the sect's difficulties in managing conflicts over authenticity in the United States and Brazil, where there is a large number of Japanese immigrants, as opposed to the lack of problems in Europe, where there has been only a small Japanese diaspora.

Sōtōshū has sent a total of thirteen missionaries since it began its missionary activities in Brazil in 1955. These missionaries were for the most part recent graduates of Komazawa University (the Sōtōshū university in Tokyo) and were sent overseas for three to five years to acquire experience. Most of them were part of the temple-household system and went to Brazil to assist immigrants in times of death by performing funerary rituals and ancestor worship. Here I will not give a detailed history of all these missionaries, but I have chosen some who are emblematic of Sōtōshū's predicament and who are still connected in some way or another to Brazil.

A good example of this kind of *kaikyōshi* is Zendō Matsunaga. Matsunaga was sent to Brazil in 1959, where he lived until he was transferred in 1964 to Zenshūji, on the island of Kaua'i, in Hawai'i.[50] Upon arriving at Busshinji in São Paulo City to assist Ryōhan Shingū *sōkan*, he was soon sent to the west of the state, where most immigrants were. Matsunaga established himself in the town of Pompéia but would visit all the other towns built along the Sorocabana Railroad. The train lines had been the main means of transportation during the expansion of coffee farming into the west at the beginning of the twentieth century, and by the 1940s the Japanese immigrants had settled in the towns along them. Matsunaga was soon to realize that the Zenshū *dankasan* (Zen congregation) was small and therefore

FIGURE 7
Matsunaga *rōshi*, Tokyo, 2005.

the Sōtō congregation celebrated Buddhist rituals such as *o-bon* (Memorial Day) and *hanamatsuri* (Buddha's birthday) together with other Japanese Buddhist denominations. Moreover, the Japanese community had already adopted Brazilian religious rituals—they also celebrated the Catholic All Souls Day (November 2), for, as I mentioned earlier, many Japanese had converted to Catholicism in an attempt to be accepted in the country.

Sōtōshū sent *kaikyōshi* to Brazil, but this did not mean Sōtōshū paid them a salary while in the mission. Matsunaga, like other *kaikyōshi* sent overseas, had to find the means to support himself amongst his congregation, which in this case was composed mainly of small farmers and merchants. Matsunaga smiled when he told me in an interview how the *dankasan* would give him proper clothes to wear, food, and treats. In fact, he commented that the congregation knew his Buddhist apparel would be reason for frowns and possible discrimination against him in a strictly Catholic country. His black robes and shaved head were before long changed to a white linen suit and a white Panama hat donated by the congregation. But that was not enough. In the beginning, the congregation still did not feel comfortable with his shaved head—Matsunaga had to let his hair grow. He told me the same situation happened when he moved to Hawai'i. This illustrates how *kaikyōshi* embodied the process of negotiation and hybridization that occurred when Zen Buddhism encountered other cultures. The classes Matsunaga taught at the *kaikan* (the community hall) of each town provided another source of income. Matsunaga reminisced,

> I would stay in Pompéia for one-third of the month and then travel around to Marília, Lucélia and Tupã or go to São Paulo city to report to the *sōkan*. Gradually my acquaintance increased and they asked me to stay longer in Pompéia. The number of students in my Japanese language class, *ikebana* (flower arrangement), *odori* (dance), and *chanoyu* (tea ceremony) also increased and I was giving two or three classes a month. Once a year we had a flower arrangement exhibition. I taught Japanese language for children as their parents had a hard time trying to understand what the children were saying because they learned Portuguese in regular school. Finally, on Sundays I had a Buddhist service for children in the morning and one for the adults in the afternoon. With all these classes, some of the Japanese who had converted to Catholicism started coming too![51]

It is clear from his memories that expanding Sōtōshū in Brazil in the late 1950s and early 1960s meant allowing for nonsectarianism and giving the immigrants a space to perform and learn about their ethnic identity. The *kaikan* and *kaikyōshi* alike functioned as solid pillars of their culture and as embodiments of their homeland. As a result, even Japanese converts to Catholicism took up the activities carried by the Sōtōshū *kaikyōshi*, and their presence was, in turn, readily accepted because of their ethnicity. It is noteworthy that since its establishment, Busshinji, like so many other Japanese Buddhist temples outside Japan, has also served as a cultural center where missionaries teach Japanese language, arts, and crafts such as *ikebana* and pottery as a way of maintaining community ties.[52]

KAIKYŌSHI WORKING WITH NON-JAPANESE BRAZILIANS

After Matsunaga left for Hawai'i, new missionaries continued to be sent by Sōtō-shū to cater to the Japanese community. In 1968, Sōtōshū sent Ryōtan Tokuda (aka

FIGURE 8
Tokuda *sensei* in Nagoya, 2000.

Kyūji Igarashi) to work at Busshinji Temple in São Paulo City. There he would be-come a teacher for the immigrants' children at the Mahayana Elementary School, situated on the temple grounds, and assist in the temple's administration.

Tokuda was a different kind of *kaikyōshi* altogether. Not belonging to a temple family, he became a Sōtō Zen monk due to a calling, not an obligation to in-herit his father's temple. He had been in the Japanese army, but after a while had deep doubts about it. He tried to find answers in religion and read many books on Christianity, Buddhism, and Zen Buddhism. In 1958, while reading books by D. T. Suzuki (whose completed works he collected thereafter) and particularly Eugen Herrigel's *Zen in the Art of Archery* (in Japanese),[53] he decided Zen Buddhism was the way to go. After having what he called "spiritual experiences," where he felt the clear calling for monkhood, Tokuda did his first *sesshin* (retreat) at Ryūtakuji, a temple of the Rinzai sect. This is not surprising since Suzuki advocated the Rin-zai tradition. However, when Tokuda decided to enter Komazawa University, he found his interests very different from his colleagues.

In the first year of the university, I had the need to practice *zazen*. At Komazawa there is *zazen*, but the first year students don't need to do it. I wanted to sit, but many colleagues who were monks didn't understand that. They used to say to me: "Next year you'll have to sit, why sit now?"[54]

This incident reveals the influence Suzuki and modern Zen had not only in the West, but in Japan as well. Evidence of such influence is Tokuda's expectation that *zazen* would play a central role in Sōtōshū's educational system, as it does in the Western Zen practice. He further told me that in 1968, when the opportunity came to go to Brazil, he knew he wanted to stay in Brazil as long as possible, learn Portuguese, and "sit with Brazilians." Paramount to this decision was the fact that he was, as mentioned earlier, on the fringe of his own sect since he did not belong to a temple family, and that his first contact with Zen happened through the literature produced for a Western audience in which the issues of meditation and enlightenment were more highly regarded than ceremonial practices. Moreover, Suzuki's influence ran deeper: Tokuda was also fascinated by early Christian mystics, for he understood the ecstatic state mentioned by Saint John of the Cross and Maister Eckhart as the experience of enlightenment in Zen. Tokuda saw no difference between West and East concerning this state of ecstasy and regarded the Christian experience of union with God as the same as *satori* (enlightenment). Indeed, Tokuda wrote,

As Saint John of the Cross said: the night of senses, the night of spirit, the night of soul. Through this internal voyage, we leave the exterior world and begin to work with our inner world, diving into our subconscious. When we get to the bottom of this darkness, there is a union with God, with Love. To this experience, Zen gives the name enlightenment, or *satori*.[55]

Tokuda's interpretation seems to derive directly from Suzuki's bid to equate Zen and Christian mysticism to respond to the challenge of Christian/Western discursive superiority. For Suzuki, because Zen was free from religious, cultural, and philosophical traditions, Buddhists and Christians alike could practice it. Indeed, Suzuki asserts, "Eckhart, [and] Zen . . . can be grouped together as belonging to the great school of mysticism" and "I am sure Eckhart had a *satori*."[56]

Tokuda's bridging of Catholic and Buddhist beliefs undoubtedly allowed him to be readily accepted by non-Japanese Brazilians who already had a *zazenkai* (sitting group) at Busshinji Temple. After four years of difficulties in Busshinji because of his views, Tokuda decided to leave the temple but to stay in Brazil leading his group of Brazilian followers. Soon afterward, he had to leave Sōtōshū also, as his making a living as a shiatsu, acupuncture, and herbal practitioner was not readily accepted by the Sōtō headquarters in Tokyo. However, he continued to be very active in spreading Zen in the country. In the past thirty years Tokuda has established more than fifteen centers and ordained more than thirty people; four of them have trained in main Sōtō monasteries in Japan such as Zuiōji and Eiheiji. Tokuda left Brazil for France in the 1990s but continued to return to Brazil for a period of three months every year to oversee his Zen centers and ordain new disciples. In 2002 he decided to move back to Brazil to establish a monastery.

Keeping in mind Lopez's description of the modern Buddhist leader, Tokuda certainly fits this category. His marginality in Japan contrasted with his importance in Brazil, his conviction that Zen is the essence of all religious experience, be it Eastern or Western, his frequent associations between Zen and Christianity, his lack of monastic training, his belief that Zen had degenerated in Japan (voiced frequently by him and his disciples), his cosmopolitanism (working in France, Brazil, and Argentina), and finally his placing meditation as a central practice all make him a prototype of a modern Zen monk. Furthermore, Tokuda's Japanese identity and association with institutional Zen (even if he calls it degenerate) has given an aura of "authenticity" to his Zen discourse, which in turn made him a prominent figure in Brazilian Zen circles.

As a last point of comparison between how institutional/traditional and modern *kaikyōshi* related to their followers, it is noteworthy that while Matsunaga made a living teaching Japanese arts and language to the Japanese community, Tokuda offered alternative medicine to his non-Japanese-Brazilian audience. In Brazil, alternative medicine is frequently associated with the "ancient wisdom of the East," as is Zen Buddhism, hence a Zen priest connected with acupuncture and Chinese herbs did not raise any eyebrows; quite the contrary, it fulfilled his followers' expectations.

A NEW *SŌKAN* ARRIVES: OPEN CONFLICT

After many years without a *sōkan* for South America, Sōtōshū finally sent Daigyō Moriyama *rōshi* to Busshinji Temple in 1993. Between 1970 and 1973, Moriyama had been the abbot of Sōkōji, the Sōtōshū temple in San Francisco. There he substituted for Shunryū Suzuki *rōshi* (1904–1971), a *kaikyōshi* forced to resign from his post as abbot because his activities with his non-Japanese-American students were not accepted by the Japanese community. Although Moriyama worked in the temple and Suzuki was managing his newly established San Francisco Zen Center, they maintained close contact. When interviewed, Moriyama *rōshi* told me he shared Suzuki's ideas of foreigners having "a beginner's mind" (*shoshin*), that is, "one which is empty and ready for new things."[57] This is how Moriyama put his discontent with Japanese Zen and his hopes for Brazil.

> In Japan, monks are more interested in social practices and money to be received for services rendered to the community, such as funerals and worship of ancestors, than spiritual work. That is why I put my energy in a foreign country; here [in Brazil] Zen Buddhism *can be created again in a purer way.* . . . Traditional Buddhist countries are losing the essence of Buddhism; I think religions are created, evolve and degrade, and this is happening in Japan now. I feel that here the same thing that I witnessed in California is taking place: in Brazil there is a kind of energy that I don't find in Japan.[58]

This resembles the words of Shunryū Suzuki *rōshi*: "I came to America to bring the *pure way* of Zen Buddhism."[59] Moriyama's words were translated into actions, and after three years working as *sōkan* at Busshinji, he underwent the same problem Suzuki had at Sōkōji in 1969. The Japanese congregation was not happy with his preference for monastic Zen practices and non-Japanese Brazilians and pressed Sōtōshū to dismiss him. As mission temples belong to the congregation rather than to the priest, as is the norm in Japan, the congregation had the right to do so. In 1995, Moriyama *rōshi* was ousted from the temple and from his post at Sōtōshū. He welcomed the change and took his non-Japanese-Brazilian students with him, establishing three new Zen groups, one in São Paulo City, another in Campinas (a major city of São Paulo State), and another in Porto Alegre (the capital of Rio Grande do Sul State). Today he lives in Porto Alegre and, together with his *sangha*, is building a monastery in the countryside. Although he lives in Brazil, his international connections are strong: his oldest disciple runs a Zen center in France, he travels often to Argentina and Uruguay to oversee other groups of students, and he has a German disciple assisting him in Brazil.

Like Tokuda, Moriyama markedly subscribes to the modern/Western Zen discourse. His evocation of a "pure," "authentic," "original" Zen, which is to be found in the Buddha's and Dōgen's enlightenment experience and which is lost in Japan, is all too familiar. In addition, his disciples, like other Western Zen followers, blur the boundaries between laity and monkhood since he places *zazen* and *sesshin* at the core of Zen. Finally, if we accept Lopez's vision of modern Bud-

FIGURE 9
Moriyama *rōshi* and followers in a retreat in Porto Alegre (Rio Grande do Sul State).

dhism having its own lineage, doctrine, and practices, we could say that although Shunryū Suzuki did not give transmission to Moriyama, Suzuki was surely a strong influence in his thought. By giving teachings and transmission in Brazil and overseas and having close contact with other non-Japanese Buddhist schools in Porto Alegre City, Moriyama is producing his own lineage of modern/Western Zen.

THE SUBSTITUTE: A NON-JAPANESE-BRAZILIAN WOMAN

Ironically, Moriyama *rōshi*'s successor and newly appointed abbess was a married, non-Japanese-Brazilian nun. Claudia Dias de Souza Batista was ordained in Los Angeles under Taizan Maezumi *rōshi* (d. 1995) in 1983, when she received the Buddhist name of Koen/Coen. In the same year, she left for Japan, where she spent the next twelve years, eight of them at Aichi Senmon Nisōdō in Nagoya.[60] Coen took the position of abbess at Busshinji in 1995, a post she was able to hold until January 2001.

Although she experienced many obstacles—including her ethnic background, gender, and marital status—she slowly gained the respect of the community. Soon after her arrival at Busshinji, she began enforcing all of the activities more strictly than they had been before, and at the same time worked hard at preserving the rituals that the Japanese community expected to be performed. Looking back, one non-Japanese-Brazilian practitioner observed,

> When Moriyama was in charge of the temple, he tried to adapt Japanese Zen to Brazilian culture. It was more flexible. With Coen, as she had recently arrived from Japan, she tried to maintain the patterns and rules by which she had lived there. She tried to establish the rhythm, behavior and discipline of the Japanese practice.[61]

I suggest that because Moriyama was an "authentic" Japanese and a male, he did not have to prove himself worthy of his position at the temple; he even made a point of not fitting their expectations. For instance, he told me in an interview in São Paulo in December 2000 that the congregation expected him to be dressed in fine brocade, but he more often than not wore monk's working clothes and carried a backpack around. On the other hand, Coen had to work at being accepted by the Japanese-Brazilian community. That included being sometimes more Japanese than the Japanese themselves, that is, being strict, respecting the congregation's expectations, and speaking Japanese fluently. In an interview conducted in March 2000, when she was still the head of Busshinji, Coen told me,

> At first, when I was officiating rituals here in Busshinji they would comment: "*gaijin, gaijin*" [foreigner, foreigner], but when I started speaking Japanese and talking about Buddhism, their attitude changed. I guess the apparent discrimination against *gaijin* is because they are not sure if we know their way of life, culture, tradition, and so on. Slowly people would start saying to me: "so and so are *gaijin*, aren't they, *sensei?*" They even felt a bit embarrassed because I lived in Japan for twelve years and some of them didn't even know how to read Japanese. Some arrived in Brazil really young and felt I knew more of their culture or was more Japanese than them. Nowadays many come to me and say they want me to officiate at the mass [*sic*],[62] it is pretty embarrassing sometimes. There are other monks and they choose me. They say: "we want you and we want you to speak Portuguese after you speak in Japanese."

Indeed, by speaking Japanese and Portuguese fluently, she was a successful intermediary among the Japanese, Japanese-Brazilian, and non-Japanese-Brazilian communities. Furthermore, it was her competence in both Japanese and Brazilian cultures that prompted Sōtōshū Shūmuchō to send her to Brazil as a missionary because the new generations did not speak Japanese and felt alienated from the temple, which as I noted earlier made the number of members fall dramatically. This proved to be the right policy since many young Japanese Brazilians would come to Busshinji to a grandparent's funeral and upon listening to her preaching in Portuguese would feel a connection with Buddhism.

Although Coen's language skills and attitude helped her to become accepted, her gender was a difficult obstacle. Buddhism has had a long history of discrimination against women, and that was no different in Japan.[63] Until the Meiji era, the head temples refused admission to women. When monks and nuns were allowed to marry and choose tonsure (1872 and 1873, respectively), monks were able to adopt the new behavior, while nuns who married and did not shave their heads were not considered nuns by society. Because women are still expected to take care of the family in the first place, those who married were "naturally" expected to abandon nunhood.[64] As a result, while married monks make up the vast majority of Japanese monks, as I mentioned earlier, nuns have maintained an ascetic life. However, since one of the features of modern Buddhism is precisely the active and visible role of women as ordained nuns and teachers, Coen was readily accepted by the non-Japanese-Brazilian congregation. If Coen's gender was problematic to the Japanese-Brazilian congregation, her status as a married woman should surely make things worse. Yet since her husband was a Japanese monk, things were a bit easier, as he actually circumvented this gender status issue by reminding the community through his behavior toward her that he was, in fact, hierarchically under her (due to his fewer years of training). Consequently, he helped her to be regarded as worthy of the position she held in the temple. But things were not easy at first. According to Coen,

> At first the congregation thought a woman officiating ceremonies as strange; they thought only men could do it. There were commentaries such as, "this is a big temple; it is not a nun's temple." This is the kind of discrimination nuns suffered in Japan; only small temples were given to nuns. Nowadays, nuns do everything monks do in Japan. Of course in practice things are a bit different, since it is a society that is not totally egalitarian. But there is a strong movement against discrimination in Japan and particularly at Sōtōshū. But the Japanese community here still sees things as Japanese people did before World War II. Information does not reach here. I was the first non-Japanese and the first woman to become president of

the Federation of the Buddhist Sects of Brazil. This was a way to be accepted in the Japanese community, because by accepting me the monks from other schools were saying that I had a high level of understanding of Buddhism.[65]

But Coen did not stop at asserting her own status. Upon arriving at the temple she realized there were some Japanese-Brazilian nuns who had never been allowed to officiate ceremonies and had been confined to ringing the bells, making tea, arranging flowers, and participating in the *baika* (a women's group that chants and plays bells during rituals). She told me these women were too old to learn how to officiate ceremonies, but nonetheless Coen asked them to participate by bringing incense, chanting, and playing the drums, and allowed them to wear *okesa*, the formal robes, which they owned but were not authorized to wear. Asserting the position of nuns in the temple was not the only thing that may have brought discontent and her final downfall in the beginning of 2001. She also told me,

> Women didn't vote here! The *fujinkai* [women's association] was forbidden to vote until 1998, when the new board was due to be elected. In 1998, on the election day the president got together with the board and reaffirmed *fujinkai* didn't vote. Then I realized the women had never voted in the temple! So I checked the bylaws and there was nothing there about it — so on that election day I said that everyone would vote. The women didn't even think that was good, they were worried and didn't know what to do. We won that election and for the first time in the history of the temple the old board lost. Even Brazilians started to vote. Only people who paid a yearly fee voted, but no one ever asked the Brazilians to pay it, so they didn't know about it. The old board was offended and went to Japan to say they should send somebody here to substitute for us because it was dangerous to leave the temple in our hands. And in reality the temple was doing really well, the number of adherents was increasing; there were more masses [sic], more people for lectures, study groups, and *zazen*.

The story with which I chose to open this chapter depicts the tense moment in March 2000 when the new *sōkan* had arrived for a first visit to oversee the election. For the next ten months the presence of both the *sōkan* and Coen in the temple — respectively as the superintendent for South America and as Busshinji's abbess — exacerbated the conflict to the point that the situation became untenable. To make matters worse, the rift reached the Japanese immigrant press and

FIGURE 10
Coen *sensei*.

even the mainstream press, as Coen was well known by the Brazilian media. She
was dismissed in January 2001. Like all the previous missionaries who lost their
positions, she took her students with her when she left. However, unlike others,
Coen established a new temple (Tenzui Zen Dōjō), not a Zen center in São Paulo
City. Some Japanese-Brazilian families also followed her to the new temple.

    Tenzui Zen Dōjō is a good example of how Zen has become creolized in Bra-
zil, that is, how the boundaries between traditional and modern/Western Zen are
blurred. Coen managed to interest non-Japanese Brazilians and (like them, sometimes nominally Catholic) Japanese Brazilians in "Japanese" rituals—such as funerals, memorial rites, *higan*, and *o-bon*. She also engaged them in "Westerners'
Zen" practices such as *zazen* and *sesshin* and in "Catholic" activities such as All
Souls Day and weddings. Coen is presently in charge of another center in Rio de
Janeiro that is managed on a daily basis by a non-Japanese-Brazilian student of hers
and hence dedicated solely to meditation. She also participates in interreligious
meetings, gives public lectures, has established a sitting group at the São Paulo City

Assembly of Councils, and leads very visible walking meditations in the city's public parks on Sunday mornings. Her charisma has led her to be frequently sought after by the media so that she is now routinely recognized in the streets of São Paulo.

RECOUPMENT: REGAINING CONTROL OF THE TEMPLE

While studying the arrival of Buddhism in Germany, Baumann deployed the term "recoupment" as one of five modes for transplanting a religion to a new sociocultural context.[66] They include contact, confrontation and conflict, ambiguity and alignment, recoupment (reorientation), and innovative self-development. Baumann explains that the process of transplanting a particular religion does not need to cover all these modes and need not necessarily occur in this sequence. "Recoupment," or reorientation, is a critique of the ambiguities that have arisen due to the need to blur the boundaries between the new religion and the host culture. Once accepted, the foreign religion then tries to reduce the ambiguities in order to regain its traditional identity.

I contend that Kōichi Miyoshi, the new *sōkan*, is part of such a process of "recoupment." If charisma and smooth transit among non-Japanese Brazilians and mainstream media are the qualities that brought Coen to the limelight, the new *sōkan* sent by Sōtōshū, had the opposite task—to keep a low profile and, in the process, hand Busshinji back to the old and traditional Japanese-Brazilian board, who in fact established and has always funded the temple through *dāna* (donations). For a start, although he had been in Hawai'i for thirty-three years (first as a *kaikyōshi* at Shobōji and then as the abbot of Zenshūji), Miyoshi never learned to speak English. Therefore, communication at Busshinji has been restored to the way it was during Shingū *rōshi*'s time (1956–1983)—most activities are solely in Japanese. When they are directed to a mainly non-Japanese-Brazilian audience, Japanese-Brazilian monks function as translators. Since Miyoshi's installation, because of the Buddhist boom of the late 1990s, new non-Japanese-Brazilian adherents have arrived and constituted a new *zazen* group, taking part in *sesshin* and *jukai* (lay ordinations). Miyoshi's lack of language skills is not an obstacle because non-Japanese Brazilians at the temple justify the situation by invoking the Zen belief that communication with a master should be a matter of *ishin-denshin* (heart/mind-to-heart/mind transmission).[67]

However, when I sat through a *hōji* (memorial) rite in 2001, Miyoshi preached in Japanese, and no translation was offered. The young Japanese Brazilians who were present showed no interest, keeping their eyes on the floor or on the walls

FIGURE 11
Miyoshi *rōshi* at Busshinji Temple (courtesy
Vitória Ang).

most of the time. While for people interested in monastic Zen the preaching in
Japanese may add to the exoticism and obscurity of Zen, thus making it a desirable religion, for Japanese descendants who have to sit through a long ritual it
can mean a further step toward rejecting the religion. Certainly this exodus is not
particular to Zen in Brazil: it occurs in other Japanese Buddhist schools in Brazil and the United States.[68] Language skills are so important in attracting young
people that in an interview I conducted with Coen *sensei* in March 2000, she attributed her appointment to Busshinji in 1995 to her fluency in Portuguese. In her
words,

> I studied in Japan for twelve years. They [Sōtōshū] asked me to return be-
> cause the Japanese community at the temple was agonizing with the lack of
> monks who spoke Portuguese. The young people of the congregation were
> leaving the temple because they couldn't understand what was being said.

Therefore, the appointment of a Japanese *sōkan* who does not speak either English or Portuguese shows the power the Japanese-Brazilian congregation exercises over Busshinji, as well as the strength of the process of "recoupment."

In addition, the *sōkan*, like all other *kaikyōshi* I have discussed, exemplifies the way missionaries carry ideas when they rotate from country to country. For instance, the group preparing for *jukai* follows a method used by the *sōkan* in Hawai'i: every student has a notebook where they write down the number of *zazen* performed, *sūtra* chanted, and the amount of *dāna* given. The novelty is not only the presence of the notebook (with Coen *sensei* there was a two-year course before ordination), but also the presence of *dāna*, that is, merit making through donations. I will explore *dāna* at Busshinji in more detail in chapter 5; here, suffice to say that merit making is the central practice for devout immigrants, whereas it is usually ignored by non-Japanese adherents for whom meditation is the "authentic," central activity. *Dāna* expresses the dependence of missionaries and temples on the local communities. Therefore, the inclusion of *dāna* in the lay ordination process indicates an overlapping, which bridges the typical separation between the two congregations.

COMPANY MEN AND FREE AGENTS

What can one learn from the lives of these *kaikyōshi* in Brazil and the sort of tribulations they went through? Nattier has pointed to the fact that there have been no scholarly studies on Zen missionaries who went to the United States, and such studies could raise "interesting issues for the study of cross-cultural religious transmission."[69] She argues that there have been two types of *kaikyōshi*.

> [The] "company man" (armed with tracts and doctrinal treatises provided by the home church, supported financially by this institution, and perhaps subject to recall if his form of propagation does not meet their specifications), and the "free agent" (who moves to a new country of his own accord, disseminates his religion as he sees fit, and is constrained only by his own need to make a living.[70]

From the lives of the five *kaikyōshi* depicted above I have shown that Nattier's categories were not quite so clear-cut in Brazil. All the missionaries belonged to and were sent by Sōtōshū to Brazil. Hence in Nattier's sense they were all "company men." However, since they did not receive a stipend from the institution and because the temple was funded by the community (through *dāna*), they were subject to the congregation's approval while living in Brazil. When the congregation decided the *kaikyōshi*'s attitudes were not acceptable, as in the cases of Ryōtan Tokuda, Daigyō Moriyama, and Coen de Souza, they lost their posts. Moriyama's case is even more revealing of the congregation's powers because he held the high position of *sōkan* for South America. I suggest that Tokuda, Moriyama, and Coen cannot be considered totally "free agents," since they did not arrive independently in Brazil and had to answer to the congregation's needs. When conflicts surfaced, they were dismissed and had their affiliation to Sōtōshū severed (in the cases of Tokuda and Moriyama). Only then did they become "free agents" and "disseminate their religion as they saw fit," as Nattier put it.

Like Lopez, Sharf has noted that "one feature shared by virtually all of the figures responsible for the Western interest in Zen is their relatively marginal status within the Japanese Zen establishment."[71] Nattier adds, "[T]hese men were, for the most part, genuine mavericks, deeply dissatisfied with the current state of Buddhism in their own country and eager to establish what they saw as 'true Zen' in a virgin mission field."[72]

Sharf and Nattier paint an accurate portrait of Tokuda and Moriyama and their desire to leave Japan for Brazil. Both *kaikyōshi* held a marginal status in their own country. The former did not belong to a temple family and chose not to marry into one—as is the norm in Japan to acquire a position in the institution—but rather left the country to preach his own Zen Buddhism to foreigners. The latter, albeit having his own temple in Japan (Zuigakuin, in Yamanashi Prefecture), has chosen marginality by not offering the regular set of services to the surrounding community. This choice is revealed in a leaflet advertising Zuigakuin to prospective Brazilian students. One reads,

> Zuigakuin (Zen Buddhist Center for Cultural Exchange) temple was founded in 1978 by Daigyō Moriyama and differs from other Zen temples in two aspects: it intends to re-establish Dōgen's Zen practice and it offers Western students access to this practice.

Coen's is a slightly different case, since she reveres Sōtōshū's authority and does not wish to leave the institution. Not being Japanese, she needs its seal of approval to legitimate her own "authenticity." However, her new temple, which has *zazen* and traditional calendrical rites at its core, further complicates the clear-cut picture of traditional Zen on the one hand and modern Zen on the other.

In contrast, Zendō Matsunaga was meaningful for the Japanese community (who even today hold him in high esteem), as he functioned as an important symbolic connection between the immigrants and their homeland. He did not, however, engage in spreading Zen outside the ethnic enclave. This attitude can be attributed to the fact that in the early 1960s, when Matsunaga lived in Brazil, there were very few non-Japanese Brazilians interested in Zen Buddhism. He was and still is part of Sōtōshū's establishment, currently holding a central position in the institution as the head of the international department at Eiheiji.

Kōichi Miyoshi may be placed in the same category—"company men"—as Matsunaga. Although he does cater to non-Japanese Brazilians and Japanese Brazilians interested in *zazen*, since (unlike Matsunaga) he has arrived at a time when Brazil is undergoing a Buddhist boom, his main task is to work for the Japanese immigrants and descendants who own the temple. His almost monthly visits to Japan to oversee his own Japanese temple and his absence from the non-Japanese-Brazilian Buddhist circuit has reduced Busshinji to the low profile it used to have before 1993, when Moriyama arrived.

These two groups of missionaries reflect the tensions that at times evolved into open clashes between Japanese traditional practices and Western expectations of Zen informed by modern/Western Zen. Matsunaga and Miyoshi have been able to continue their careers inside the institution because they delivered what the Japanese congregation overseas expected of them. Coen managed to keep her connection with the institution by accepting Sōtōshū's injunctions. Tokuda and Moriyama may not have had a long career at Sōtōshū, but both, together with Coen, have been "genuine mavericks" for the expansion of Zen amongst non-Japanese Brazilians.

BUSSHINJI'S PREDICAMENT AND THE FUTURE

In the light of so many conflicts, one cannot help but ask what will become of the Sōtōshū's mission in Brazil when the old Japanese immigrant congregation, who financially supports the temple through funeral and memorial rituals, dies out. Since young Japanese Brazilians are not interested in belonging to the temple any more, how will Busshinji survive its own predicament? This is neither a situation peculiar to the Zen sect nor to Brazil. Other Japanese Buddhist schools in Brazil and in Hawai'i and elsewhere in the United States have also been alarmed by the dwindling number of the congregation and the difficulties in attracting new generations of Japanese Brazilians and Japanese Americans. All studies identified the same problems: the lack of Japanese missionaries who speak Portuguese/English, the assimilation into Brazilian/North American ways, and the conversion to Christianity.

If the "slow bleeding," as Tanabe writes, has been taking place in most of the schools, Sōtōshū's siding with the old Japanese congregation, since the temples belong to them, has only deepened the crisis.[73] However, in recent years Sōtōshū has realized the threat to the mission and has adopted a more inclusive attitude. For instance, when, in 1995, in a bid to attract a new generation of Japanese Brazilians, the temple's board of directors asked a Sōtōshū Shūmuchō representative to publish a Portuguese version of Zen no Tomo (a magazine published by the headquarters and distributed in the temple), Sōtōshū promptly assented. A thousand copies of Caminho Zen (Zen path) have since started to be sent to Busshinji every quarter. The same need had been felt in the United States before, where Japanese descendants were given an English version called Zen Quarterly (later renamed Zen Friends). Another change has been the readmission of Tokuda into the sect. In 2000, Sōtōshū recognized his nonstop proselytizing work and installed him as the official resident kaikyōshi of Eitaiji, a new international temple Tokuda had founded in the south of France to be the basis of Sōtōshū in Europe. I believe keeping Coen sensei as a missionary after the intense and public crisis of her dismissal was also part of this effort to secure fronts to attract new members.

When I asked kaikyōshi who still work in Brazil about their future plans, all but Coen sensei had surprisingly similar goals: the establishment of monasteries for the training of monks and nuns from Brazil, South America, and even Japan. After living in France for ten years, Tokuda moved back briefly to Brazil in 2002 to establish Zen Horyuzan Eisho-Ji, a monastery dedicated to the formation of monks in Pirinópolis, central Brazil. Moriyama and his students are presently working at building a monastery significantly called International Buddhist Monastery Dōgen Zenji in Rio Grande do Sul State. Miyoshi told me in 2002 that he is working with Sōtōshū to gather funds for the construction of a monastery as well as a center for Zen studies and for proselytization on a plot of land behind Busshinji Temple. When I asked a Japanese-Brazilian monk at Busshinji how he perceived the current crisis, he told me,

> The Pure Land schools must be more worried than, for instance, the Shingon school, which is esoteric Buddhism and therefore receives lots of non-Japanese Brazilians who want to solve spiritual problems. In a Zen temple, one can have correlated practices to support the temple such as ikebana [flower arrangement], tea ceremony, and so forth. Then we wouldn't depend on ancestor rites for funds. A temple shouldn't depend solely on performing masses. Then, the dankasan [congregation] would have to be responsible to the temple. Right now, the non-Japanese-Brazilian dankasan is

very irresponsible because the Japanese-Brazilian congregation supports the temple. If funding generated by funerals and memorials disappears, I don't believe Zen will die in Brazil, but the new congregation will have to start thinking of ways to fund the temple. For instance, in Mogi [Zengenji] the congregation built a social club that is let for weddings and karaoke and is a significant source of income. You know, things are always changing. [For instance] during Shingū *rōshi*'s time most of the monks were retired Japanese Brazilians, now younger people are choosing this path.[74]

I posed this same question to the representative of Sōtōshū Shūmuchō in Japan in 2000. He gave me another surprising answer: "We need more non-Japanese Brazilians to come here to train as priests so that they can go back and spread Zen in Brazil." Considering the previous conflicts, I am sure the old Japanese immigrants would be more than a little shocked. The answer nevertheless reveals Sōtōshū's attempt at some flexibility in dealing with the crisis.

CONCLUSION

In the first part of this chapter I showed how Japanese immigration has played a strong role in the discussions around national identity and the future of Brazil in the late nineteenth century and the first half of the twentieth century. The desire to enter modernity led Brazilian elites to construct the Japanese as white and as an asset to Brazil. Japan's rise as an economic and military power made it into an example to be followed, either by copying Japanese policies or by having Japanese immigrants in Brazil.

The same desire for modernity prompted Brazilian elites to adopt the Zen that had been packaged to assert Japan's own modernity vis-à-vis Western cultural hegemony. Not surprisingly, when Sōtōshū *kaikyōshi* who subscribed to this modern/Western Zen arrived in Brazil, they found a group of followers who were eager to practice this European and North American Zen. The fact that both kinds of *kaikyōshi* (traditionalist and modernist) were sent by Sōtōshū—and thus invested with "authenticity"—created conflicts that reflected on Sōtōshū itself. The "dualistic discourse" Reader alluded to was created in the negotiation between traditional Japanese and modern/Western Zen. Throughout its history, Sōtōshū has always adopted a policy of flexibility and adaptation as a means of surviving new trends. Whereas in the fourteenth and fifteenth centuries it embraced popular practices, in the twentieth century, when it was confronted with modern/Western Zen, it incorporated the recent phenomenon of the centrality of meditation in its practices. It may well be fortunate that Sōtōshū had Dōgen as a patriarch who preached meditation so that it could accommodate meditation among its practices. Other Japanese Buddhist schools in Brazil, such the Jōdo Shinshū, have had to create meditation sessions due to the high demand for them and due to accusations by non-Japanese Brazilians of not being "authentic" Buddhism. The English historian Eric Hobsbawm has rightly argued that traditions are invented when there are rapid changes either on the demand or supply side so that the old tradition and their institutional carriers no longer prove sufficiently adaptable.[75] Adaptability to changing times has proved a successful formula for Sōtōshū's survival.

Another significant issue pertaining to Zen in Brazil, which will be further explored in the next chapters, is its strong globalizing trend. Through the rotation of *kaikyōshi* in overseas missions and their international groups of disciples (in the case of modern/Western Zen *kaikyōshi*), these missionaries actively participated in this globalizing process carrying and exchanging ideas and Zen practices into Western countries as well as Japan itself.

In the following chapter I will continue to discuss the practice of Brazilian elites of emulating metropolitan centers as a key to modernity. In this chapter I analyzed it in relation to Japanese immigration concerning the construction of national identity and the conflicts created by the adoption by non-Japanese Brazilian of modern/Western Zen. In the next chapter I will analyze this desire for modernity through culture, particularly looking at the role of Orientalism in the construction of Japan, Buddhism in general, and Zen in particular. While in this chapter I looked at the Sōtō missionaries' attitudes, in the next I will discuss the role of non-Japanese-Brazilian intellectuals in spreading Zen.

2 | Non-Japanese Brazilians and the Orientalist Shaping of Zen

The head of Sōtō Zen (or any Japanese Buddhist school) is like a prince, a Japanese prince. I experienced this when I was lecturing at the university in Londrina.[1] There are two Buddhist temples there: Higashi Honganji and Nishi Honganji. When the head of the Higashi Honganji came from Japan, a prince too, they invited me for the ceremony since they knew I was connected to Buddhism and was a lecturer at the university. It was a fantastic experience! The way "the prince" behaved was totally different. The way he conducted the ceremony, his gestures, his movements, the way he looked at me, his elegant ways, it was . . . They are connected to the imperial family, so they are treated like princes of the imperial household in Japan. He was incredibly aristocratic! So unlike the Brazilian Japanese here![2]

In this chapter I will examine how European Orientalist imaginings mediated the Brazilian cultural elite's perceptions of Japan, Buddhism in general, and Zen. Rather than viewing Japanese immigrant communities in Brazil as a source of the "exotic East," Brazilian artists and intellectuals—and eventually the general public—have been inspired either indirectly by ideas of Orientalism originating from cultural centers in the West such as France, England, and the United States or directly through assumptions about the "authenticity" of Japan itself.[3] As a result, Zen was never confined to the narrow boundaries of Sōtōshū's temples in Brazil, but has been disseminated throughout elite culture.

In this light, I start by examining the history of the reception of foreign products and ideas into Brazil. I contend that such a situation derives from what Said has referred to as the discourse of "Romantic Orientalism" (a nostalgic yearning for a pure and pristine past) as well as from a deeply rooted set of class distinctions in Brazilian society. While the Brazilian cultural elite were drawn toward fantasies of lost wisdom in ancient Japanese classical ages, they did not view Japanese immigrants in Brazil as legitimate carriers of this heritage. These immigrants were seen either as inhabitants of a "modern" and degraded Japan and hence lacking in "authenticity" or as lacking in artistic and cultural refinement by virtue of their status as peasants at the time of their arrival in Brazil. For the same reasons, non-Japanese Brazilians very seldom turned to Japanese-Brazilian religious practices and beliefs and did so only if they matched their own imaginary of Zen.

MISPLACED IDEAS: FASCINATION, COPY, AND STRUGGLE FOR AUTHENTICITY

> We Brazilians and other Latin Americans constantly experience the artificial, inauthentic and imitative nature of our cultural life. An essential element in our critical thought since independence, it has been variously interpreted from romantic, naturalist, modernist, right-wing, left-wing, cosmopolitan and nationalist points of view, so we may suppose that the problem is enduring and deeply rooted.[4]

Roberto Schwarz, a well-known Brazilian literary critic, identifies the origin of this predicament of "inauthenticity" in Brazil's Declaration of Independence in 1822, when the newly created empire adopted the British parliamentary system, along with republican ideas of the French revolution, but kept the colonial system of slavery.[5] In this context, equality, civil liberties, and the separation between public and private were juxtaposed with the slave trade, clientelism,[6] and large agricultural estates. This explicit "contradiction between the real Brazil and the ideological prestige of the countries used as models" has since been at the core of the discussions of national identity and culture (such as those between nationalists versus internationalists) and has taken different forms.[7]

According to Schwarz, in the nineteenth century the discussion ranged from those who thought the colonial system should be supplanted by new foreign ideas to those who identified the colonial system with the "real," "original/authentic/genuine" Brazil that should be protected against the uncritical imitation of foreign models. Although slavery was abolished in 1888 and Brazil became a republic the following year, harsh inequalities persisted, and questions of which foreign ideas had a real place in Brazil and which were just imitative or mimicry were constantly on the agenda. In the 1920s, the modernist movement tackled these questions in a different way. Instead of regarding this disjuncture between rural patriarchy and bourgeois ideology as problematic, Oswald de Andrade (1890–1954)—one of the most important leaders of the Brazilian modernist movement—offered a different response to the perceived problem of Brazilian cultural dependency. In his *Manifesto Antropofágico* (1928), he imagined the possibility of "cannibalizing" European metropolitan culture and thereby absorbing it into local culture. The outcome of these "digested" foreign influences would be something singular and new. Andrade's witty Shakespearean pun in the manifesto was the perfect metaphor of such cultural cannibalism: "Tupi or not Tupi, that is the question!"—the Tupi in question being the name of a Brazilian indigenous group and their language.

By invoking the Tupi, the first inhabitants of Brazil, Andrade is clearly not only questioning how Brazilian culture is construed, but also the building of a national identity.[8]

In the next decades, the dominant nationalism of the Vargas regime (1932–1945 and 1950–1954) and the subsequent ideology of industrial development of the 1950s kept the question of national identity vis-à-vis foreign culture alive. In the early 1960s, the rapid development of the mass media, the internationalization of capital, and the associated commodification of social relations further exposed the country to foreign ideas. The United States took over Europe as the primary source of culture, models of behavior, and worldview.[9] Like the Antropofágico movement that argued for a local primitivism and "cultural irreverence in place of subaltern obfuscation,"[10] the 1960s and 1970s produced a similar "cannibalistic" movement that manifested itself mainly in music, but also in fine arts, literature, film, theatre, and poetry. Following the footsteps of the Antropofágico movement, the Tropicália movement advocated the use of foreign, avant-garde ideas of counterculture combined with local themes to create innovative, distinctively Brazilian arts. Schwarz shows that such "hankering for the latest products of advanced countries" has been disseminated in the whole society, be they popular culture products or academia's new doctrines and theories.[11] For instance, Rodriguez has shown that the question of whether there exists an original Latin American and, by the same token, Brazilian philosophy has been tormenting many Latin American philosophers since the nineteenth century.[12] Indeed, it was not only literary critics and philosophers who were concerned about the autochthonous viability and valence of Brazilian culture. As I will show in this chapter, writers and poets also agonized about the originality of their ideas and work.

Schwarz, however, has identified a viable and interesting way out of this national and historical preoccupation with originality. He concludes his article by saying that copying is a false problem if one realizes that the original and the copy, that is, the foreign and the national, are not real oppositions but are deeply interconnected. Imitation entails translation and the consequent generation of "misplaced ideas," which are distinctively Brazilian. Such a view draws attention to the inherent instability of the "original"—a point noted by Benjamin, who problematizes the relationship between the original and the (translated) copy by showing how the original lives on through its growth or "afterlife" in translation.[13] In a similar way, Derrida has argued that the process of translating or copying an original will "truly be a moment in the growth of the original" and that "if the original calls for a complement, it is because at the origin it was not there without fault, full, complete, total, identical to itself."[14] Of course, the process of copying "for-

eign" repertoires of cultural codes, imagery, and ideas is always framed by historically specific relations of hierarchy and asymmetry.[15] From this perspective, the
idea that Brazil would only mimic what was created overseas obscures two facts.
First, since the thirst for the latest foreign product or idea is part of the same process by which advanced countries develop and are enriched, it masks the power
relations that are in play between the global and the local. As Schwarz notes, the
requirement of "creation *ex nihilo*" is a myth, as ideas evolve from ideas, which are
meshed in power relations. In an increasingly globalized world, the global flows
and patterns of cultural influence and absorption are inevitably enmeshed in what
Massey calls a "power-geometry" that produces uneven effects on the local spaces
over which they traverse.[16] Second, there are elements of dynamism in Brazilian
culture "which display both originality and lack of originality."[17]

Indeed, in the beginning of the twentieth century, the cultural exchange
between Europe, particularly France, and Brazil also occurred in the opposite direction. Many avant-garde European artists, poets, and writers such as the Italian futurist Filippo Tommaso Marinetti, the French poets Paul Claudel and Blaise
Cendrars, and the composer Darius Milhaud traveled to Brazil to interact with
Brazilian avant-garde artists and poets. This exchange was even more meaningful
when we know that Claudel had been a diplomat in China and Japan and wrote
some texts on Ch'an and Zen. There are no documents that I am aware of that
clearly state that Claudel exchanged views on these subjects with Brazilian intellectuals, but it is very likely that they read Claudel's works due to his impending
trip and the fact that he was a well-known poet in Brazil.[18]

The complex and dynamic relationship between the original and copy, global
and local, foreign and national offers a useful framework for understanding how
and why ideas about Buddhism, Zen, and Japan that emerged in Europe and the
United States made their way into Brazilian culture initially in the academic and
intellectual setting and subsequently in popular culture in the 1990s. In this context, I will address the historical literary production that deals with the "Orient,"
Japan, Japanese poetic forms, Buddhism, and Zen.

BRAZILIAN ORIENTALISM: THE "EXOTIC EAST"
IN BRAZILIAN LITERATURE

As early as the nineteenth century, writers such as Fagundes Varella (1841–1875),
Machado de Assis (1839–1908), and Raimundo Correia (1860–1911) were drawn
to European ideas of orientalism as a source of images of exoticism, wisdom, sen-

suality, and peace. This was in spite of the fact that they themselves inhabited a land constructed as exotic in the European imagination. In his poem "Oriental," Fagundes Varella urges his beloved to flee with him "to the delicious Ganges plains," while in "Ideal" he sets his beloved in "the land of the Chinese empire, in a palace made of red porcelain, on a Japanese blue throne."[19]

In 1914, the Brazilian philosopher R. de Farias Brito addressed Buddhism in his *O Mundo Interno* (The internal world). In this book, Christianity and Buddhism were presented as the two most important world religions since they formed the basis of the two greatest world civilizations—the Occident and the Orient. Farias Brito thought his era was marked by religious crisis and loss of faith as a result of the discoveries of science. Nevertheless, by advocating the notion that religion was the moral basis of society and that it was philosophy in practice, Farias Brito argued that religion should still be the most important preoccupation of the human spirit. For him,

> The religious problem may only be solved by a new religion which can satisfy the present aspirations of the human spirit. [This new doctrine] shall be the outcome of a fusion between Orient and Occident, purifying the best in each civilization in a universal synthesis that will establish the spiritual unity of humankind. It will be a battle between Christianity and Buddhism, resulting in something completely new.[20]

The word "purifying" is crucial here. For the philosopher, the new doctrine should expurgate "false dogmas and interpretations" that were imposed through the ages and thus be in accordance with the new discoveries of science. Christianity and Buddhism, being religions founded by human beings, were suited for such a task. Farias Brito is clearly influenced by nineteenth-century European Buddhist scholars who, in seeking an alternative to Christianity, constructed Buddhism as "an agnostic, rationalist, ethical movement [which could become] a foundation for morality in everyday life."[21] In this context, Buddhism could be regarded as scientific and in accord with modern times since ritualistic and devotional practices and beliefs were thought of as superimposed cultural accretions that corrupted Buddhism over time. Because these European scholars privileged texts over actual practices, they also considered Buddhism a philosophy and not a religion per se.[22] Indeed, drawing his knowledge of Buddhism from Charles B. Renouvier (1815–1903, *Philosophie Analitique de L'Histoire*) and Hermann Oldenberg (1854–1920, *Le Bouddha*), Farias Brito criticizes the former for regarding Buddhism as a religion of despair. On the contrary, he affirms that Buddhism is neither materialistic nor nihilistic, but "an idealistic religion, derived from a deep and elevated philosophy of the spirit."[23]

Similarly, the importation of European philosophical ideas influenced some Brazilian poets at the turn of the century. The School of Recife (1863–1916) was a cultural movement that brought together scholars, legislators, philosophers, sociologists, and poets of northeast Brazil in debates concerning the theories of Spencer, Heckel, Hartmann, Schopenhauer, and Kant. However, it was not only Heckel's monism and Spencer's evolutionism that became the central ideas for combating the "old" theological debates; the ideas of spiritualism were also deployed. Living in this cultural milieu, some poets participated in the School of Recife writing "scientific poetry." Augusto dos Anjos (1884–1914), one the best known poets of the time, used evolutionism, monism, philosophical materialism, and sometimes spiritualism as frameworks for articulating his favorite themes of death, nonbeing, longing, and matter and spirit. Three of his poems—"Budismo Moderno" (Modern buddhism), "Revelação" (Revelation), and "Cismas do Destino" (Preoccupations of destiny)—allude to Buddha. In the first poem, Anjos works with the concepts of nothingness and death as dissolution or decomposition. In "Revelação," Buddha is opposed to a sybarite, and in the last poem Buddha is regarded as dwelling in peace. The themes of nihilism, dissolution after death, luxury in contrast to frugality, and peace associated with the Buddha and Buddhism show the influence of ideas of Buddhism produced in the nineteenth century by European Buddhologists.[24]

THE CONSTRUCTION OF JAPAN IN THE BRAZILIAN IMAGINARY

In the early twentieth century, Brazilians acquired familiarity with Japan through newspaper articles and books written by the Portuguese writer Wenceslau de Moraes (1854–1929). In contrast to authors who never traveled to the "East," Moraes wrote extensively in Portuguese about his firsthand experience of the "Orient." After having lived in Macau, of which he wrote many reports for Portuguese newspapers, he moved to Japan in 1898, where he became the Portuguese consul general at Kobe. Like Lafcadio Hearn (1850–1904), who wrote for an English-speaking audience, Moraes' writings depict Japanese everyday life and his love for the country. His works include *Dai-Nippon*, published in Lisbon in 1897, *Bon-Odori* (1916), *Oyoné e Ko-Haru* (1923), *Relance da Alma Japonesa* (Grasping the Japanese soul, 1924), *Cartas do Japão* (Letters from Japan, 1927), and *O Culto do Chá* (The cult of tea).

Although this material was available in Portuguese, France was the main source of ideas on Japan. The Brazilian elite in the nineteenth century and the first half of the twentieth century were heavily influenced by French culture through education, fashion, and travel. Speaking French fluently, adopting the newest French fad, and sending their sons to study or just live in the country before starting a career was seen as de rigueur for the Brazilian elite. Pierre Loti (1850–1923), the well-known novelist of exotica and author of *Mme Chrysanthème* (1886), together with Anatole France and J. K. Huysmans, was widely read by this sector of society.[25] In 1908, films with Sadayakko, the Japanese dancer-actress famous in Europe and North America at the end of the century, were well received in Rio de Janeiro. In 1920 an exhibition of Japanese art held in São Paulo clearly echoed the Parisian "Japan boom."[26]

Analyzing the reception of three Japanese opera singers who performed *Madama Butterfly* in Brazil in the first half of the twentieth century (1921, 1924, 1936, and 1940), Hosokawa observed, "No doubt Parisian interest in Japan was a stronger impact on the opera-goers than the presence of a small Japanese colony in the city."[27] Hosokawa notes that Brazilian journalists were more concerned with the Japanese opera singers' physical appearance than their artistic talent, focusing at length on their prettiness, smallness, and charm in their reviews. Due to these singers' ethnic origin, journalists readily identified them with the traits of the characters they played, as if they were incarnated Madama Butterflies themselves. Moreover, heavily influenced by French *japonaiserie*, reviewers employed French adjectives such as *petite femme*, *mignon*, and *poupée* to describe these female artists, not unlike Loti's *Mme Chrysanthème*. Hosokawa argues that by repeatedly regarding the Japanese singers as miniature, they made them manageable, not threatening to the Western observer, "imbued with intimacy, passion and desirability. . . . Miniature is associated with nostalgia and evokes a pristine past, lost objects and irretrievable land."[28]

Hosokawa's analysis shows that French Orientalism profoundly shaped the way many non-Japanese Brazilians regarded Japan in the first quarter of the twentieth century. This was the case despite the fact that Japanese immigration to Brazil had started in 1908—and by 1930 there were close to sixty thousand Japanese immigrants in the country—and that, moreover, this community was soon to become the largest Japanese expatriate community in the world. There are two main reasons for this: France was perceived to be the center of high culture for Brazilians and for the world in general and therefore had the cultural capital that Japan lacked;[29] and the Japanese in Brazil, by contrast, were of peasant origin, mostly living in rural areas. The few who lived in the cities worked as small shopkeepers, laundrymen, small retail traders of foodstuffs, and so on. Because of the deep-rooted presence of slavery in Brazilian history, manual labor of any sort has been traditionally associated with African Brazilians and disenfranchised classes. The Brazilian anthropologist Ruben Oliven observes,

> In Brazil, labor—particularly manual labor—is held in low esteem. In Portuguese one word for "to work" is "mourejar," branding it as something that should be left to the Moors; in Brazil a racist expression refers to hard work as "black man's work," a direct reference to slavery. Even after the abolition of slavery [1889] and the introduction of waged labor in factories, labor was still not valued, because the social order continued to be extremely excluding.[30]

Thus only those who have had a formal education and work using their acquired "knowledge" are to be considered middle or upper class. Even if the Japanese owned property in urban and rural areas, they still did not enjoy social prestige and status in Brazilian society, since their work was strongly associated with manual labor.[31] Therefore, in the eyes of Brazilians, they, too, lacked the necessary cultural capital to be regarded as a source of knowledge of Japan.

HAIKU AND ZEN

A good illustration of the European mediation of the flow of ideas on and from Japan, as well as its consequent Orientalist tendency and eventual association with Zen, can be found in haiku, the Japanese seventeen-syllable poem (three lines of 5-7-5 syllables). Haiku has evolved throughout the twentieth century in Brazil to become a popular form of poetry. According to a Brazilian literary critic, as a source of knowledge of Japanese culture it has been matched only by the interest in martial arts in the country.[32] Haiku arrived in Brazil first in French translations and subsequently English ones through the diaries of European travelers. These very short poems were then regarded as exotic curiosities akin to the Japanese elaborate etiquette, the diminutive sake cups, and the communal bath. Paul-Louis Couchoud's *Sages et Poetes d'Asie* and Julien Vocance's (pseud. Joseph Seguin) *Art Poétique* (1921) were the main sources of knowledge of haiku in Brazil at the beginning of the twentieth century.[33] Wenceslau de Moraes was the first to translate haiku into his mother tongue, albeit in a very loose format more akin to Portuguese poetic forms. However, Brazilian poets did not take much notice of Moraes' haiku, favoring instead the French translations.

Afrânio Peixoto (1876–1947) was one of the first Brazilian poets to attempt to compose haiku, which he learned about from reading Couchoud's translations.[34] However, this poetic form would become renowned in Brazil only in the 1930s through the work of the celebrated poet Guilherme de Almeida (1890-1969). Like his predecessors, Almeida learned about haiku first through French translations. He later engaged with the Japanese-Brazilian community as well, meeting a group of haiku practitioners in São Paulo City and helping establish and preside over the Aliança Cultural Brasil-Japão, a cultural center for the Japanese-Brazilian community.

In the 1950s and 1960s there was a second wave of interest in haiku, which — like the earlier one — drew its understanding not from the Japanese-Brazilian community, but from the translations and writings of others, in this case, Ernest Fenollosa (1853-1908). Fenollosa's *The Chinese Written Character* was posthumously published in 1919 by the American poet Ezra Pound (1885-1972) and was very influential among Brazilian poets from 1955 onward. Fenollosa's and Pound's notion that the ideogram was the core Chinese and Japanese understanding of the world, since it constructed meaning through juxtaposition and montage, informed the newly founded avant-garde Concretista movement established by Augusto and Haroldo de Campos and Décio Pignatari.

While this avant-garde movement associated haiku with the "exotic" Chinese character (kanji), the next generation of poets, from the early 1970s until the last decades of the twentieth century, identified it strongly with Zen, a connection derived from the works of Reginald Blyth, Alan Watts, D. T. Suzuki, and Jack Kerouac. In fact, Suzuki dedicates a whole chapter of his *Zen and Japanese Culture* [35] to the relationship between Zen and haiku. Paulo Leminski (1944-1989), who popularized Brazilian Zen haiku, praised Zen's paradoxical, non-Cartesian understanding of the world. For him, haiku was a way to evoke the Japanese notion of *dō* (the way) present in so many other Japanese Zen arts such as kendō (the way of the sword), *kadō* (the way of the flowers), and *chadō* (the way of tea). Because Leminski strongly emphasized the connection between Zen and haiku, he was called the "Zen disciple of Bashō" by Haroldo de Campos, the Concretista poet most interested in Japanese culture and haiku. In the 1980s and 1990s, through his talks and books, as well as poems turned into popular songs, Leminski became a highly influential source of ideas on Zen for the intellectual, upper middle class of Brazil. Attempting to explain why Brazilians were so fascinated by haiku, one Brazilian literary critic has pointed to

> a search for an imaginary Japan filled with Zen, feudal ethics and old contemplative wisdom. In other words, the Japan that exists in the Brazilian

contemporary *imaginaire* seems to be laden with a lot of nostalgia, idealization of a pre-industrial world and life under the Tokugawa regime. In sum, there is still a lot of exoticism as there has always been.[36]

Indeed, haiku is a good example of how the global cultural flows from Europe and North America shaped non-Japanese-Brazilian perception of Japan and Zen. However, haiku may also be used to unveil how the two groups — non-Japanese Brazilians and Japanese Brazilians — related to each other. The strong visibility (in books, newspapers, and lectures) of non-Japanese Brazilians writing haiku overshadows the fact that Japanese immigrants, albeit of peasant origin, had been composing haiku since their arrival in Brazil. Hidezaku Masuda Goga, a Japanese-Brazilian poet, has argued that the first haiku was composed on board the *Kasato-Maru* itself — the first ship to arrive in Brazil from Japan in 1908. Since then, haiku clubs and regional and national contests have evolved.[37] Migrant newspapers published in Brazil such as the *Shūkan Nambei* (South American weekly) and *Brasil Jihō* (The Brazil review), established in 1916 and 1924, respectively, had as many pages dedicated to poetry as they did to news stories. Hence Japanese immigrants and descendants would have been a source of knowledge of haiku for non-Japanese Brazilians if the latter had sought them out.

While non-Japanese Brazilians introduced new rhythm to the haiku, and some even added a title where this form of poetry does not have one, they strove to keep the connection between haiku, Zen, and Tokugawa Japan. Japanese Brazilians, on the other hand, maintained the haiku format but introduced Brazilian *kigo*, that is, seasonal words relating to the fauna and flora of the new country. Thus since haiku arrived in Brazil, the former group has sought to retain their idea of Japan as an essentialized, unchanging, and exotic source of Zen and lost wisdom, while the latter has adapted what they understood as the core of the poem, its seasonal feeling, to the Brazilian environment. Indeed, Franchetti has remarked that Japanese Brazilians have constantly been amused and baffled to find the ubiquitous presence of Zen and the overemphasis on the Chinese character in non-Japanese Brazilians' haiku.[38]

Certainly, there are fewer Japanese Brazilians who compose haiku than non-Japanese Brazilians, but the lack of integration between the two groups of poets reveals two facts. First, their understanding of Japan, haiku, and Zen came from quite distinct sources. Whereas non-Japanese Brazilians absorbed the flow of ideas and images of Japan from Western metropolitan centers of culture, Japanese Brazilians embodied or inherited them. Second, the system of class distinction in Brazil prevented the local Japanese and Japanese Brazilians from being seen as bearers of what non-Japanese Brazilians considered high culture even if the former did compose haiku. Both these factors—different sources of inflows and class distinction—are significant if one is to understand the gap and struggle between both groups concerning the authenticity of Japanese culture and, as I will show, their religious practices and beliefs.

INTELLECTUALS AS COSMOPOLITANS: RECONVERTING CULTURAL CAPITAL ACCUMULATED OVERSEAS

I would like to return here, briefly, to the (false) predicament of Brazilian culture—namely the debate as to whether Brazilian culture is a copy or an "authentic original"—analyzed by Schwartz and others in the beginning of this chapter. The examples reported so far of how Brazil related to Japan, Buddhism, and Zen have shown how cultural flows originating in Europe and North America have strongly influenced Brazilian culture. In the 1920s, the Modernist movement and Andrade's *Manifesto Antropofágico* attempted a discourse of resistance to European trends by reclaiming the figure of the cannibal who could "absorb" and "digest" powerful foreign flows and, in turn, produce a national culture. But the writers, poets, and artists fascinated by Japan and Zen were not interested in producing a counterdiscourse to these flows and asserting a local culture. Indeed, as I argued earlier in this chapter, the binary opposition between a copy and an "authentic original" is a false one, since new indigenized cultural forms emerge from sources that are already "impure." In other words, global flows have always influenced and, in turn, been localized in Brazilian society, and the origins of these flows are themselves "impure." I contend that the same principle and pattern of influence and exchange applies to Zen in Brazil. That is, the need to translate Zen into Portuguese and into Brazilian culture guaranteed that it was creolized locally and in very particular ways. I would further argue that much as Brazilian artists, poets, and intellectuals emulated European Orientalist trends in the past, from the late 1950s onward, elite intellectuals saw their knowledge of Zen not as a form of cultural resistance, but rather as a tool enabling them to demonstrate both their role in Brazilian society as translators and interpreters of overseas avant-garde movements *and* their prestigious position as cosmopolitans. These claims gave them the cultural capital necessary to reinforce and maintain their own class status in the country.

In chapter 4 I will discuss in more detail how habitus, lifestyle, taste, and the media have played a determining role in the choice of Buddhism and Zen by upper middle-class Brazilians since the 1990s. Here I would like to shed light on how this process of imbuing Zen with prestige and cultural capital was initiated in the late 1950s by a small group of intellectuals who deployed their knowledge of Zen as a marker of social distinction. While in the 1990s the dynamic of popularization within consumer culture allowed the media to play a powerful role in interpreting Buddhism and Zen to a wider audience, in the late 1950s non-Japanese-Brazilian cosmopolitan intellectuals were the sole arbiters of how Zen and Buddhism should be represented and understood.

Bourdieu has shown that social identity is asserted and maintained through difference, which in turn is visible in people's habitus. According to Bourdieu, habitus is the system of classification (the structuring structure) and the principle through which objectively classifiable judgments are made (the structured structure). Through this means, social classes would be defined by their habitus, that is, by their internalized unconscious dispositions as well as their relational position in a structure of taste. In other words, a social group would be identifiable by having similar choices in taste derived from a particular habitus situated in this system of correlation and distinction. Importantly, this system is eminently hierarchical so that the tastes of the upper classes carry prestige while the tastes of lower, disenfranchised classes are regarded as vulgar. Because tastes do not have an intrinsic value, the dominant classes who hold economic and/or cultural capital make theirs rare and unreachable (in either economic or cultural ways) so that they may successfully imbue them with prestige. Conversely, the tastes of the poorest fractions of society are regarded as common and identified with vulgarity, for they are easily accessible. This entails a constant effort by the upper classes to maintain social distance by always creating new, rarer tastes and imposing artificial scarcity of products consumed by them. On the other hand, as Featherstone puts it, there is a constant attempt by "lower groups to emulate and usurp the tastes of higher groups, causing the latter to respond by adopting new tastes which will re-establish and maintain the original distance."[39]

In such a structured and structuring system, Bourdieu places intellectuals as part of the dominated fraction of the dominant class, for they possess a high volume of cultural capital but do not readily possess economic capital. Their cultural capital is valuable because it is ultimately converted into symbolic capital, and in doing so it accords them prestige and recognition that in turn gives them social power. By striving to retain a monopoly in the production, judgment, and hierarchy of symbolic capital, intellectuals attempt to secure their dominant position within the structure of society.

Similarly, I contend that when Brazilian intellectuals translated books and wrote newspaper articles about Zen and Buddhism, when they traveled overseas to visit Buddhist places to meet either European and North American Zen scholars or Japanese Zen masters, they were creating new, rare, and exotic tastes, which would establish their role as bearers of a symbolic capital. Once this knowledge was translated into Portuguese, these intellectuals acquired social and even "mystic" power in Brazil, for their knowledge dealt with matters of sacred and lost wisdom from the Orient. Featherstone has pointed out that intellectuals already have a sacred authority derived from their possession of a high volume of cultural capital.[40] When some of these non-Japanese-Brazilian intellectuals were ordained Zen monks/nuns (some even became full-fledged missionaries), the symbiotic relation was complete: not only did they hold the intellectual and thus Western knowledge of Zen, but also the esoteric and practical knowledge of the Eastern masters themselves. Both kinds of cultural capital legitimated their writings and their status in a field where scarcity and monopoly of knowledge prevailed.

So far I have examined the role of non-Japanese-Brazilian intellectuals as translators and interpreters. The other side of the coin is their role as cosmopolitans. Hannerz has argued that not everyone who travels to foreign lands is a cosmopolitan. To be considered a cosmopolitan one has to move freely out of and back into one's own culture, be competent and able to participate in alien cultures, and enjoy one's status as master of the new culture(s). Accordingly, for Hannerz, tourists (who are merely spectators and not participants of the new culture), people in exile (who may not move freely in and out one's culture), and labor immigrants (who are surrounded but not immersed in the foreign culture) may not be called "cosmopolitans." For him, more than any other group, cosmopolitanism is associated with the intellectual class, a privileged group which "has an advantageous point of departure" to move and engage in other cultures around the world.[41]

Although I concur with Hannerz in associating cosmopolitans with intellectuals, there are two important points that I believe he has neglected. First, despite asserting at the opening of his article that world cultures are interconnected, Hannerz sets a clear distinction between cosmopolitans and locals. For him, "people like the cosmopolitans have a special part in bringing a degree of coherence . . . to all the variously distributed structures of meaning. . . . If there were only locals in the world, world culture would be no more than the sum of its separate parts."[42] In a strong critique of Hannerz's notion of cosmopolitanism, Robbins points out that "if it is no longer feasible to think of cultures as distinct entities . . . but as mobile, fluid, hybrid and inclusive," there is no reason for Hannerz to see locals as separated from cosmopolitans.[43] Robbins contends that there are multiple cosmopolitanisms and these are not the monopoly of Western intellectuals and travelers, but arise whenever there is intercultural contact and negotiation.

Clifford has argued for travel and contact as complex and pervasive phenomena of human experience.[44] If this is so, the focus of the anthropological "field" should shift from dwellings as sole locations of culture to encompass travel, that is, practices of displacement, histories of people in transit, places of contact, encounter, and translation as well. Clifford is not calling for bounded territories to be replaced by borders, margins, and edges as sites of anthropological research. He is not calling for the figure of the "native" to be replaced by the "traveler," but for anthropologists to focus on the complex and dynamic relationship between both. By the same token, since for Clifford culture is at the same time "rooted" and "routed," sites of dwelling and travel, then the concept of cosmopolitanism needs to be expanded beyond Western intellectuals to incorporate "locals" who are themselves part of an increasingly interconnected world. In such a world, the boundaries between the cosmopolitan and the local become blurred.

Significantly, despite maintaining the distinction between cosmopolitans and locals throughout his article, at one point Hannerz does concede that the recent media explosion has made "just about everybody a little cosmopolitan," creating the possibility of "becoming a cosmopolitan without going away at all."[45] My research findings echo Hannerz's in the sense that one may distinguish between cosmopolitans and locals in Brazil until the mid-1980s, but thereafter the boundaries between the two groups become indistinct. Until the 1980s, only bearers of economic and cultural capital, that is, the economic elite and intellectuals who were able to travel overseas and be conversant in foreign languages, could be considered cosmopolitan. They were the main translators and interpreters of foreign cultures. However, the severe economic and social crisis of the 1980s saw for the first time in Brazilian history a diasporic movement into the United States, Europe, and Japan. In 1990, the country opened up to foreign imports, and the subsequent pegging of the Brazilian currency to the U.S. dollar allowed a large number of middle-class people to travel abroad for the first time. In the 1990s, transnational workers, tourists, students, and the media joined intellectuals as carriers of intensely desired knowledge of foreign cultures. Unlike Hannerz, I believe transnational workers, tourists, and students can be regarded as cosmopolitans in the sense that they bring knowledge of cultural products from the metropolitan centers into Brazil—Robbins' "multiple cosmopolitanisms" and Clifford's notions of culture as "rooted and routed" should be accounted for here. Moreover, Brazilian transnational workers (particularly Japanese Brazilians working in Japan) have a history of frequently leaving and returning to Brazil for periods of time during which they try, many unsuccessfully, to reestablish themselves in the country.[46] During their comings and goings they bring with them different worldviews, commodities, foods, and so forth. In sum, if one can speak of intellectuals and the economic elite being the cosmopolitans par excellence in previous years in Brazil, from the 1990s onward the domain of cosmopolitanism was enlarged to encompass upper middle- and middle-class Brazilians.

A second critique that can be directed toward Hannerz's discussion of cosmopolitans is that he does not situate them either historically or geographically. According to him, they are basically free-willed travelers who even at home are cosmopolitan, as they are "unusual" for their fellow locals.[47] Robbins has noted that this claim for universality, independence, and detachment from affiliations, commitments, and bonds is flawed as it does not reveal the situatedness of the traveler.[48] The idea of situatedness is particularly important in view of the fact that the Brazilian intellectual elite who travel overseas do not do so indiscriminately. Instead, they travel to specific locales in different historical moments, and they do so because there is something to gain from it at that particular moment—namely cultural capital, a hard currency to be redeemed back home that will help them maintain their status. At the same time that their travel and knowledge ensure that they assert their place in the social hierarchy at home, it also guarantees that they are seen as equal in relation to their peers overseas, giving them a sense of multiple, transnational belonging. Bourdieu has called this process "reconversion of capital," a term that refers to those strategies employed by any sector of society to reconvert their economic and symbolic capital within transnational circuits.[49] Learning languages and skills that carry kudos, familiarizing oneself with the latest fashion and lifestyle produced in metropolitan areas, reading the latest books produced in these areas, and so forth are all strategies of reconversion of capital for the Brazilian elite intellectuals.

In this context, while France was the main producer and disseminator of meaning for Brazilian society up until World War II, the United States took its place thereafter. It is not a coincidence that intellectuals and the economic elite would learn French and later English and would emulate and travel to these geographically and historically situated cultures. When Japan became a strong economic power in the 1980s, it became a more frequent destination for Brazilian students, tourists, intellectuals, and transnational workers. Knowledge about its culture and language became such a highly valued currency that attitudes toward Japanese descendants in Brazil became more positive, contrasting starkly with the way they were previously regarded.

This phenomenon is, of course, not specific to Brazil. It is part and parcel of the complex relations of power among countries that seek to appropriate the culture of metropolitan centers. However, "centers" and "peripheries" have relational locations; as in a rhizome, centers may become peripheries and vice-versa. For instance, because from the 1960s to the mid-1990s Brazil was not a primary producer and disseminator of meaning about Buddhism, intellectuals had to travel and read in foreign languages to be able to acquire knowledge. However, this picture changed considerably in the late 1990s, when Buddhism experienced a rapid expansion and the country—while still maintaining its peripheral location—became a node for the production and dissemination of information about Zen to Latin America, Portugal, and even to traditional centers such as France and the United States. In conclusion, inequalities of wealth and power that divide the world, assigning distinct places for the acquisition of cultural capital, have to be accounted for if one is to understand why elite Brazilians travel to specific locales at different historical moments. Accordingly, places of travel for cosmopolitan Brazilians may differ greatly from those of developed-world cosmopolitans, since the cultural capital to be gained in each case is also situated and constructed.

NON-JAPANESE-BRAZILIAN INTELLECTUALS: BRIDGING THE LOCAL AND THE GLOBAL

Before D. T. Suzuki's *Introduction to Zen Buddhism* was translated into Portuguese in 1961, non-Japanese-Brazilian intellectuals could learn about Zen from articles and translations (from English and French) by the journalist Nelson Coelho published in *Jornal do Brasil*, a leading newspaper from Rio de Janeiro. Coelho was a foreign correspondent based in New York from 1956 to 1958. Living in a cultural milieu where Zen was fashionable and "beat," Coelho himself became interested in the new trend through reading Suzuki, Hermann Hesse, Eugen Herrigel, R. H. Blyth, Carl Jung, and Alan Watts. The Sunday edition of *Jornal do Brasil* was well known for its reporting on avant-garde movements. Coelho told me that the two main topics at the time were his articles on Zen and articles by poets of the Concretista movement who, as noted earlier, were also fascinated by haiku, the ideogram, and ultimately Zen. According to Coelho, his weekly stories published from 1957 to 1961 sparked an intense wave of interest in Zen Buddhism among non-Japanese-Brazilian intellectuals. Such was the enthusiasm for Zen, Coelho pointed out in an interview, that although the owner of the newspaper was a devout Catholic, she was excited by the novelty and the artistic side of Zen and thus allowed the weekly translations of Zen texts, kōan, and commentaries. I would add that Zen would not have posed a threat to her religious convictions as it was pictured as a philosophical path to self-knowledge. Coelho has himself remarked,

As soon as Busshinji Temple was established in São Paulo, I started to frequent it. However, after a few sitting sessions, I quit. I was fascinated by Zen theory but sitting still and silent for a whole hour lacked meaning, it did not provide what I was looking for. I was looking for an active way of doing Zen, but the temple did not hold any kendō or tea ceremony classes.[50]

During the interview and in his book, Coelho emphasized his role as the person responsible for the introduction of Zen into Brazil.[51] Clearly, this gave him prestige and cultural capital in Brazilian society as his name became associated with Zen.

Another intellectual instrumental in the spread of Zen Buddhist ideas in Brazil was Murillo Nunes de Azevedo. Azevedo was deeply influenced by the ideas of the Theosophical Society, where he had acted as president of the Brazilian chapter for nine years. In 1955, Azevedo reestablished the Sociedade Budista do Brasil (Buddhist Society of Brazil), which had dissolved soon after it had first been founded in 1923 by Theosophists in Rio de Janeiro. As professor at the Pontifical Catholic University in Rio de Janeiro, Azevedo taught philosophy of the Far East, published reports on Theosophy and Theravada, Tibetan, and Zen Buddhism for *Correio da Manhã*, a Rio de Janeiro-based newspaper, wrote books on Buddhism, and organized a collection of translations called *Luz da Ásia* (Light of Asia) for Civilização Brasileira, a well-known publishing house in Brazil. In this collection Azevedo published twenty books dedicated to Eastern philosophies. Among them was Suzuki's *Introduction to Zen Buddhism*, which Azevedo translated into Portuguese in 1961. The book was still frequently cited and highly regarded as a source of understanding of Zen in the interviews that I conducted among Zen practitioners in the late 1990s.

In 1966, Azevedo traveled extensively to India (where he visited the Dalai Lama), Thailand (for the World Buddhist Conference, where he met Christmas Humphreys), and Japan. He wrote reports for *Correio da Manhã* as he traveled. In Tokyo, Azevedo had a meeting with Rōsen Takashina *zenji*, the abbot of Eiheiji and Sōjiji, the head temples of Sōtōshū. Takashina *zenji* had been to Brazil in 1955 to survey the country for the possibility of sending a Sōtōshū mission and again in 1964 for the commemorations of the first decade of Sōtōshū activities. Azevedo's description of this meeting between him and the *zenji* is very similar to the ones given by other Westerners who encounter Japanese Zen masters. He is self-deprecating in portraying himself as the Western man who wears a suit, sits uncomfortably on tatami mats, and shows off his "knowledge" of Zen, thus displaying his ego. On the other hand, the *zenji* is the wise, silent, and vigorous ninety-two-year-old Oriental master. Most of the meeting occurs "beyond words" as he is served green tea "without sugar . . . slowly drunk as is appropriate for the old etiquette of tea ceremony."[52] When the master finally speaks, Azevedo claims he initiates a *mondō*[53] and asks him what he had understood by Zen. At the cue, Azevedo writes that he used his "pseudo-wisdom" to reply "full of himself as an intellectual who likes to shine." The *zenji* retaliated with a "short and quick" paradoxical question to which Azevedo could not reply, but only bow in deep reverence. At the end of the meeting, "a monk brought in a tray upon which there was a paper written in Japanese that declared that from that moment onwards I was a monk, a Sōtōshū missionary for Brazil and that I had received the Buddhist name 'Reirin Jodo.'"[54] Azevedo lacked the preparation and formal education needed, whether for a Japanese or a non-Japanese Brazilian, to become a monk or nun. But Sōtōshū realized that he occupied a strategic position as a university professor with good standing in society and as a writer and a translator, enabling him to contribute to the spread of Zen in Brazil.

Both Coelho's and Azevedo's stories demonstrate that Brazil was not isolated from the strands of Buddhism existing in Europe and North America. Although Buddhism in the 1960s and 1970s in Brazil was a much smaller and more confined movement than in the late 1990s, it was very much connected with overseas Western strands, as intellectuals who traveled and wrote newspaper articles and books functioned as translators and interpreters of these trends to a Brazilian audience.

Other intellectuals followed a similar path. Their initial encounter with Buddhism and Zen was through imported literature, which then led them to seek a place to practice; they found it in Busshinji in São Paulo. In order to cater to the demands of non-Japanese Brazilians, in 1961 Ryōhan Shingū, the *sōkan* in charge at the time, created a Zen meditation group (*zazenkai*) that met every Saturday. His interpreter was Ricardo Gonçalves, then a history student at the prestigious University of São Paulo. Unlike other intellectuals, Gonçalves had been interested in Japan from an early age because of his contact with Japanese-Brazilian children at school. By the time he started university he spoke Japanese fluently and began to frequent Busshinji. Later on his language skills allowed him to participate with fellow Japanese in the first course organized at Busshinji for the training of *shudōshi* (local monks who would assist overseas Japanese missionaries). His role as translator of Japanese and Portuguese was paramount in spreading Zen amongst non-Japanese Brazilians and second- and third-generation Japanese Brazilians, as many of these did not understand Japanese. Thus not only did Gonçalves preach and celebrate funerary and memorial rites at the temple and at residences of the Japanese-Brazilian community, but he also acted as a translator for Shingū *rōshi* when his university colleagues and other intellectuals frequented the temple, at lectures given by the *rōshi*, or whenever a high official from Sōtōshū arrived in Brazil.[55] In 1967, he published *Textos Budistas e Zen Budistas*, a seminal book where he translated Mahāyāna and Zen Buddhist texts. This book is still cited as a source of knowledge on Zen by many Brazilian Zen students and is frequently included in Buddhist e-mail lists.

In making Zen accessible to Brazilians, Gonçalves helped to break down the language barrier that had been the main obstacle to the proselytization of Buddhism in Brazil. Until very recently, when Brazilians of non-Japanese descent sought association with other Japanese Buddhist schools, they were redirected to Busshinji, because "they speak Portuguese there, and it is the place for non-Japanese Brazilians," as some non-Japanese-Brazilian adherents told me. Nowadays, Japanese Pure Land Buddhist schools (Jōdo Shinshū and Jōdo Shū) also have Japanese-Brazilian monks who speak Portuguese and even some non-Japanese-Brazilian monks ordained in the tradition.[56] Azevedo and Gonçalves are also responsible for the non-Japanese-Brazilian interest in Pure Land Buddhism. Both Gonçalves (in 1971) and Azevedo (in 1972) left Zen Buddhism in favor of other Japanese Buddhist schools. Gonçalves was reordained in the Shingon tradition after a ten-month residency in Japan in 1973, but after returning to Brazil he felt there was no support for his work as a missionary at the school's branch in São Paulo. He continued to teach Buddhism to Theosophists with Azevedo in Rio de Janeiro while getting closer to the Jōdo Shinshū Ōtani-ha (True Pure Land Ōtani branch), the school responsible for establishing the Higashi Honganji temple in São Paulo. In 1979, he started working at this school's Institute for Missionary Studies, a center dedicated to the translation of texts and development of strategies for preaching in Brazil. In 1981, he was reordained a monk in the Jōdo Shinshū tradition during a third trip to Japan. He has since been working as a missionary at this school and has sent three non-Japanese Brazilians to train as missionaries in the school's quarters in Japan.[57]

Being a close friend of Gonçalves, Azevedo followed his steps: he went to Japan a second time with Gonçalves to become ordained in the Shingon tradition and upon returning to Brazil also left this school, as he felt it had syncretized Afro-Brazilian rituals and was not following the message of Kūkai, its founder. Since then, Azevedo has associated himself with Jōdo Shinshū (Nishi Honganji), and in 1982 he became a missionary for this school during a third trip to Japan. He stated in an interview that "this school gives me freedom to speak about Theosophy, Christianity, and whatever I wish. It is in fact an ecumenical school."[58]

The trajectories of these two cosmopolitan intellectuals are meaningful for two reasons. They reveal the difference between monks and laity, which is maintained in Japan but is elided in Brazil. As followers of modern Buddhism, these men were able to act as laypeople (by changing affiliations whenever it suited them), as well as continue to be monks. In addition, they illuminate the constitution of a specific representation of Buddhism in the country, as most of the subsequent generations of Brazilian adherents either studied under Azevedo and Gonçalves or read their books. Although Brazilians and Japanese do follow several religions during a lifetime, Japanese do not usually change affiliations to traditional Buddhist schools, as these are assigned by family tradition. If they do change, it is not usually as a result of a spiritual quest, but rather because of a move to urban areas and disengagement from the rural, traditional family temple.[59] By contrast, according to the Brazilian sociologist Reginaldo Prandi, one-fourth of the adult Brazilian population has sought religions other than the one s/he has been born into either in time of affliction, or as an answer to a deeper, spiritual quest.[60] Moreover, in adhering to other religions, Brazilians may drop Catholicism altogether or simply add these religions to their Catholic worldview.

It is worth noting that Azevedo and Gonçalves went further than most Brazilians, as they became fully ordained in three different traditional Buddhist schools, receiving three different Buddhist names. In Japan, such switching of schools would not be readily accepted, because traditionally a disciple (*deshi*) is supposed to follow a master/teacher (*sensei*) indefinitely.[61] Aware of the disapproval with which his "hopping" around may be viewed, Gonçalves justifies it in the following way:

> My status as a Western scholar of religions gave me that "approach from a distance" mentioned by Lévi-Strauss, which allows me to view Buddhism through different lenses than those of my Japanese colleagues. The latter seldom experience Buddhism outside the school in which they were born and raised. The fact that I was trained in several schools, such as Zen and Shingon, before establishing myself in Shin Buddhism, allows me an overview of Japanese Buddhism that few of my colleagues have.[62]

By invoking his status as a Western scholar, Gonçalves places himself at the same time as an outsider and insider. However, unlike the anthropologist cited by him, Gonçalves "goes native," as he becomes a fully qualified monk and missionary in all three traditions.[63] His self-conferred ability to strategically move in and out of Japanese culture as it pleases him, that is, the ability to assert his Buddhist monk identity and/or his Western scholar identity as needed, makes him a good example of the cosmopolitan.

TEACHING BUDDHISM TO A NEW GENERATION

I would like to turn now to the second important feature in the trajectories of Gonçalves and Azevedo—namely their role as teachers of a second generation of Buddhists and consequently their role as constructors of a particular representation of Buddhism in Brazil. Azevedo, like many other non-Japanese Brazilians I interviewed in the late 1990s, says he was attracted to Buddhism because of the Buddha's recommendation that one should decide whether or not to accept his teachings on the grounds of reason and discernment, not simply faith.[64] This injunction has been cited many times over as evidence that Buddhism is in accord with science and reason. Azevedo's association of rational thought with Buddhism and his deep involvement with the Theosophical Society shaped a particular universalistic and ecumenical approach to Buddhism, which is revealed in several of his published books and which he used while lecturing at the Pontifical Catholic University of Rio de Janeiro.

Some of his students at the university went on to become priests themselves, the best known of them being Gustavo Corrêa Pinto. Pinto has been active as a member of the International Association of Shin Buddhist Studies as well as a missionary of the Higashi Honganji temple in São Paulo City. In 2002, he was frequently in the media because of his project of reerecting, in an ecological reserve in central Brazil, reproductions of the Bamiyan Buddhist statues destroyed in Afghanistan. In early 2002, Pinto traveled to Japan and Dharamshala, India (to meet the Dalai Lama) to gather funds. His is an ambitious project: it involves the carving of a 108-meter-high Buddha into a mountainside (this is double the size of the Afghan ones) and the construction of Japanese, Chinese, Korean, and Tibetan Buddhist temples, a center for interreligious dialogue, a Buddhist university, as well as biology laboratories to study the area's ecosystem. The ecumenical and universalistic trend preached by Pinto's university teacher is also apparent in the project's original blueprint.

> East and West meet again, this time to promote peace. This great South American Buddha will be sculpted to unite the different Buddhist schools and deepen the dialogue among them, and by doing so reveal the unity to which they are heirs.

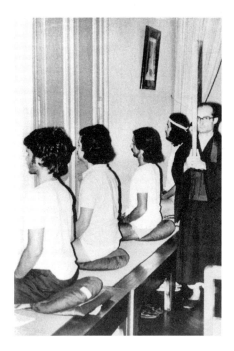

FIGURE 12
Zazen at Busshinji in the late 1970s.
Eduardo Basto de Albuquerque is standing
with *kyosaku* (wooden stick).

Gonçalves, in turn, worked as a catalyst to spread interest in Buddhism among his colleagues at the University of São Paulo and other intellectuals. Eduardo Basto de Albuquerque, who like Gonçalves also became a professor of the history of religion and an ordained Zen monk, was the first colleague to start frequenting Busshinji at Gonçalves' invitation. Basto de Albuquerque, together with other intellectuals such as Cecília Meirelles, Pedro Xisto, Orides Fontela[65] (all well-known Brazilian poets), Nelson Coelho (journalist), Gerhard Kahner (a German migrant who worked in China and became a translator), Lourenço Borges (a lawyer and founder of the Theosophical Society), and later Heródoto Barbeiro (journalist) would meet every Saturday evening for a sitting session. According to Basto de Albuquerque, in order to sit *zazen* they had to remove the wooden pews used by the Japanese congregation during memorial and funeral rituals at the Buddha hall. While this marks a clear distinction between Japanese-Brazilian and non-Japanese-Brazilian practices in the temple, there was at the time a group com-

FIGURE 13

Shingū *rōshi* (center front), Tokuda *sensei* (sitting left of Shingū), Christiano Daiju Bitti (sitting right of Shingū), and non-Japanese-Brazilian adherents at Busshinji in the late 1970s.

posed mainly of Japanese expatriates and postwar immigrants who would sit *zazen*. However, the separation between the two congregations was maintained by the Japanese having their *zazenkai* on Tuesdays, while the non-Japanese Brazilians sat *zazen* on Saturdays. Hence when the two congregations did enjoy the same activity they were still kept apart by the language barrier.

FIRST *SESSHIN* AND TASTE IN FOOD: EMBODYING HABITUS

Institutional separations did not mean a total segregation. Basto de Albuquerque told me in an interview that he participated twice in the annual seven-day *sesshin* (retreat) instituted for Japanese-Brazilian rural monks. These *sesshin* involved little *zazen* since they were intended to teach monks to perform funerary and memorial ceremonies for the Japanese-Brazilian community in the countryside, beyond the reach of the temples. He told me "they [Japanese-Brazilian monks] were like me, no one had been to Japan, or had had much previous training." Establishing *sesshin* for non-Japanese Brazilians in the mid-1970s was not an easy task; according to him,

> Ricardo [Gonçalves] and [Ryotan] Tokuda convinced the *sōkan* in charge of Busshinji, Ryōhan Shingū, to authorize a *sesshin* not in the temple in the city because it was too small, but at the headquarters of the Theosophical Society in Itapecerica da Serra, a town in the outskirts of São Paulo City. Murillo Nunes de Azevedo was the president of the society and he, being interested in Zen Buddhism, agreed to hold the *sesshin* there. The people of the society prepared the (Brazilian) food for the *sesshin*. But Shingū did not consider this a real Sōtō *sesshin* and did not attend.[66]

Basto de Albuquerque explained that Shingū's uneasiness toward the *sesshin* was due to its being held at the Theosophical Society estate and the requirement that he be a member of the society to participate. Once *sesshin* started to be held twice a year at Busshinji in the mid-1970s, Shingū actively participated in them. Basto de Albuquerque told me that up to thirty non-Japanese Brazilians and some Japanese/Japanese-Brazilian monks would take part in the *sesshin*.

It was Shingū who decided that Brazilian breakfast (coffee, milk, and fresh bread) should be served instead of the traditional *sesshin* breakfast (rice gruel and pickles), despite the fact that two participants had to leave the *sesshin* and go to the bakery every morning for bread and milk. Although the other meals were Japanese-temple style, Shingū dispensed with the traditional *ōryōki*[67] in favor of Western plates. Instead of following tradition and having the *tenzō* prepare the food (the *tenzō*, or head cook, is usually a senior monk, as it is the second level in the hierarchy of a *sesshin*), Shingū arranged for his wife and other Japanese women to do the cooking. Nonetheless, some younger non-Japanese-Brazilian participants were not content with the food arrangements. Basto de Albuquerque told me that some were scandalized to see the Japanese eating eggs and white rice. For them, brown rice and macrobiotic food was an integral part of what they imagined Zen temple food to be. He finished his anecdote with a smile: "They solved this problem by not eating any of the food offered in the *sesshin* and eating the fruit they brought with them." Tropical fruit is, of course, not served in Japanese Zen monasteries.

The choice of food in these *sesshin* is very revealing both of Shingū *sōkan*'s attempts to adapt Zen to Brazil and of the non-Japanese Brazilians' expectations of Zen. The fact that for Shingū a Brazilian breakfast was so important that he would accept people leaving the period of intense meditation and complete silence

FIGURE 14
Sesshin breakfast: Brazilian food.

to wander around the busy streets surrounding Busshinji shows his willingness to reach out to the new practitioners.[68] In addition, delegating the high position of *tenzō* to his wife and the *fujinkai* reveals first an adaptation from monastery life to temple life and second that the *sesshin* was viewed like any other social and communal activity of the temple, where members would unite in a common pursuit. Indeed, in Japan, monasteries and nunneries are separated by gender. They are a place for the training of monks and nuns, respectively, thus *sesshin* are held there, not in temples. Temples, on the other hand, are the dwellings of a monk and his family who are in charge of funeral and memorial rites, catering to the outside community.

The choice of food also reveals that some young non-Japanese Brazilians were undoubtedly influenced by counterculture ideas associating vegetarianism and macrobiotics with Zen.[69] Furthermore, Bourdieu's association between taste in food and social class may help us understand which strata of society these practitioners belonged to, since food functions as a marker of social distinction. As I discussed earlier, for Bourdieu, habitus—that is, the "internalized dispositions that generate meaningful practices and meaning-giving perceptions"—is embodied.[70] In other words, the choices of each stratum of society such as the quantity and quality of food ingested, clothes that reveal or restrain the body, the shaping of the body through exercise or lack of it, body language (the way one gestures, grimaces, restrains oneself), and so forth are all physically inscribed. Regarding food, Bourdieu has shown that the main, broad opposition between consumption by the poor of "fatty, heavy, fattening and cheap" foods, which are most filling and economical, and the "lighter and non fattening (especially fresh fruit and vegetables)" foods favored by the wealthy obscures a secondary opposition within each social group.[71] Indeed, Bourdieu reminds us that within the same sector, economic capital and cultural capital are differentiated. The higher the cultural capital one possesses, the more one is interested in consuming exotic, healthy, delicate, refined, light foods.

In the Brazilian case, these non-Japanese Brazilians demonstrated their membership of the "dominated fractions of the dominant class" precisely by demanding macrobiotic rather than what they saw as "immigrant's foods." They may not necessarily have economic capital, but their cultural capital regarding Zen is clearly based on ideas acquired from overseas. In Brazil, vegetarianism is not a mainstream practice and is usually associated with the upper, white, informed social class, who receive foreign ideas through travel, books, films, and the media—the same sector of Brazilian society that adheres to or sympathizes with Zen. For Brazilians, there is a clear distinction between vegetarianism and the tastes of necessity. These *sesshin* participants probably regarded the Japanese preparing the food as uninformed, unrefined immigrants who did not really know what Zen food should be like.

Because tastes in food are so closely associated with class, these vegetarian and macrobiotic participants kept their embodied habitus when they founded their Morro da Vargem temple in Ibiraçú (Espírito Santo State) in 1976. After spending five years training in Japan at Zuyōji Temple in Shikoku Prefecture, Christiano Daiju Bitti, one of the participants of the group, became abbot of Morro da Vargem in 1983. Currently, the monastery grows its own organic vegetables, produces its own honey, has established an ecological reserve and a center for environmental education, and until the early 1990s had a very strict food orientation. An informant told me that after many complaints by people who participated in monthly *sesshin*, meals became less spartan. Indeed, when the monastery published a book of recipes of *sesshin* meals in 1996, they included a mix of Japanese and Brazilian ovo-lacto-vegetarian dishes. The recipe for *okayu*, the rice gruel served for breakfast during *sesshin*, calls for brown rice instead of white. Because of the countercultural association between Zen and macrobiotics and vegetarianism in Brazil, this choice of ingredient is probably in accord with what the mainly non-Japanese Brazilian *sesshin* participants expected from Zen food.

The book of recipes and the taste in food call to mind the San Francisco Zen Center's many recipe books and its fashionable gourmet vegetarian restaurant (Green's) and grocery shop, whose organic food comes from Green Gulch Farm, a rural extension of the Zen Center. Two people who frequented Morro da Vargem in the late 1970s went on to live in the San Francisco Zen Center in the early 1980s. One was Odete Lara, a famous Brazilian movie star and sex symbol of the 1960s who became a Zen practitioner in the 1970s. Besides translating books by Zen masters such as Shunryū Suzuki and Thich Nhat Hanh, Lara published a book of memories of her spiritual quest, including the time she lived in this Californian Zen center.[72] These two practitioners probably contributed to the flow of knowledge from one place to the other, though the influence of counterculture on Zen and consequently on the founders of the Morro da Vargem temple predated their move to San Francisco.

CONCLUSION

Any analysis of how ideas such as Japan, Zen, and Buddhism are circulated and consumed in Brazil must entail a discussion of cultural translation as a process by which cultures are entangled and negotiate with each other. Brazilians themselves in the 1920s used the trope of "cannibalism" to deal with their anxieties concerning the copying of metropolitan originals and/or the creation of something new and innovative. One cannot speak of the foreign as "authentic" or "original" on the one hand and the national as "copy" on the other. Both are deeply interconnected in that ideas evolve from ideas; there is nothing "pure" or "pristine." Cultural dynamism, which involves hybridization and creolization, takes place when cultures meet.

Zen became a sign of prestige and symbolic capital for the Brazilian intellectual elite in complex ways. Intellectuals assiduously situated themselves as cosmopolitans who traveled to particular metropolitan cultural centers at different historical moments, such as Europe before World War II and the United States afterward, to acquire knowledge, which in turn became hard currency to be redeemed back home. I contend that the desire to accumulate cultural capital had a twofold result. First, the intellectuals' understanding of Japan, Buddhism in general, and Zen was informed by European and subsequently North American Orientalist representations, and second, Japanese immigrants present in Brazil since 1908 were seldom sought as sources of knowledge.

The way the Japanese in Brazil were overlooked is significant, since it sheds light on Brazilian society and its imaginary of Zen. The first, more obvious reason is that Japan was not a metropolitan cultural center for Brazilians until the 1980s. In addition, the Romantic Orientalist discourse and its fantasies of lost, pristine wisdom ensured that Japanese immigrants were regarded as part of a degraded, modern Japan that had lost touch with its culturally pure past. Class distinction had a strong role in this omission. Because of the deep-rooted presence of slavery in Brazilian history, manual labor has been traditionally associated with disenfranchised classes. The Japanese arrived in Brazil as peasants, and although they have ascended to the ranks of the middle class through their university-educated *nisei* and *sansei,* they are still considered lacking in refinement.

An exploration of Zen in Brazilian literature shows that an imaginary of Zen has been disseminated in Brazilian high culture through travels, translations, books, newspaper reports and articles, poetry, and the arts in general. It has been a dissemination in which the Sōtōshū school has had a relatively small role to play. Indeed, intellectuals were flirting with Zen long before the first Zen temple in Brazil was built. Sōtōshū, unlike other Japanese Buddhist schools in Brazil, was fortunate to have mainstream university lecturers, poets, writers, journalists, actors, psychoanalysts, and the like as practitioners. The visibility of these followers would guarantee a constant, if small, flow of interest in Zen by non-Japanese Brazilians. Their publications would nurture future generations when the time came for Zen to be revamped in what in North America was called "Tibetan chic," that is, the elite interest in Tibetan Buddhism that developed in the mid-1990s.

3 The Brazilian Religious Field: Where does Zen Fit In?

In January 2002 I was participating in a one-year memorial ceremony for a Japanese-Brazilian family at Tenzui Zen Dōjō, the temple Coen *sensei* had established the month before. During the ceremony, I overheard two girls who were sitting behind me whispering—one was telling the other that she was not feeling well. Immediately after that, the sick girl left her seat and went to speak to a woman sitting in the front row. This was Nícia, a Japanese-Brazilian woman who had organized this memorial rite for her mother. When both Nícia and the non-Japanese-Brazilian girl were preparing to leave the room, the girl fainted and was taken by other family members to a back room. After the ceremony, when I inquired what had happened, I was told a story that beautifully puts together many of the elements that make up this chapter. Nícia told me that the girl, a maid in her house, was a medium. Because she would "incorporate" (i.e., receive in her body) entities at any time and had no control over this process, they had been to many Afro-Brazilian and Spiritist centers to find assistance, but to no avail. On that day, she had "incorporated" the spirit of Nícia's deceased mother. Although the mother had been a devout Catholic all her life, her spirit had come back to a Buddhist ritual through an Afro-Brazilian/Spiritist type mediumship. In Nícia's words, her mother's spirit "wanted to thank the family for the beautiful 'mass' they had organized." Here, as in Brazilian society at large, many different religious beliefs and practices intermingled and had their place in their own right. While the ceremony at Tenzui Zen Dōjō was Zen Buddhist, there was room for mediumship (typically of Afro-Brazilian religions and Euro-Brazilian Spiritism) and Catholicism (in Nícia's mother's faith and words).

In this chapter, I address this religious world so that I can place Zen in its milieu and profile its sympathizers and adherents. By doing so, I aim to understand why and on what terms Zen has been accepted in the country. I argue that modern Buddhism—constructed by Asian elites as compatible with science and thus superior to Christianity—was adopted by Brazilian intellectual elites in opposition to what was perceived as a mystical, hierarchical, dogmatic, superstitious, and hence traditional and "backward" Catholic Church, the religious tradition into which they were born. Through in-depth interviews and a survey conducted among adherents and sympathizers, I learned that most adherents had a history of shunning Catholicism and some of being Marxist militants in the 1960s and 1970s.

Nevertheless, we should keep in mind that modernity and tradition coexist and are deeply connected in Latin America and Brazil, as I discussed in the introduction. The Brazilian religious field is particularly well known for its exuberance due to hybridizations, overlappings, juxtapositions, and creolizations of diverse religious practices, although religious choices and creolizations are often class based.

In relation to Zen Buddhism, I will show in this chapter that Spiritism and Umbanda facilitated the understanding of Buddhism, as they themselves were informed by Buddhist ideas derived from beliefs of the Theosophical Society. Furthermore, the process of industrialization and modernization set in motion in the 1930s brought a modern religious landscape to Brazilian society by the 1980s. Contrary to the thesis of secularization, as first argued by Weber using the metaphor of the "iron cage" of modernity,[1] more recent scholarship has acknowledged that the religious field remains significant in modern society.[2] In this chapter, I contend that the characteristics of this modern religious field—pluralization of faiths, privatization of choice, and turning to the self as the main source of meaning—account for the acceptance of Zen and the way it is practiced in Brazil.

EARLY CREOLIZATIONS: A PLURAL RELIGIOUS FIELD

Although Brazil is known as "the world's largest Catholic nation," this description ignores the presence of many other religions and religious practices that have been introduced and creolized in Brazil since the Portuguese arrived in 1500, bringing with them Roman Catholicism. Through the system called *padroado real* (royal patronage), through which the pope gave to the Portuguese crown the right to control all ecclesiastical activities in its colonies, church and state were unified at the outset of colonization. In this light, colonization meant evangelization. This was regarded by white European colonialists as a civilizing mission to the indigenous peoples and African slaves. In 1549, the Portuguese colonizers established the first Jesuit missions and *colégios* (schools) for the catechization of indigenous people. The next year saw the first waves of African slaves being introduced into the country. While indigenous people were under the tutelage of the Jesuits, African slaves were the property of plantation owners and hence were not directly subject to sustained catechization. African religions did face fierce persecution, but they were able to endure by adopting and creolizing Catholic beliefs. A common strategy to resist Catholicism was for slaves to worship their *orixás* (Yoruba deities) disguised as Catholic saints. This encounter between African and indigenous religious traditions with Catholicism during the colonial period (1500–1822) is significant, as it subjected Catholicism itself to a process of creolization. Popular Catholicism was created from such a convergence, adding indigenous and African beliefs, rituals, pilgrimages, observances, and festivals to the formal Catholicism of the clergy and upper classes.[3]

Adding to this field of asymmetrical power relations in which Catholicism (and its white adherents) stood at the top, Brazilian elites introduced French Kardecist Spiritism during the imperial period (1822–1889). Having enlisted intellectuals and the elite as followers, Kardecist Spiritism was in a position to establish greater legitimacy in its debate with the church. The same period also saw the introduction of Protestantism, which was carried by the first European immigrants who came to work on the coffee plantations.

With the change to a republican regime in 1889, church and state were separated (1890), and Catholicism was no longer the official religion of the country. As a consequence, in the years to come not only did the existing religious traditions expand, but new ones arrived and/or were created. Umbanda emerged in the early twentieth century as a quintessential Brazilian religious creation. It deployed elements of the main religious traditions of the country (Catholicism, Spiritism, indigenous and African traditions). At the same time, Japanese immigrants arrived, bringing Shintō and Buddhist beliefs, while esoteric traditions such as the Theosophical Society, Rosicrucianism, and Freemasonry were also making inroads in the Brazilian religious field.

Internal divisions within the Catholic Church were created in the 1960s, when Liberation Theology and the "preferential option for the poor" were preached by sectors of the Catholic Church influenced by the Vatican II Council (1962–1965). This, coupled with the church's more tolerant and pluralistic attitude, strengthened the Evangelical and Pentecostal denominations, as well as Spiritism, Candomblé, and Umbanda. In addition, Japanese New Religious Movements (NRMs) started attracting non-Japanese Brazilians in the 1960s and became a significant force in the religious field. This process paved the way for a mature spiritual marketplace in the mid-1980s as the middle classes adopted alternative spiritualities, while the disenfranchised turned to neo-Pentecostalism.

Carpenter has argued that "Brazilian religious culture has been the most pluralistic in the entire region" because, unlike the church in adjacent Spanish-speaking nations, the Brazilian Catholic Church suffered from institutional weakness.[4] This has allowed for other traditions to develop in the interstices of society. This is not to say that other religious traditions were not stigmatized and persecuted. Power relations were unbalanced in the Catholic Church's favor until as recently as 1960. One of the ways of persecuting adherents of religions other than Catholicism was through the Penal Codes of 1890 and 1940. Both prohibited unconventional practices of healing, regarded as *curandeirismo*, that is, witchcraft, sorcery, or charlatanism. Under this rubric were Spiritism and Afro-Brazilian traditions, since healing was at the core of their practices. Brazilian historian Ubiratan Machado has pointed out that the Penal Codes were inspired by Comtean Positivist aspirations to a modern society, as well as by the allopathic medical community and the Catholic Church's eagerness to protect its own interests.[5]

However, other religious traditions have always found room to survive and expand. Religions of possession (including Afro-Brazilian religions, Spiritism, Pentecostalism, neo-Pentecostalism, NRMs, and Japanese NRMs) have become so pervasive that the Brazilian anthropologist José Jorge de Carvalho contended that the Brazilian contemporary religious field should be seen as a "dispute of spirits." In other words, instead of analyzing the articulation between all other religions and the Catholic Church in terms of a vertical hierarchy, he advocated addressing the articulation amongst the diverse "marginal" religions of possession horizontally.[6] As the Catholic Church's hegemony visibly weakens (it has been steadily losing followers since 1950, with the 2000 census showing a loss of 10 percent in the past decade)[7] and Evangelicalism expands remarkably (in the last decade its followers increased by almost 100 percent), Carvalho's argument is convincing. For our purposes, however, it is worth noting that another group has expanded in the last two decades—those with "no religion." While until the 1980s they made up only 1 percent of the Brazilian population, currently they have grown to 7 percent. This expansion is significant because many people of this group have in fact moved on to alternative spiritualities and Buddhism, since for them "no religion" often means "no institutional religious affiliation." Before we delve into the constitution of the Brazilian religious field, it would be useful to briefly map the current field, as seen in table one.

Although religious choice is class based, more often than not Brazilians choose from a set of repertoires in this varied "religious basket" according to which religion best suits their needs at the time, for most see religious traditions as complementary, not mutually exclusive. This occurs because religious consumption does not necessarily mean thorough conversion. As the Brazilian sociologist of religion Reginaldo Prandi observed, "Seeking a religion in search of magical-religious assistance has become a common practice in Brazil, albeit hidden in different social classes."[8] Apart from Evangelical, Pentecostal, and neo-Pentecostal denominations, which press their adherents to shun other traditions, most Brazilians feel free to add, juxtapose, admix, integrate, fuse, and creolize different religions. According to Brazilian anthropologist Roberto da Matta, whereas the Catholic Church is

TABLE 1
The Brazilian Religious Field According to the 2000 Census

RELIGIONS	BRAZILIAN POPULATION	PERCENTAGE OF POPULATION
Roman Catholics	124,976,912	73.8
Evangelicals/Protestants (incl. traditional Evangelicals, Pentecostals, and neo-Pentecostals)	26,166,930	15.5
No religion	12,330,101	7.3
Spiritists	2,337,432	1.4
Umbandists	432,001	0.25
Buddhists	245,871	0.15
Other Eastern religions	181,578	0.11
Candomblé	139,328	0.08
Jews	101,062	0.06
Esoteric traditions	67,287	0.04
Muslims	18,592	0.01
Indigenous religions	10,724	0.01
Total	169,799,170	100

a "basic form of religion, which marks the impersonal side of our relationship with God, [other religious traditions] evince personal, familiar, intimate and direct ways of communication between this and the other world." Therefore, this complementarity, which "for a North American Calvinist, an English Puritan, or a Catholic Frenchman would be a sign of superstition or even cynicism and ignorance, for us it is a way of amplifying our possibilities of protection."[9]

Given this complex, plural, and porous religious universe, it is not surprising that Zen Buddhism found a place in the country. Indeed, not only did the early plurality of the Brazilian religious field facilitate the introduction of Zen within a small sector of society—namely the white, upper middle-class intellectuals—but also, the conspicuous New Age movement of the mid-1980s and 1990s paved the way for the expansion of interest in Buddhism in the late 1990s among a larger stratum of society—the white, upper- and middle-class professionals.

KARMA AND REINCARNATION: SPIRITIST AND
AFRO-BRAZILIAN UNDERSTANDINGS

I believe the main contributors to the early and wide acceptance of the concepts of karma and reincarnation in Brazil were Kardecist Spiritism and Umbanda. Significantly, by deploying a scientific discourse affirming its tenets, Spiritism has drawn followers from much the same sector of society as Zen. Indeed, Brazilian sociologist Lísias Nogueira Negrão noted, "Spiritism is a literate religion. More than a religion, Spiritism claims to be science, philosophy. Because of its high powers of persuasion in deploying logic, it is adopted by higher educated social classes."[10] Currently, Spiritism is so widespread in the country that according to Carvalho, "In many aspects, the Spiritist world-view became part of the national ethos, as much as Catholicism, and more recently Protestantism."[11] The latest census data showed that Spiritism is still expanding: while in 1991 it had 1.6 million followers, by 2000 the number had increased to 2.3 million. Umbanda, on the other hand, is less widespread (432,000 in 2000), and the majority of its adherents come from the lower middle class. However, there is one Umbanda lineage that strategically places its origins in the "Orient" (mainly India) in order to acquire prestige and legitimacy. Significantly, its followers come from the same sectors of society as Zen adherents. Therefore, when Zen arrived in the early 1960s, and later when it spread more widely in the 1990s, it encountered a base in which it could germinate and develop.

French Spiritism was first introduced by the Brazilian elite in the late nineteenth century. Following the same aspiration toward modernity that would drive intellectuals to adopt the U.S.-based Zen boom of the 1960s, Brazilian elites were quick to embrace the then latest French fashion. This is not surprising since, as mentioned before, France was a metropolitan center in the nineteenth century no less than the United States has been since the second half of the twentieth century. Spiritism or Kardecism—as it is known in Brazil due to its founder Hippolyte Rivail's pen name, Allan Kardec (1804–1869)—was itself a synthesis of many religious practices such as Catholicism, Protestantism, and occult philosophies that flourished in eighteenth- and nineteenth-century Europe, such as Swedenborgianism, Mesmerism, Rosicrucianism, Freemasonry, and Theosophy. At the core of the Spiritist doctrine is the idea of spiritual evolution through reincarnation, as Kardec was very much influenced by the positivist ideas of the nineteenth century. According to Kardec, the spirit, created by God, would go through several reincarnations until it achieved perfection. Karma and its corollary, the law of cause and effect, would determine reincarnation: if one's actions in a past life were negative, one would reincarnate into a life of suffering (through poverty, disease, unhappiness). By contrast, if one practiced charity in a past life (a concept Kardec drew from Christianity), one would reincarnate into a life of happiness. In this context, free will plays a key role, as human beings may choose what path to take in their lives. As a result, the evolution of the spirit would depend solely on its own choice and effort.[12]

The gap between Brazilian culture and Zen Buddhism has been bridged through the creolization of Zen Buddhist ideas of karma, rebirth, and the individual's responsibility for his/her own enlightenment (*jiriki*)[13] with Spiritist concepts. The evidence of interviews with practitioners, newspaper and magazine stories on Zen, and discussions on e-mail lists all attests to this process. However, the apparent similarity of concepts disguises deep differences, particularly in relation to key terms such as karma and reincarnation/rebirth. For example, as I mentioned before, Spiritism sees karma as closely connected with the always-ascending evolution of the spirit, and one's actions in this life determine one's next incarnation. In contrast, in Buddhism, karma is not a deterministic concept. In general terms, karma is a "deed" that, according to the universal law of cause and effect,

> produces a fruit under certain circumstances; when it is ripe then it falls upon the one responsible. For a deed to produce fruit, it must be morally good or bad and be conditioned by a volitional impulse, in that it leaves a trace in the psyche of the doer, leads his destiny in the direction determined by the effect of the deed. Since the time of ripening generally exceeds a lifespan, the effect of the actions is necessarily one or more rebirths, which together constitute the cycle of existence.[14]

Below I reproduce two of the many discussions that take place on the Buddhist e-mail lists on the concepts of reincarnation, rebirth, and karma. The questions exemplify how Brazilians have creolized their Christian and Spiritist ideas with the novelty that Buddhism presents. The answers are by Brazilian Buddhist adherents who have been in contact with Buddhism much longer and can therefore clarify such confusion of concepts.

> Q: Can somebody explain this to me? There is no individual soul that survives death, OK, I can believe that, but then what to do with the theory of reincarnation?
>
> A: The Buddhist doctrine is very different from the Kardecist one. It is

impossible to reconcile the belief in spirits and Buddhist teachings. According to the *dharma*, body and mind are a unity which is undone at the time of death; hence there isn't an individual being that survives. Life continues in other beings; life is regarded as a process, not as a chain of individuals. These are seen as mere illusions. As such, there is no reincarnation in Buddhism, but there is rebirth.[15]

Q: In Judaism and Christianity there is guilt. Isn't it the same as negative karma? I keep hearing people telling me not to do this or that because of bad karma; this conditioning of bad and good, isn't it the same as in Judaism and Christianity?

A: No, because in Judaism and Christianity one believes there is free will; in Buddhism we think that people act impelled by conditions (cultural, parental, family, country) as well. Hence, there isn't an individual guilt. Karma is a much larger concept. No karma is completely individual; all actions influence the whole world. Changing karma is like steering a large ship: we need to hold the rudder for a long time until the ship's direction changes. That's why the training is long and hard.[16]

Another meaningful creolization takes place with Umbanda. Umbanda was created by white, middle-class Spiritists attracted by the possession rituals of the Afro-Brazilian religions in the 1920s. In a process of creolization, these practitioners superimposed Afro-Brazilian religious elements on their mainly Kardecist matrix, which in turn already had Catholic and Eastern religious elements. Accordingly, Umbanda also draws ideas from Theosophy, Hinduism, and Buddhism, reinterpreted to fit the demands of Umbanda's adherents. Because of these origins, the theory of karma and reincarnation as a way of returning to earth to evolve spiritually is an essential part of Umbanda. Spirits are seen as needing to assist human beings to develop their own karma so that they, too, shall have a better incarnation in the next life. In order to do that they descend through mediums to help human beings, who usually seek their services to solve love, work, and legal problems, or to cure diseases.[17]

In Spiritism, mediums summon up deceased ordinary human beings. By contrast, in Umbanda the medium channels spirits of the *caboclo* (a deceased indigenous person) and *preto-velho* (an elder African slave) during a trance. In addition, Umbanda's pantheon also includes spirits of African origin (particularly Exú)[18] as well as Eastern/Oriental entities. There are seven lines of entities with which to communicate. One of them is significantly called "Line of the East/Orient" or "Eso-

FIGURE 15
Japan Town in São Paulo City: a Catholic church
next to an Umbanda shop and a Japanese school.

teric Umbanda."[19] In this line, Eastern entities such as The Hindu/The Indian,
The Turk, The Jew, The Gypsy, The Chinese, The Goddess of Fortune (sometimes
interpreted as Lakshmi), and Brahma descend on mediums.

Also associated with these figures is one called The Buddha who, in contrast
to the others, is not incorporated by mediums, but is exclusively associated with
bringing good fortune, happiness, and wealth. Interestingly, the images of Buddha
that I found in Umbanda centers and in shops that cater to Afro-Brazilian traditions are, in fact, those of Hotei (Chinese: Pu Tai). Although originally regarded

FIGURE 16
Images of Buddha and "The Hindu" sold at the Umbanda shop.

in China as the future Buddha (Maitreya), Hotei is known in Japan as one of the Seven Gods of Fortune. In Brazil both Japanese and Chinese associations persist, with a Brazilian twist. In Brazil, Hotei, as one of the Seven Gods of Fortune, is regarded as the one to bring happiness and wealth to the home. In addition, it is also thought of as Buddha, but this time not Maitreya, as in China, but the historical Buddha. Moreover, one can easily find small images of this fat-bellied, happy-faced Buddha in commercial outlets, coffee shops, and some homes. This Buddha will always be placed with his back to the door, so that the happiness and wealth he brings will stay inside.

Gilberto de Exú, a Candomblé and Umbanda practitioner and intellectual who researches and writes about these religions, told me that every single Umbanda altar (*gongá*) has a Buda/Hotei, and if these altars are more elaborate, they also bear the Seven Gods of Fortune. When Brazilian anthropologist Norton Corrêa asked the head of a center in northeast Brazil why she had these images on the altar, she answered that Buddha would bring wealth and happiness and "the little Buddhas worked for him," indicating that they had the same function of other entities who work to help human beings deal with problems of this world. In the same article, Corrêa writes of another Umbanda center, one headed by the president of the Umbanda and Afro-Brazilian State Council in Rio Grande do Sul State—a

FIGURE 17
"The Buddha."

white, upper middle-class, university-educated man. Besides invoking other entities, this center also invokes Brahma, Shiva, and Vishnu for sessions, and the head
of the center claims that the Oriental Line "has to do with Zen, the Himalayas
and Buddhism."[20]

This man's wife, who used to receive an entity called Brahmayana, has become a Zen practitioner at the Zen center of Porto Alegre (Rio Grande do Sul
State) headed by Moriyama *rōshi*. Like many other Brazilian Zen practitioners I
interviewed, she told me, "Umbanda was one of the many religions I visited. Spiritism, African traditions, Seichō-no-ie, Hinduism, and Buddhism were the other
ones." When asked what authors influenced her choice of religions, she mentioned
Krishnamurti, Osho, Helena Blavatsky, Zen authors (Philip Kapleau, D. T. Suzuki,
Thich Nhat Hanh, Seung Sahn, and Shunryū Suzuki), and Tibetan Buddhists
(Dalai Lama, Tarthang Tulku, Lama Yeshe, Zopa Rimpoche, Chögyan Trungpa,
and Lama Surya Dass), as well as Mircea Eliade and Gandhi. She said she read all
these authors in Portuguese, as she does not know any other language. Her easy

transit among different religious traditions and her readings epitomize the typical Brazilian Zen adherent.

India and the mythic "Orient" have always fascinated Umbanda practitioners. Gilberto de Exú mentioned that books by Blavatsky and Lobsang Rampa were mandatory reads for Umbanda practitioners in the 1950s and 1960s: "All these authors were a huge success. Everyone wanted to open *chakras*, talked about vibrations and so forth."[21] Corrêa explains the creation of the Line of the Orient as a strategy by these white, middle-class, well-educated Brazilians to counter the stigma that Afro-Brazilian traditions have even today. Since these religions are viewed as "primitive," "barbaric," "witchcraft," and "religion of blacks," they have packaged Umbanda as a scientific tradition (much as Spiritists do) that has its roots not in Africa, but in the "Orient."[22] Given the pervasiveness of what Said called Romantic Orientalism in Brazil, with its ideas of a "pristine wisdom of the Orient," it is clear that this association between Umbanda and the Orient anoints the former with the prestige of the latter. Gilberto de Exú corroborates this.

> Maybe what happened was a substitution of the *caboclo*—the native Indian, who among upper classes is considered ignorant, less important— by these Oriental entities considered evolved, enlightened, without karma. In poorer areas, where a more orthodox African Umbanda prevails, the opposite takes place, as the *caboclo* and *exú* predominate among other entities.[23]

To be sure, Spiritism is more widely disseminated in the country than Umbanda. It is noteworthy, however, that like Zen the Line of the Orient received its legitimation and prestige from its association with the "Orient" as a place of pristine wisdom. Along with Spiritism and Umbanda, other esoteric traditions arrived at the turn of the century to pave the way for the diffusion of a Buddhist worldview in Brazil. Círculo Esotérico da Comunhão do Pensamento (Esoteric Association for the Communion of Thought), an association for the study and dissemination of Hindu philosophy, was, for instance, founded in São Paulo in 1908. Later it established Editora Pensamento, a publishing company for esoteric, Eastern religious, and philosophical books that expanded considerably in the late 1980s and 1990s due to the Brazilian New Age and alternative spiritualities boom. The Círculo Esotérico is a Brazilian creation originating from Kardecist, Rosicrucian, and Freemasonry influences. By invoking Parabrhahmam, Ishvara, Elifas Lévi, Vivekananda, and other masters, it attests to a religious diversity that does not stem from Christian roots and that has been bearing fruit in the country for a century.[24]

In addition, the Theosophical Society was established in São Paulo City in 1919 and in Rio de Janeiro in 1923. As I showed in chapter 2, there has always been a close association between Buddhism and Theosophy in the country. The Sociedade Budista do Brasil (Buddhist Society of Brazil) was founded in 1923 by Theosophists in Rio de Janeiro. It was soon dissolved but later reestablished by Theosophists in 1955—the new founder, Murillo Nunes de Azevedo, was concurrently president of the Theosophical Society. In assessing how these esoteric traditions influenced the Brazilian religious field, Carvalho has argued that

> these esoteric traditions, which are already a century old in the country, have traversed and influenced our religious field much more than can be seen at first sight. They have expanded our religious culture, spreading the world of Oriental religions, particularly of Hindu tradition, considered by the majority of the esoteric groups (particularly the Theosophists) as the deepest religious root of humanity.[25]

I have given a lengthy explanation of the associations among Spiritism, Umbanda, the "Orient," and Buddhist and Hindu concepts (derived from Theosophy and other occultist traditions) because they are most important for an understanding of where Zen fits in this fluid and ever-changing religious field. Put simply, when the first Zen texts were introduced in the country in the 1960s, concepts that had long been in the Brazilian imaginary carried by Spiritists, Umbandists, and a host of Eastern and Occultist traditions, which arrived in the country from the nineteenth century onward, were recognized in Buddhism.

WHEN WILL SECULARIZATION COME?

The process of the modernization of society induced by the Reformation and the Enlightenment led many Western social scientists to think that religion would be displaced by science as a source of meaning. In the early twentieth century, Weber argued that Protestantism, with its shunning of rituals and veneration of rationality, would become a victim of its own making—it would perish like other religions. According to him, the increased rationalization of human action and its counterpart—disenchantment of the world—would lead to a similarly increasing process of secularization of society. In this light, secularization would be both this process of rationalization and disenchantment and the result of this process.[26] In the following decades, sociologists of religion such as Bryan Wilson, Peter Berger, Thomas Luckman, and Karel Dobbelaere argued that the more modernized, industrialized, urbanized, and rationalized a society, the more religion would be devalued and marginalized. Secularization theory, as it became known, argued that modernization and secularization would go hand in hand, science would replace religion as a meaning-making source, there would be a decline in individual religiousness, and, finally, once a society became secularized, the process would be irreversible.[27]

More recently, however, social scientists have rejected secularization theory by arguing that it was more a matter of "wishful thinking," "a myth," and "a prophesy"[28] and never consistent with reality. Writing in 1965, Martin was an early voice against the concept of secularization, but from the mid-1980s onward other scholars started claiming weaknesses in the theory. Swatos and Christiano have observed that secularization theory and evolutionism are deeply connected, for proponents of the theory saw religion as belonging "to some prior level of human evolution, [leaving it] now uselessly appended to the modern cultural repertoire."[29] Furthermore, the data do not corroborate this unilinear theory of evolution from religion toward secularity. For example, Stark and Finke have shown that religion has not declined in the United States. Their data reveal the contrary; the rate of church membership there has increased threefold in the last 150 years.[30] In addition, not only have NRMs appeared and expanded in so-called secularized societies, but religion itself has become a vital political force in the world.

In light of the above arguments, it is clear that what is taking place is neither secularization nor its opposite (a trend toward reenchantment), but change, transformation, and adaptation of religions to the new conditions of modernity. What are these changes and adaptations? We may observe increased religious pluralism, the establishment of a religious marketplace, private religious choice, and turning to the self as a source of meaning. Some characteristics of modernity have shaped these changes. For example, the separation of state and church has made religious affiliation optional. Urbanization, migration, mass education, and mass media, all intensified by the advent of globalization, have further increased pluralism and competition among different religious worldviews.[31] As a result, in this marketplace religions cannot impose but have to market themselves. The central feature of the religious marketplace is that "consumers" are free to pick and choose amongst diverse religions.

One of the first scholars to analyze this religious marketplace was Peter Berger. Although at the time Berger saw the constitution of this marketplace as a sign of secularization, he accurately identified its characteristics. For him, the crucial consequence of the existence of a pluralistic religious situation was that "religious contents become subjects of fashion."[32] Such a marketplace was established in Brazil in the 1980s and 1990s, as a result of earlier rapid industrialization, expansion of mass media, overseas migrations, and globalization.

ESTABLISHING A SPIRITUAL MARKETPLACE: THE WEAKENING OF THE CATHOLIC HEGEMONY

> In the second half of the twentieth century, the Brazilian religious universe has changed in degree and scope, and at a pace never before seen in our history . . . particularly in the areas where the country is modernized and has established rational and secular patterns. This process of expansion of Pentecostalism, Spiritism, and Umbanda is the corollary of the decline and erosion of the traditionally dominating religion—Catholicism.[33]

The increase in the number of Buddhist centers and practitioners in Brazil is another facet of the decline of the Catholic Church in the last decade of the twentieth century. Admittedly, Buddhism is a minor shareholder in this process. Protestant religions (particularly Pentecostal and neo-Pentecostal denominations) and NRMs, which appeal to disenfranchised classes, have the larger share of this market.[34] Brazilian sociologists of religion Antônio Pierucci and Reginaldo Prandi have argued that the expansion of Evangelical, Pentecostal, and mediumship religions is a consequence of the modernizing and secularizing trends of the church following Vatican II. The shift to a more tolerant attitude to other religions after Vatican II facilitated the expansion of religious pluralism. Pierucci and Prandi add another significant reason for "migration" away from the Catholic Church. According to them, while the Catholic Church ironically made its "preferential option for the poor"—which in Brazil took the form of Liberation Theology and the Comunidades Eclesiais de Base (Base Communities)—it was this very action that made it less attractive to that sector of society.[35] By emphasizing politics, social issues, and collective interests while stripping itself of the sacred, miracles, and healing practices, the church lost ground to religious traditions that emphasize the latter.

The Catholic Church is very much aware of this migration to other religions of healing. At the Twenty-Ninth General Assembly of the National Conference of Brazilian Bishops (CNBB) in 1991, it was decided that the church should focus on mysticism and healing, alleging that they were old practices that the church had left behind. This new direction gave strength to the Catholic Charismatic movement, which had arrived in Brazil in the early 1970s but became successful among the middle classes only in the 1990s, when it was emphasized by the church as a response to the Protestant explosion.[36]

However, the church continues to struggle with its loss of followers in Brazil. In January 2003, during a meeting between the pope and CNBB's bishops of São Paulo State, the pope attributed the loss of followers to pluralism and privatization of choice while calling for clear-cut boundaries between the church and other religions. In his words,

> There is a tendency to level religions and diverse spiritual experiences according to a minimum common denominator, as if they were equivalent and each person would be free to follow any of the several paths of salvation. Although these manifestations are typical of the Brazilian people, creativity and spontaneity in the celebrations should not alter rites and texts.[37]

More recently, at CNBB's Forty-First General Assembly in May 2003, there was a heated response to a study conducted by scholars at the Pontifical University of Rio de Janeiro that indicated that in 2010 there will be only 65 percent declared Catholics, a downturn of 9 percent from the 2000 census. According to the study, these "lost" Catholics would migrate to Evangelical churches or become atheists. In addition, the study predicted an increase in the number of Brazilians who affirm they have faith but are not affiliated with any religious tradition. According to the newspaper report, CNBB has since asked participants to contribute ideas on how to strengthen followers' commitment to the church.[38]

Prandi sees the move away from the Catholic Church as a consequence of both its secularizing trend of the past forty years and of the exclusion of the disenfranchised classes from the country's modernity project. Subscribing to secularization theory, he claims that because "the majority of the population was kept away from scientific thought, [and] from modes of behavior that imply a rational choice," they are prone to seek solutions for their problems in magic healings, and miracles.[39] He goes on to assert that

> although religion seems to take a step *back*, it is actually society itself that does so [since] it is not able to solve its own deep structural problems. So deep are these problems that society is forced to turn to religious plurality and thus finds the answers to problems that afflict its population closer to magic and farther from politics. . . . The success of religion and the crisis of society are two sides of the same coin. The well-educated upper and middle

classes, as "representatives" of a disenchanted world, constitute a social limit to the propagation of non-rationalized religion beyond a certain point.[40]

What, then, should we make of the explosion of alternative spiritualities among university-educated segments of the middle and professional classes? The presence of this highly educated group as part of the religious migration indicates that it is modernity itself—with its plurality of religions, constitution of a market-place, and privatization of choice—that fosters a burgeoning religious field. Since Prandi and Pierucci, in common with most Brazilian scholars of religion, focus their research on disenfranchised classes, their analysis is limited by their field-work findings. There is some irony in the fact that Prandi and Pierucci lecture at the prestigious University of São Paulo alongside academic colleagues who were among the first Brazilians to practice and spread Zen.

Indeed, in the past two decades so many New Age practices have become conspicuous in Brazil that Hess described the Californian New Age reality as bland compared to the Brazilian one.[41] The New Age trend became evident in the late 1980s, when there was a remarkable increase in sales of esoteric books, and this very category—"esoteric"—became commonplace in bookstores and bestseller listings in the press. By the 1990s, there was a booming network of shops, seminars, therapies, workshops, courses, therapeutic clinics, bookstores, and even consulting firms. In addition, since the 1960s Japanese NRMs such as Seichō-no-ie, Sekai Kyūsei Kyō, Sōka Gakkai, Ōmoto, Tenrikyō, Risshō Kōseikai, Perfect Liberty Kyōdan (PL), and Seikai Mahikari Bumei Kyōdan, which arrived in Brazil with the Japanese immigrants, have become highly successful among non-Japanese Brazilians. Research shows that in the 1990s about 90 percent of the followers of Seichō-no-ie, PL, Sōka Gakkai, and Sekai Kyūseikyō were non-Japanese Brazilians.[42]

As well as Japanese Buddhist schools, Korean Zen, and Vietnamese Zen (Thich Nhath Hanh visited Brazil in 2000), Chinese, Taiwanese (Fo Kuang Shan), Thai, and Sinhalese traditions of Buddhism have been increasingly present in Brazil over the last decade. In 2003, Fo Kuang Shan opened a four-million-dollar monastery (the largest one in South America) on the outskirts of São Paulo City. The monastery offers food, martial arts, and ethics classes to the surrounding slum dwellers. It is also implementing a university to join its three other universities in the world: two in Taiwan and one in the United States. Korean Zen has become better known among non-Korean Brazilians since Heila and Rodney Downey—disciples of the Zen master Seung Sahn and heads of a dharma center in South

Africa—have started visiting Brazil for lectures and retreats in the past two years. Heila Downey was previously a student of Philip Kapleau, a teacher of Japanese Zen, in Rochester, New York. These unexpected connections between Brazil and South Africa and Brazil and Taiwan are good illustrations of the globalizing trends of Buddhism.

To be sure, Tibetan Buddhism has been the main carrier of Buddhism since the 1990s. This trend was informed by "Tibetan chic," a fashionable movement extensively reported in the São Paulo and Rio de Janeiro media. There are many examples of the rapid expansion of Tibetan Buddhism in the country among elite sectors of society. A significant one is Lama Michel, an upper-class Brazilian boy who was recognized as a *tulku* (reincarnated lama) in 1993.[43] Since then, he has lived in the Tibetan monastery of Sera Me in India but goes to Brazil frequently for talks, and teachings, and to publicize his books. Another example is Chagdud Rinpoche, a well-known Tibetan Lama of the Nyingma school. Having fled Tibet for India in 1959, he subsequently moved to the United States in 1983, and in 1994 he relocated permanently to the south of Brazil (Rio Grande do Sul State). In 1993, in one of his previous trips to the country, he first created a dharma center in São Paulo City that is now run by a North American female disciple (Lama Tsering). Since then, four other centers of his have been established in Brazil. When Rinpoche passed away in December 2002, the news was reported in the mainstream national media as well as in Buddhist magazines for an English-speaking audience such as *Buddhadharma*.[44]

A final example, one with an interesting twist to it, is the Brazilian Lama Segyu Rinpoche. He used to be a medium in Umbanda in Rio de Janeiro City when he had visions, and like Lama Michel, he was later identified as a *tulku*. He went on to become the abbot of the Tibetan monastery Sed-Gyued Datsang in Nepal as well as the director of the Healing Buddha Foundation Segyu Gaden Dhargye in Sebastopol, California. In 2000 he established a center (Je Tsongkhapa) in Porto Alegre, the capital of Rio Grande do Sul State. Having been a healer in the Umbanda tradition, he continued to use many of its techniques (salt and herbal baths, incense for purifications) after he became a lama.[45]

All of these examples corroborate the fact that Buddhism in Brazil is not isolated from overseas trends, and, furthermore, that Brazil is not only a recipient of such trends, but an exporter as well. Indeed, Lama Michel is expected to succeed Lama Gangchen, his Tibetan mentor, as the head of the Lama Gangchen World Peace Foundation, a network of mainly European centers whose headquarters are in Milan. In addition, by living permanently in Brazil, Chagdud Rinpoche made his network of North American centers directly subordinate to the headquarters in Brazil. Finally, Lama Segyu is "exporting" new healing techniques to the United States and Nepal by creolizing Umbanda and Tibetan healing methods. Faced with such a highly plural religious field, Carpenter described it in the following terms.

> Brazil is the home of the world's largest Catholic population, as well as to more Pentecostals, Spiritists, and adherents of traditions derived from African religions than can be found in any other country in the world. Moreover, there are more followers of the cluster of traditions known as Japanese New Religions in Brazil than in any other country outside Japan. Brazil's religious economy is unquestionably the most diversified in all of Latin America and it is within this thoroughly eclectic religiocultural milieu that esotericism has been making inroads during the boom period [1980s and 1990s].[46]

Carpenter argued that this fully fledged spiritual marketplace was possible not only because of the Catholic Church's decline in the last quarter of the twentieth century, but also because of key roles played by mainstream cultural producers such as publishing companies, the press, and television. My own interviews and fieldwork observations corroborate Carpenter's argument. A profile of adherents will show that culture industries in the form of newspaper and magazine reports, books, and Hollywood movies did play a key role in spreading knowledge of Zen Buddhism.

MAPPING THE RELIGIOUS FIELD IN NUMBERS: MIGRATIONS, MULTIPLE RELIGIOUS AFFILIATIONS, AND CREOLIZATIONS

As I stated at the beginning of this chapter, statistics available on religion from the 2000 census (see table 1) show that the great majority of Brazilians (74 percent) come from Catholic families. What these figures do not show is the extent to which people move from one religion to another or adopt multiple religious affiliations and simultaneously follow the practices of each religion. Others eclectically combine elements of different traditions.[47] Statistics and surveys can give us a general idea of the field, but they lack the refinement of in-depth research. Therefore, while looking at the census data it is important to keep in mind that because the majority of Brazilians are baptized, they will answer "Catholic" when asked what religious tradition they are affiliated with. However, that does not necessarily mean they actively practice Catholicism nor — if they do — that they practice only Catholicism or that their Catholicism is devoid of elements of other religions.

Good historical examples of multiple religious affiliations but self-identification as Catholics are African slaves who were baptized into Catholicism but continued to practice their native religions and Japanese immigrants who converted to Catholicism as a means of being accepted into the country while not abandoning their own religions.

Brazilian anthropologist Carlos Rodrigues Brandão has given a more recent example of this phenomenon of multiple affiliations. He has argued that in Brazil people draw upon the religion most suitable for tackling their particular problem at the time. Through his fieldwork he met a woman who organized Catholic pilgrimages, but upon entering her house he noticed Jehovah's Witness books beside the Catholic Bible. She explained,

> [I have all these books] because religion is like that: I am Catholic, my parents are Catholic, I have organized twenty-five pilgrimages, and have made promises to Our Lady. But, professor, there are some problems, some modern diseases that the Catholic Church does not solve, because it is an older church. So, these more modern things we deal with in the divine temple, because they [Jehovah's Witnesses] are people who showed up now. They are new, some even speak English; they are prepared for these [new] things. Now, I continue to be Catholic. But there was a neighbor who wanted to steal my husband, so I went to Umbanda, because these things between man and woman we can't ask Nossa Senhora de Aparecida [Our Lady of the Apparition, the patron saint of Brazil], we can't ask Jesus [for help]. This is an Orixá fight, it is Pomba-Gira, it is Exú.[48]

Surveys and census data may lack refinement, but they can be used as pointers to the phenomenon under study. Indeed, a survey conducted in São Paulo City in 1995 points to a burgeoning culture of religious migration.[49] It showed that 26 percent of the Brazilian adult population gravitated to a religion different from the one they were born into. In addition, the survey also showed that one in ten converted residents of São Paulo City had her/his new religion for a year or less, while three in ten residents had it for up to three years. Here the data produce a revealing picture of the Brazilian religious field, as shown in table 2.

From this picture, it is clear that while Spiritists and Catholics belong to the upper echelons of society, Evangelicals and Pentecostals come from the lower sectors. These survey numbers show the weakening of the Catholic Church's hegemony and the establishment of a religious marketplace where the church, though still in a position of strength, has to compete with other religious traditions.

TABLE 2

The Correlation of Religious Adherence, Ethnic Background, and Education in the City of São Paulo in 1995

RELIGION	WHITE %	AFRO-BRAZILIANS %	TERTIARY EDUCATION %
Catholicism	60	40	13
Spiritism	73	27	34
Afro-Brazilian religions	54	46	13
Evangelicalism	52	48	5
Pentecostalism	50	50	2

Source: Reginaldo Prandi, "Religião Paga, Conversão e Serviço," in *A Realidade Social das Religiões no Brasil: Religião Sociedade e Política*, ed. A. Pierucci and R. Prandi (São Paulo: USP/Hucitec, 1996), 266.

Where do Zen followers and sympathizers fit in this competitive market-place? A survey I conducted among Zen practitioners in the cities of São Paulo, Rio de Janeiro, Ouro Preto, and Porto Alegre in 1998 and 1999 corroborates the data that a quarter of the population has moved to a different religion than the one they were born into.[50] Out of a total of eighty respondents, the majority (sixty-six) came from Catholic families. The remaining fourteen respondents were equally distributed among Jewish, Spiritist, Evangelical, Protestant, the Church of World Messianity (Sekai Kyūsei Kyō, a Japanese NRM), and nonreligious backgrounds. Of these eighty respondents practicing Zen Buddhism, twenty had moved from the religion of their upbringing to other religions before adopting Zen Buddhism. Some (nine) had been affiliated with Spiritism, but the majority also combined the religion of their upbringing with other religions, such as Protestantism, Theosophy, Rosicrucianism, the Church of World Messianity, Daoism, Nichiren Buddhism, Tibetan Buddhism, and what some respondents referred as "non-conventional religions." Eleven of these twenty "migrants" still practiced other religions while regularly practicing Zen meditation at their Zen center or temple. In addition, their upper middle-class status is apparent in the results: of the eighty respondents, seventy-one had tertiary education, and their professions ranged from medical doctors, psychologists, psychiatrists, actors, businesspeople, architects, engineers, journalists, teachers, and professors.

Finally, when asked if they considered themselves to be Buddhists, thirty-eight respondents said "yes" while eleven answered "not yet," "sort of," or "almost." This is a hard question for Brazilians, as they consider Zen Buddhism and Buddhism in general mostly a philosophy rather than a religion. One respondent gave a very revealing response: "If one who practices *zazen* is considered Buddhist, then I am a Buddhist." This is a common view of modern Buddhism: while there is no requirement to learn the scriptures or perform other Buddhist practices, meditation is supposed to be the key element that denotes who is a Buddhist. The "not yet" Buddhists could be classified as "sympathizers," a term Tweed has used in his research on Buddhism in the United States for "those who have some sympathy for a religion but do not embrace it exclusively or fully. When asked, they would not identify themselves as Buddhists. They would say they are Methodists, or Jewish, or unaffiliated."[51]

Brazilians, considering Zen Buddhism more a philosophy, often view it as a meditation technique for stress relief. Coen *sensei*, the former head nun of Busshinji Temple, supported this view in an interview for the O *Estado de São Paulo* newspaper: "It's not necessary to be a Buddhist to practice this kind of meditation. The temple offers several lectures for those who wish to learn this activity, even if they have no intention of becoming Buddhist."[52] In the same report, one practitioner said, "Zen Buddhism is a way to awaken my sensibility without denying my Catholic religion." As a result, being a Buddhist does not exclude professing other religions. Many Brazilians continue being Catholic while adopting Buddhism. The survey I conducted showed that if asked which religion they profess, it is most likely they will say Catholicism (since they were baptized) or no religion (if they do not actively adhere to any institutional religion) even though they might have adopted Buddhism as a way of life. Christiano Daiju Bitti, the non-Japanese-Brazilian abbot of Morro da Vargem Temple, reinforced this point in an interview for the weekly national magazine *IstoÉ*.

> If a Catholic considers his/her religion as a study of himself/herself, then he/she is also a Buddhist. Catholic priests, who were initiated in Buddhism, told me that after that they had a better understanding of the Bible. Buddhism has neither the intention to challenge adherents nor to convert them. People loosen up because we are not challenging anything. We just want to strengthen the faith of the Brazilian people.[53]

The borders of religious traditions in Brazil are very porous indeed. A survey conducted in 1988 by Brazilian anthropologists of religion Luiz Eduardo Soares and Leandro Piquet Carneiro showed that when Catholics who attended church once a week were asked if they believed in reincarnation, 46 percent said yes.[54] Since reincarnation is not part of the Catholic doctrine, one can see how permeable the borders of the Catholic world are in Brazil. Conversely, the survey also showed that 90 percent of the people classified as of "no religion" declared they believed in God, 60 percent declared they believed in heaven, 44 percent believed in hell, and 40 percent believed in reincarnation. These last responses can be interpreted by arguing that people who identified themselves as having "no religion" are in fact not formally associated with an institutional religion but still have a personal faith. These are most probably people who would follow alternative religions, picking and mixing according to their needs and interests at the time. A survey conducted by the agency Vox Populi in 1996 revealed that 59 percent of the Brazilian population believes in the existence of spirits, a concept accepted only by Spiritism and Afro-Brazilian religions such as Umbanda and Candomblé.[55] Undoubtedly, while the Catholic worldview has spread beyond its borders, the same is true for other religions in relation to Catholicism.

Japanese-Brazilian and non-Japanese-Brazilian Buddhists also participate in this phenomenon of borrowing beliefs and worldviews from diverse religious traditions. I will deal extensively with this phenomenon in chapter 5; here it is sufficient to give some examples. For instance, a message posted in February 2002 on a Brazilian Buddhist e-mail list illustrates how new religious concepts are superimposed onto a preexisting (in this case Catholic) matrix. One messenger asked, "Is there any reference to the Trinity in the Buddhist schools?" Another messenger answered, "Not that I am aware of. [But] There is the Buddha, the Dharma and the Sangha"[56] On the other hand, Japanese Brazilians at Busshinji constantly refer to the *sōkan* as *bispo* (bishop) and the memorials as "mass." Indeed, because this phenomenon is so pervasive, many higher religious officials work actively to reinforce and patrol religious boundaries. In 2000, on the Honmon Butsuryū (a branch of the Nichiren school) web site (no longer active), there was the following injunction: "Say temple, not church; ritual, not mass; priest, not father; thank Gohonzon, not thank God!" But Catholicism is not the only influence that spills over into Buddhism. Ricardo Gonçalves, the non-Japanese-Brazilian Jōdo Shinshū priest mentioned in chapter 2, has pointed out that

> the notable feature of the congregation is that its members combine elements of Buddhism, New Religions, popular Catholicism and even Afro-Brazilian religions in a syncretic whole. This syncretism is reflected in the adherents' behavior—many times they come to the temple carrying talismans and symbols of New Religions—and in the language they use, a mixture of Japanese and Portuguese, where the temple is called "the Church," the monks are called "father," and the *hōji* is called "mass." Some followers

get to the point of asking the monks to undo *trabalhos de macumba* [Afro-Brazilian evil spells] that they believe were cast upon them.[57]

FROM RUCKSACK TO *RAKUSU*: MODERN BUDDHISM, NEW AGE, AND ZEN ADHERENTS

The expansion of Zen Buddhism in the West is historically associated with the counterculture movement of the 1960s and with its subsequent development, the New Age.[58] Bellah has pointed out that Asian religions, and especially Zen, had the deepest influence on countercultural spirituality. In his words,

> In many ways Asian spirituality provided a more thorough contrast to the rejected utilitarian individualism than did biblical religion. To external achievement it posed inner experience; to the exploitation of nature, harmony with nature; to impersonal organization, an intense relation with the guru. *Mahāyāna* Buddhism, particularly in the form of Zen, provided the most pervasive religious influence on the counterculture; but elements from Taoism, Hinduism, and Sufism were also influential.[59]

Researching the associations between British Buddhism and New Age, Cush traced them not only to counterculture, but also to a nineteenth-century common ancestor—Theosophy. This brings to mind the connection between Zen and the Theosophical Society in Brazil, discussed in chapter 2. Cush points to similarities between Buddhism and New Age. These included

> a lack of dogmatism and a stress on the need for the individual to be their own authority, the use of meditation to alter and improve consciousness, the idea that religious traditions, teachings and practices are a means to an end, a raft to be used, not sacred in themselves, a stress on the human potential rather than on an external deity, and finally, the unity and interdependence of all things leading to a concern with ecology.[60]

Significantly, these purportedly Buddhist features present in the counterculture as well as in New Age were part of modern Buddhism, constructed by the interaction of Asian and Western elites from the nineteenth century onward as a way to counter the threat of Westernization. My own interviews and daily monitoring of Brazilian e-mail lists indicated that the discourse of modern Buddhism is ever present in Brazil. In an interview, one practitioner explained his adoption of Zen with these words:

What called my attention to Zen was mainly its simplicity. Zen is very much this *experience of meditation,* it's to *practice* and *observe* what happens in your daily life. Zen does not make this separation, as the majority of other religions do, between the religious place, where you practice (the temple, the church), and your normal, daily life. Zen puts these two things together. The practice is not only when you do *zazen,* but it is also something you'll practice in your daily life.[61]

By deploying the terms "experience," "practice," and "observe," this follower subscribes to modern Buddhist discourse, which regards Zen, and more precisely meditation, as a scientific tool for learning about the inner self. In addition, I found through my interviews that the United States is a significant source of ideas on Zen, through the media, books,[62] movies,[63] and travels. All of the people interviewed described their first contact with Zen through books. English is more accessible to Brazilians than Japanese, and hence most of the books on Zen available in Portuguese were originally published in the United States. Moreover, because these practitioners come from the intellectual upper middle class and the vast majority are university-graduate liberal professionals, many read the books in English before they are translated. Some buy books on Zen on the Internet at the Amazon web site and/or subscribe to American Buddhist magazines such as *Tricycle* and *Shambala Sun.* In addition, there are frequent suggestions of web sites in English, as well as translations of passages of books, on the e-mail lists. Following this trend of the globalization of North American Zen, some practitioners even choose to travel to Zen centers in the United States or feel that America is more attuned to their own practice than Japanese Zen. In their own words,

[When I was] In San Francisco, I felt Zen was more incorporated into U.S. culture [than in Brazil]. There the abbot seems to have Zen already blended in his personality, emotion, action, intellect, and in his whole being. So much so that the lectures aren't on classical texts. There the monks are American and the community is already forty years old. So they have a local color, the main core of Zen was preserved, but it is not so much Japanese.[64]

After I arrived home from a *sesshin,* I looked up a book about the experience of *zazen* by an American nun, Charlotte *Joko* Beck. Her talks with her disciples were published in two volumes. She is also a Westerner, so she understands what goes on in the mind of a Westerner who has embraced

Zen Buddhism. She speaks as we do; we understand what she says about the psychic processes, about the psychology of a Western person, in this case of a Brazilian person. I really didn't feel any difference. The American style of Zen is closer to ours.[65]

In addition, the New Age Brazilian boom of the 1980s helped spread this modern Buddhist discourse to an audience larger than the sphere of Zen adherents. Many examples could be given, but four should suffice. First, Paulo Coelho, the best-selling Brazilian esoteric writer, frequently writes Zen stories in his Sunday column for the widely read *Folha de São Paulo* newspaper. Second, in 1987–1988, TV Globo aired a *telenovela* (soap opera) called "Mandala," which dealt with alternative spirituality. One of the characters was a former Brazilian playboy who returned from Tibet as a Buddhist monk. Third, in 1990 the International Holistic University of Brasília (Unipaz) was established as a branch of the Université Holistique Internationale of Paris. Zen is taught at Unipaz, and Morro da Vargem Temple is one of the recommended sites for students to conduct their final-semester research. Finally, a disciple of Tokuda *sensei* opened Kanguendō, a Zen spa in Rio de Janeiro, where the visitor can enjoy organic food, healing therapies (acupuncture, shiatsu, and so forth), swimming pool exercises, and Zen meditation.

Although the New Age movement played a significant role in the acceptance and expansion of Zen in Brazil, not all Zen practitioners subscribe fully to its worldview. Through my fieldwork I found that there is what could be called a "continuum" in the spectrum of adherence. From this perspective, people may stand at one end of the continuum by being sympathizers, displaying very little knowledge and practice of Zen (for instance, just decorating their home with "Zen" motifs or reading a book or two about it) and creolizing it with other New Age practices. Indeed, many people I interviewed identified several New Age practices that they frequently associated with Zen Buddhism—practices of healing (yoga, shiatsu, *do in*, tai chi chuan, and acupuncture), eating habits (vegetarianism and macrobiotics), practices of self-understanding (many kinds of psychotherapy and astrology), martial arts (aikidō, karate, and kendō), and other alternative religions (the Rajneesh movement).[66] Moving toward the middle of this continuum, Zen adherents may sometimes meditate at home and/or at a Zen center or temple, read books, occasionally go to Buddhist talks, and participate in e-mail lists on the Internet. Approaching the other end of the continuum, they may become serious adherents and take lay ordination (*jukai*). Finally, they may stand on the other extremity of the continuum by receiving full ordination, becoming a monk/nun, and going on to study in Japan. Of course, New Age or fashion may be the catalyst for an interest and subsequently a more serious dedication to Zen by people at any stage of this spectrum. For instance, Christiano Daiju Bitti, the abbot of Morro da Vargem Temple, first became interested in macrobiotics and communitarian life in the early 1970s before starting *zazen* practice at Busshinji and subsequently training in Zuiōji in Japan for five years. Thus there are different degrees of understanding, creolization, and practice—all depending on individual choice.

MODERN BUDDHISM AND DISENCHANTMENT
WITH CATHOLICISM

The expansion of alternative spiritualities and Buddhism in Brazil demonstrates that the country underwent a process leading to religious modernity, with pluralization and privatization of faiths. However, according to Brazilian anthropologist Luis Eduardo Soares, the recent burgeoning of alternative spiritualities among the urban middle class points to other significant developments in Brazilian history, apart from the phenomena analyzed earlier of increased religious plurality and weakening of the Catholic hegemony. Soares argues that one important reason for the expansion of alternative spiritualities is dissatisfaction with religious experiences of childhood and youth, imposed by family or social pressure. Second, the end of dictatorship has aided in alleviating deep-seated tensions, allowing the introduction of new themes in social life.[67] The shift to democracy in the late 1980s meant that politics became one of many sites of self-realization and change. Finally, increasing poverty, corruption, violence, and devaluation of life has led on the one hand to a revival of an interest in ethics, and on the other to "individual experimentations through therapies, esoteric disciplines or alternative practices." Soares observes that these two directions (toward ethics as well as alternative practices) "express an ample recognition by intellectuals and middle classes that the traditional moral and religious model—prudish, hypocritical, authoritarian and sexist—has exhausted itself."[68]

Soares' arguments corroborate my own in relation to Zen Buddhist Brazilians. As I will show in chapter 4, the need for a clear set of humanistic ethical values to counterbalance rampant violence, crime, and corruption in the 1990s has led sectors of the upper middle classes to turn to Buddhism. For now, it is worth addressing the second direction—the quest for alternative spirituality to counter the dissatisfaction with religious experiences of childhood and youth. Most of my interviewees told me that what drove them to leave Catholicism and seek a more meaningful religious practice was their disappointment in religion in their youth coupled with the belief that the traditional moral and religious model was not suitable for tackling "real life." As I have noted earlier, the vast majority of the people interviewed were Catholics before they started to "shop around" in the religious marketplace and find Zen Buddhism. They explained their disenchantment with Catholicism in various ways, such as its dogmatism, its separation from daily life and its problems, its hierarchical organization, its attitude toward nature, its superstitions, and its almighty God. Notably, these were the same themes present in the modern Buddhist discourse and cited by Bellah and Cush as part of counterculture and New Age movements in the United States and the United Kingdom, respectively. I argue that Brazilian Zen followers adopted modern Buddhism as a viable alternative to Catholicism. Indeed, one practitioner, who was an ophthalmologist, told me,

> I have a Catholic background; I used to go to church till first communion. You go more because of your parents' influence. But after that, never again, because the Catholic Church is very divorced from daily life. I guess that's why Zen is so interesting. Christianity is too separated from reality. Zen is not; it is a very practical thing, very down-to-earth on how to face difficulties. Its pragmatism attracted me.[69]

Moreover, the Catholic attitude toward nature is another important reason for the adoption of Buddhism. The "spiritualization" of nature and the consequent concern with ecology are some of the main themes of contemporary spirituality. Likewise, Buddhists regard nature and all sentient beings as sacred, as they contain Buddha-nature. One practitioner, who is a university lecturer, related Catholicism to the destruction of the planet and told me that the Buddhist attitude toward nature was one of the reasons she left Catholicism for Buddhism. In her words,

> Buddhism has a distinctive trait if compared to Christianity. For Buddhism there is life in all the elements of nature besides human beings themselves. There is life in the plants, rocks, mountains, and water, in everything. But in Christianity things are different. I realized this reading Genesis, which deals with creation. There it says God created the animals to serve human beings. That shocked me. Human beings took their ethnocentrism too far. They subjugated animals and plants. Today we are watching the destruction of the planet. Buddhism has a different way of approaching this problem. And this is fundamental for me. To integrate nature is for me a spirituality that has to do with my life story.[70]

This vision is supported by Sōtōshū itself, since it is aware of this trend in contemporary spirituality in the West. Its *Zen Quarterly* magazine, which is distributed in Brazil, frequently addresses ecological issues. In one issue, the editorial read,

> As we approach the twenty-first century with the mindfulness of compassion and non-violence, our Buddhist challenge is to cultivate the Buddhist teachings that will stop the crimes against the environment and will reform our money-oriented world.[71]

Therefore, by uniting nature and human beings under the banner of Buddha-nature, as well as by offering a religious model perceived as less rigid and less dogmatic, Zen was able to present itself as an appealing alternative to the traditional Catholic religious model.

QUEST CULTURE: SPIRITUALITY AS A JOURNEY

The failure of the traditional religious model to address the aspirations of some upper- and upper middle-class sectors of society has meant that they had to seek new sources of meaning. Writing in relation to this phenomenon, Soares has attempted to profile the Brazilian alternative religious follower, whom he calls an *andarilho* (journeyer). In his words,

> S/he is in permanent dislocation among ways of addressing spirituality in the name of an always-renewed quest for mystical experiences. Hence, there is nothing more coherent than inconstancy. Devotion to beliefs and rituals takes place under the banner of *experience*. Having an indefinite itinerary built as s/he goes, the New Age wanderer walks alone [and] tends to recognize the essence of her/his utopia and the nature of her/his devotion in the quest itself.[72]

Deploying similar tropes, Roof described North American baby-boomer religious adherence as a quest culture, which emphasizes personal experience over inherited faith.[73] According to Roof, for boomers, spirituality is regarded as a journey of the self toward finding an individualized, authentic identity. Since the self plays such a central role in religious choice, terms such as "experience, fulfillment, happiness and inner peace" traverse this religious discourse. In the name of these values, and in the search for individual identity, the individual makes his/her own combination of picking, choosing, mixing, hybridizing, and creolizing from different religious traditions according to her/his needs in her/his "spiritual journey." Furthermore, like Soares in relation to Brazil, Roof identifies the open acknowledgment of doubt as one of this quest culture's main characteristics. According to him, "the loss of faith in the secular alternatives—in progress, science, therapy, politics, consumption" shows that for this generation uncertainty encompasses not only religion, but also most social institutions.[74] Such mistrust of institutions paves the way for exploration and experimentation with new beliefs. Finally, according to Roof, because the boomers comprise seventy-six million North Americans, they were able to establish social, moral, and political values influencing lifestyle, taste, belief, and consciousness.

The influence of the baby boomers' lifestyle, taste, beliefs, and consciousness has been felt beyond the borders of the United States and into Brazil, as Soares' typology of the alternative religious follower indicated. In his study of alternative spiritualities in Brazil, Carpenter observed that "esoteric networks thriving of late in São Paulo, Rio de Janeiro, and other Brazilian urban centers in many ways seem more attuned to the highly individualistic 'seeker' culture and 'self-spirituality' of postmodern Western Europe and North America than to the traditionally communitarian religious culture of Latin America."[75] Moreover, like their U.S. counterparts, Brazilian "seekers" belong to middle and upper classes and are highly literate. There is a certain degree of inevitability in this because adhering to alternative spiritualities involves not only the high financial cost of buying books and accessories, participating in seminars or classes, and undergoing healing therapies, but also being in touch with foreign trends. On the whole, these common trends could be summarized as a significant concern for ecology and the life of the planet, spirituality as a journey/pilgrimage/quest to seek the inner self or the God within, regarding the individual as the final arbiter of spiritual truth (derived from a mistrust of institutions), and finally the lack of a lifelong commitment to religious/spiritual choices.

THE ALMIGHTY INDIVIDUAL, OR "I DON'T NEED HERMENEUTICS"

I will finally focus on these trends and their influence on the Zen practitioners I interviewed. I argue that empowering the self as the final religious authority is one of the key factors leading to the choice of Zen. Most people interviewed particularly mentioned their Catholic background with its almighty God as a reason for their shunning of Catholicism. They praised the authority of the individual to interpret the scriptures by frequently quoting the Kālāma *sutra*, a discourse of the Buddha in which he warns the audience not to be influenced by expertise or teachers, but to rely on their own experience for the assessment of truth. Hayes has observed that this is the most frequently cited *sūtra* and that people frequently say that they were first attracted to Buddhism by this text.[76] As in Brazil, he notes that there are heated debates on North American e-mail lists on the issue of personal authority versus teacher's authority in the practice of Buddhism. One practitioner, a professor at the University of São Paulo, told me in an interview,

> [In Zen] I don't need an interpretation; I don't need hermeneutics, some-body telling me which is the correct way. It is Zen itself that says: "Don't let the *sutra* command you, you must be in command."[77]

If the individual has the final authority to say whether something is meaning-ful, then s/he may choose elements from different traditions and synthesize them in her/his own way. As I showed earlier in this chapter, religious pluralism is the re-sult of a mistrust of institutions, which in turn shifts the source of meaning making to the self. Pluralism is very much part of Zen in Brazil, and it is justified using the Buddhist idea of nonattachment. The famous Zen saying "If you see the Buddha on the road, kill the Buddha" is interpreted by practitioners as the impossibility for one religion to be the permanent answer to their spiritual needs. One adherent praises Zen Buddhism as a religion that does not request loyalty in such terms.

> You have to keep picking the little things you believe in and they will work for you as a step to go further. Then you will leave things behind when you have no use for them anymore. You shouldn't say, "I believe in this. . . ." It's interesting because the monk himself said this. "You cannot get attached to Zen Buddhism."[78]

This calls to mind the idea that the teachings are not sacred, but skillful means (*upāya*) that could be abandoned at will once they have fulfilled their role. As Sharf observes, "The rhetoric of *upāya* provided Western enthusiasts with the tool they needed to shape Buddhism to their own liking."[79] Importantly, if scrip-tures, rituals, and institutions are mere boats to reach the other shore, they then can be regarded as cultural accretions, or outer forms of one univocal universal essence, a view advocated by modern Buddhism. From this perspective one can "migrate" to different Buddhist schools, be affiliated with several Buddhist schools or/and other religions at the same time depending on one's current needs. Messages on e-mail lists frequently address this topic, praising migrations as enriching experiences. Here I convey two of these messages from an intense discussion that took place in April 2003.

> Someone asked the difference between Zen and Tibetan Buddhism. Padma Dorje (Nyingma) and Guenshō (Zen) answered: "the color of the robes." What are they saying with that? That Buddha's teachings are one, that there is one goal: enlightenment. . . . The diversity of *methods* helps all beings to follow on the footsteps of Buddha.[80]

> Tokuda-san himself was Rinzai and then moved on to Sōtō. Sometimes we migrate because of disappointments regarding the centers/temples, or searching for new challenges, or to acquire more knowledge, or simply to feel better. . . . Buddhism offers these options here in the West. We are very lucky as we have options which aren't connected to the culture of each country of origin. Unlike us, there people were dogmatically associated with schools because of family ties; they had no option.[81]

From this perspective some Brazilians participate in meditation at a Tibetan Buddhist center, at a Theravada one, as well as at a Japanese Zen center, particularly when Buddhist teachers come from abroad. Because they are the two main strains of Buddhism in the country, there is a common assumption that Zen is for people who prefer the lack of ritual and color, while Tibetan Buddhism is for people who appreciate the opposite. An adherent who previously followed Umbanda explained the difference between the two.

> I don't like Tibetan Buddhism because of the excessive ritualism (I associate it with Umbanda). That's why I stayed in Zen. I think I can be considered a non-orthodox Buddhist. Paraphrasing Alan Watts, I follow my own path.[82]

This woman's words significantly illustrate how the themes of authority of the individual, spirituality as journey, and quest culture are part of Zen in Brazil. These themes are also found in the Buddhisms of the United States. Tweed coined the term "shoppers" to denote those North American Buddhists who "shop, purchasing a bit of this and consuming a bit of that, but never buying it all."[83] However, such shopping is not aleatory. In an interview, a non-Japanese-Brazilian Zen teacher who doubles as a business consultant giving Buddhist talks in corporations explained that the difference between Tibetan and Zen Buddhism lies in their different methods of reaching the same enlightenment. Using a modernizing worldview, where religious rituals and superstitions are placed hierarchically beneath science, he calls Tibetan Buddhism "popular Buddhism," while Zen, which according to modern Buddhism is devoid of ritual and akin to science, would be "elite" Buddhism. He goes on to predict that because Tibetan Buddhism is so ritualized and mystical it will expand faster in Brazil, while Zen will be restricted to elites, who desire a more direct, and thus harder, path to enlightenment. His views have recently reached a wider audience as he has secured a place on the e-mail lists as a spokesperson for Zen (neither Coen *sensei* nor the Japanese missionaries write on the e-mail lists). In this interview, he told me,

> I am a skeptic, of a rationalist mind, a business administrator. I write about economics, I am interested in science. I am not a man of faith and technically could not be called religious. In fact, I could be called an atheist. If a student comes into my *zendō* and asks about astrology, . . . I send him to Vajrayāna,[84] because it is the right place for her/him. Vajrayāna has more rituals, initiations, these mystical aspects that are absent in Zen. Thus, for different people there are different methods. But in essence, there is no difference because there are no alterations in the philosophical discourse.[85]

Whereas this Zen teacher stands closer to the end of the continuum that subscribes fully to Zen (even if he does not think going to Japan is necessary, since he told me that there he would learn only cultural accretions, not the essence of Buddhism), other Brazilian Buddhists stand at the opposite end of the continuum. They pick and mix elements from Afro-Brazilian religions with the justification that all deities are equivalent, as they are only "energy." This message was posted in January 2001, and the messenger would surely have been referred to Vajrayāna if he had met the Zen teacher previously mentioned.

> I have this habit of always comparing and relating different beliefs. If a Buddhist deity REALLY exists (as form, energy and an archetype) why can't saints or deities of other religions exist in the same way? I liked the explanation given by somebody in another message. He said that the Buddhas and deities are not Buddhists, but they manifest themselves in this way to help Buddhists. Hence, they can manifest themselves as Iemanjá,[86] Our Lady, Shiva, Angels, etc. . . . In sum, they are "beings" (I prefer energies) that help us humans in the best way possible so that we can under-

stand them (they try to speak "our language"). In this way, Tara[87] can be the same "power" that is manifested in Our Lady and vice versa. Actually, none of them exist and at the same time both exist, and they exist inside of us too![88]

Thus for this follower not only all different Buddhist traditions have a univocal, universal essence, but also deities of all religions are equivalent, as they are "energy." Here it is worth going back to alternative spiritualities, as energy is a common denominator present in nature, body, and spirit empowering these elements with the sacredness of life. In this context, Carvalho has argued that "Christ is understood as a divine principle (as Buddha nature) and Jesus as an incarnation, an avatar, a historical manifestation of the deity, equivalent to Buddha Shākyamuni, Krishna, Zoroaster, and Mohammed.[89] Understandably, for a country deeply steeped in Catholicism, many interviewees as well as messengers to the Buddhist lists regard Buddha and Jesus as enlightened beings and thus equivalent. Books that associate both traditions such as the ones by the Vietnamese Buddhist monk Thich Nhat Hahn are always mentioned as evidence of their interchangeability.

While turning to the self as the source of meaning has meant individuals could synthesize their own religious journey, it has also meant that people who once were averse to religion have become attracted to it. As in the United States, many Brazilians who were leftist and Marxist in the 1970s have turned to spirituality as a source of meaning. Many of my interviewees had been Marxists but told me they were drawn to Zen because of Zen's reliance not on an external god but on the individual's responsibility for her/his own life. All were intellectuals who, in one way or another, were associated with university life. One particular follower is a good representative of this intellectual strand of Brazilians who became interested in Buddhism in the 1960s, spent the 1970s as Marxists, and went back to Buddhism in the 1980s. In an interview he told me,

> I am fifty, and have been observing Buddhist flows reaching us Brazilians and Americans in general since the 1960s. I met the poet Paulo Leminsky in 1968, when we were all Marxists. We'd read the beatniks, Alan Watts and the great Buddhist master from the University of Kyoto who was the small and wise Teitaro Suzuki. In the 1970s, I studied philosophy at USP [University of São Paulo] and spent the whole decade as a Marxist. In 1978, I got tired of all this and went to live alone on a farm. There I started to read the wonderful work by Teitaro Suzuki, *Essays on Zen Buddhism*. I also read many books by the spiritual leader and great intellectual Alan

Watts. Both were very important for my generation. In 1982, I went to live with an indigenous group and took just two books: the complete works of Fernando Pessoa and a small translation of *Zen and the Unconscious* by Suzuki. The time I spent with indigenous people and Zen taught me to live in the present moment.[90]

While the disappearance of an external god, particularly the Catholic God, has attracted this group to Zen, their mistrust of institutions has made it difficult for many of them to fully belong to Sōtōshū by taking lay ordination. One adherent who is a university professor said that to become ordained was like getting married in the church, which she had never done, as she did not need to formalize her emotional commitment. Another adherent, who is a video maker, noted,

> I haven't been [lay] ordained and will never be. I can't belong to any institution. *Zazen* is great, but it didn't need to be part of a religion. Really, the only thing that bothers me in Zen is this need to have Japan and religion in the package.[91]

Here, we can see once more the themes of Buddhist universalism disconnected from Japanese cultural accretions and of Zen not being a religion but an individual experience that does not require the association with institutional tradition advocated by modern Buddhism, and particularly by D. T. Suzuki in regard to Zen. Moreover, one can perceive the strong opposition to Catholicism as a significant institution when the above interviewee compared ordination to marriage in the church. Indeed, because Zen gives this freedom to participate without necessarily subscribing to it wholly, it can attract those people who had left Catholicism behind. In modern Brazil, it is the "almighty individual" who experiments, tests, chooses, and adds elements to her/his religion(s) of choice. Modern Zen, with its emphases on experience rather than doctrinal belief, responsibility of the individual for his/her own realization, and the personal testing of this method of realization, attracts people who have left Catholicism, regarded as authoritarian, hierarchical, superstitious, dogmatic, and distant from daily life.

CONCLUSION

While in chapters 1 and 2 I showed how an imaginary of Zen arrived in Brazil carried by Japanese immigrants, Japanese missionaries, and cosmopolitan intellectuals, respectively, in this chapter I have looked at how it spread at a grass-roots level among Zen practitioners. I showed that by deploying their own diverse religious matrices as a basis for a new Buddhist vocabulary, Brazilians creatively transformed modern Buddhist discourse acquired overseas, actively breaching the divisions between tradition and modernity. Indeed, in the first vignette and throughout the chapter, I provided ethnographic evidence of *how* modernity—with its features of religious pluralism, privatization of choice, mistrust of institutions, and a turn to the self as a source of meaning—is deeply articulated with tradition in the use of Catholic, Afro-Brazilian, Spiritist, and alternative-spiritualities beliefs as lenses through which to grasp it.

As Brazilian anthropologist Ruben Oliven noted, "Possibly the peculiarity of Brazilian society lies precisely in its capacity to take on those aspects of modernity that are of interest to it and to transform them into something suited to its own needs, in which the modern interacts with the traditional, the rational with the emotional and the formal with the personal."[92] Despite such interactions taking place locally, the drive to adopt European and North American modernities is intensely spread among the population. For upper- and upper middle-class Brazilians, who maintain closer contact with these localities through travel, the Internet, books, movies, and media, it seems that modernity is just around the corner and, furthermore, that either "traditional" Buddhist masters or "modern" North American/European Buddhist teachers can take them there.

In the next chapter I will address the role of the culture industries, particularly the printed media, in packaging Buddhism as fashionable, modern, and thus desirable for the upper echelons of society. To this end, I will analyze global flows into the country while looking at how their localization is efficacious in creating and preserving social distinction.

4 The Brazilian Imaginary of Zen: Global Influences, Rhizomatic Forms

In 1997 the glossy, upmarket Brazilian magazine *Casa Vogue*, a local version of *Vogue Living*, featured a cover story on "Zen Style." The magazine invited twelve prominent Brazilian architects and interior decorators to produce designs that evoked ambiences of "Zen." Each professional was asked to define the qualities of this "Zen Style." The story was reported under the heading "Zen Style: More than a Decorating Style, It is a Life Style." The list of attributes provided by the twelve professionals continued along the same lines.

> Zen has to do with culture, refinement, and it is contemporary; it reflects a particular mood; it is poetic because it incorporates all elements of life; it is quality above all; it seeks the essence; it has to do with visual simplicity, it is functional—it is here to be used; it is monastic but not poor; it is not decorative; Zen accessories are powerful because they carry memories and stories within themselves; Zen ambiences are monochromatic.[1]

The cover of the magazine featured the interior design chosen as the quintessential expression of a "Zen ambience": it portrayed a white-grayish room displaying three-dimensional white artwork on the back wall, wooden sculptures resembling thin, dry tree trunks on the right-hand side, immaculate white pillows on a dark wooden Indian bed in the center of the room, some African black-and-white rugs complete with a traditional African guitar leaning on the side of the bed, and finally, a long, shallow, dark wooden bowl placed on the floor containing two items: a small loaf of French bread broken into two and ruffled, recently read newspapers. Bland yellowish light fell on two particular spots: the white artwork on the back wall and the loaf of bread on the floor.

ZEN STYLE—A LIFESTYLE? IMAGINED WORLDS

What makes *Casa Vogue* and some of the most prominent Brazilian interior decorators think Zen is a lifestyle? Where do the ideas of refinement, high culture, and monasticism (but not, as one designer was quick to note, poverty), which are associated with Zen, come from? Where do the African accessories and the bread fit in? What about the newspapers? Why was Zen associated with anything more than religion in the first place?

FIGURE 18
Cover of *Casa Vogue:* Zen Style (1997).

This story weaves together many of the different threads that have entangled Zen in Brazil. I will argue that it exemplifies the way Zen is associated there with urban cosmopolitanism, class distinction through taste, and the construction of the imagined worlds of the exotic other. I contend that the constructed Zen ambience on the cover of *Casa Vogue,* and indeed all other images and ideas of Zen produced, circulated, and consumed in Brazil, shed light on the sectors of society that produce, circulate, and consume such ideas and images. Appadurai has argued that because of the recent massive globalization of the media and migration, the imagination does not belong solely to the fields of art, myth, and ritual anymore.[2] He asserts that "imagination is now central to all forms of agency, is itself a social fact, and is the key component of the new global order."[3] He observes, moreover, that this collective, shared imagination creates transnational communities. If that is so, one has to look for answers to the question of the association of Zen with high culture and lifestyle in the genealogy of global flows of the imaginary of Zen and their creolization with the local Brazilian imaginary.

GLOBAL FLOWS AND SITUATED IMAGINARIES

Many authors have discussed the implications of the intensification of global flows of people, images, information, technology, commodities, and capital for the nation-state.[4] Deploying the idea of rhizome developed by the French poststructuralist theorists Gilles Deleuze and Felix Guattari, Appadurai asserts that the West is just one of the nodes from which global cultural flows emanate. Like a rhizome, the global cultural economy does not spread from one particular center, but moves around in a chaotic and unpredictable pattern.[5]

In order to examine such transnational cultural flows, he proposes a system of five overlapping dimensions of the global cultural economy: ethnoscapes, mediascapes, technoscapes, finanscapes, and ideoscapes. Current cultural traffic would take place in and through the disjunctures among these five "scapes." Appadurai points out that such "scapes" are not objective, but are constructed by the actors according to their historical, linguistic, and political location. In this context, the different locations Brazilians occupy in society and their different exposures to global cultural flows inform the way they construct their "imagined world" of Zen Buddhism. A brief illustration of this point is the fact that while Zen Buddhism is portrayed as evil by Pentecostal preachers,[6] it is regarded as chic by trendsetters, as philosophical and/or meditational by white upper-class practitioners, and as a religion that involves devotion by Japanese immigrants and descendants.

In previous chapters I have addressed ethnoscape in the form of Japanese Zen Buddhist missionaries in Brazil, non-Japanese-Brazilian neophytes training in Japan, Buddhist sympathizers on pilgrimage tours, and intellectuals traveling and translating texts on Buddhism. I have also shown that Appadurai's notion of rhizome is useful in describing the way global flows carry Zen Buddhism to and from Brazil. Although the United States is a strong source of information and ideas on Zen and Buddhism in general, it is not the sole producer of this cultural traffic. Not only do Brazilian Zen Buddhists seek to establish the authenticity of their practices in various centers including Japan, the United States, and Europe, but Brazilian Zen is also "exported" to other areas of the world. Having missionaries, novices, adherents, and tourists on the move across Brazil, Japan, the United States, and Europe in the past decades has opened a window for cross-pollination among the diverse schools and masters, which in turn shapes the way Brazilians relate to Zen Buddhism. In this chapter I address mediascapes (cultural industries) and techno-scapes (the Internet) and analyze the construction of a Brazilian imaginary of Zen through them.

MEDIASCAPES: "BUDDHA IS POP"

While all "scapes" contribute to the process of constructing an imaginary of Zen Buddhism in Brazil, the mediascape, which produces and conveys images, infor-mation, and ideas throughout the world, has an especially prominent role. The in-creasing visibility of Buddhism among the intellectual, middle- and upper middle-class sectors of Brazilian society in the 1990s is very much due to the frequency and the way Buddhism is represented in the media, be it foreign or local. The 1990s wit-nessed Hollywood's increasing fascination with Buddhism. Such films as *The Little Buddha* (1993), *Kundun* (1997), and *Seven Years in Tibet* (1997), and more recently the non-Hollywood movies *The Cup* (2000) and *Samsāra* (2002), did not go un-noticed by this audience, and neither did the Free Tibet concerts by the U.S. rock group the Beastie Boys, nor the international celebrities who have called them-selves Buddhists, nor yet the trend North American media designated "Tibetan chic."

Locally, *Casa Vogue* is not alone in its depiction of Zen. Since the Brazilian media is very much influenced by the North American one, from 1997 onward—the year that two of the three Hollywood films were released and *Time*'s cover story featured an extensive report on Buddhism in the United States showcasing Brad Pitt in his role in *Seven Years in Tibet*—all major Brazilian magazines and news-papers began regularly running stories on Buddhism. Indeed, this report is a good example of how ideas circulate and arrive in Brazil. I remember being at a major bookstore in São Paulo (FNAC) when I saw a group of teenage girls giggling and reading *Time*. That was surprising not only because the content of the magazine is not usually appealing to teenage girls, but also because of the language barrier. When I got closer to the stand where the magazine was displayed, I realized they were in fact reveling in Pitt's picture on the cover. They would probably see the film because of him, and by doing so they would gain exposure to a Hollywood imaginary of Tibet.

Following *Time*'s report, most Brazilian magazine and newspaper stories attempted to introduce Buddhism to an unfamiliar audience: they started by giving a basic explanation of Buddhist concepts, schools, and deities, mentioning the Dalai Lama and pointing out international celebrities who adhere to Buddhism. From then on, most of the stories featured interviews with national celebrities (from actors to politicians) who are Buddhists. Another common format focused on meditation as a technique for a better quality of life and improvement of attention, and hence productivity, in the workplace. For instance, the cover report of the national weekly magazine *IstoÉ* featured an article titled "Meditation: How to Use This Ancient Technique to Overcome the Economic Crisis, Escape Daily Stress, Improve Your Concentration, and Make Difficult Decisions."[7] In the media, going to the gym may qualify as a Zen experience. In 2001, *IstoÉ* ran a story titled "Zen Fitness" in which it revealed a new fashionable class given at upmarket gyms: Zen gymnastics.[8] Reading the story, one discovers that "Zen gymnastics" is, in fact, a general term for classes that integrate body and mind, such as the "prajna ball" and "chi ball," described as Indian and Chinese breathing exercises, respectively. Significantly, in attempting to make the classes more appealing and fashionable, the story also mentioned that the number of gyms offering them in the United States had doubled in the last four years.

Ideas commonly associated with Zen in the media are happiness, peace, tranquility, well-being, simplicity, harmony, and meditation on the one hand and modern, fashionable, and trendy on the other. Most telling, in flipping through *Folha de São Paulo,* a major Brazilian newspaper, one can regularly find the word "Zen" being used as an adjective.[9] It appears mainly in the social column, where Zen is used to connote cool, savvy, cosmopolitan, and chic people. It is noteworthy that these people described as "Zen" are not necessarily rich, but ones who are generally thought to possess some form of cultural capital. Adding to the trend, Paulo Coelho, the now world-famous Brazilian New Age writer, also has a Sunday column in *Folha de São Paulo* where he writes about popular occultism, mysticism, and Buddhism. He usually recounts traditional stories/dialogues between Zen masters and disciples, disseminating these tales into mainstream society.

It is significant that the term "Zen" has been a common part of the Brazilian vocabulary of upper middle classes in Brazil since the 1960s Zen boom. To call someone "Zen" is to say this person is calm, collected, and peaceful. For instance, Itamar Franco, a well-known politician running for president in the 2002 election, used this colloquial expression several times in the media, claiming he was in a "Zen phase" of his campaign, by which he intended to reassure voters of his confidence.[10] The usual imaginary of Zen as tranquility and inner peace is juxta-

FIGURE 19
"Buddha Is Pop," Buddhist MTV presenter and daughter (*Folha de São Paulo*, July 2001 Alexandre Schneider/Folha Imagen).

posed with the notion that Zen encompasses all Oriental, exotic beliefs, practices, and techniques employed to achieve this state. Hence newspaper and magazine stories frequently carry titles involving the term "Zen" that in fact deal with other schools of Buddhism (most commonly Tibetan Buddhism), yoga, tai chi chuan, feng shui, crystals, and so on. In June 1998, *Elle* ran a story titled "Zen Wave" but featuring mainly Tibetan Buddhism.[11] The title of a report in the June 1998 issue of the national magazine *Veja* makes these two juxtaposed meanings readily apparent: "Seeking Zen: The Quest for Oriental Exercises Increases."[12] Likewise, the

FIGURE 20
Claudia Raia, Buddhist soap opera star (*IstoÉ*, May 2001).

Folha de São Paulo web site has a link called "Everything's Alright, Everything's Zen" (Tudo Bem, Tudo Zen), adopting the common usage of the word Zen as a synonym for peace and tranquility.[13] On this site many alternative practices and world religions are discussed. Apart from the print media, there have also been some TV programs on Buddhism. They basically show interviews with Buddhist monks, nuns, and followers in Brazil—either Brazilian or of foreign origin. Such programs have attracted the attention of the public as well.

Since the late 1990s, along with the "media infatuation" with Buddhism, there has been a publishing boom in Buddhist books. Following the two visits by the Dalai Lama to Brazil in 1992 and 1999, many of his books have been translated into Portuguese. In June 2001, they accounted for 40 percent of the sales of nonfiction books in Rio de Janeiro and São Paulo (the two most populous and developed cities in Brazil). The Dalai Lama's *The Art of Happiness: A Handbook of Living* (1999) has topped the best sellers' list since it was translated in June 2000. In fact, this book alone sold 185,000 copies by July 2001 and became the publishing company's biggest seller since its establishment in 1975.[14] On August 12, 2000, a long article in the leading newspaper *Jornal do Brasil* titled "The Soft and Sweet Eastern Invasion: The Interest in Eastern Philosophy Increases and Unfolds a Series of New Book Releases Heralded by the Dalai Lama's New Book" comments on the boom in books on Eastern philosophy, particularly Buddhism, due to a great demand by readers. In addition, it reports on the growing interest in Buddhist psychology among Rio de Janeiro and São Paulo psychoanalysts, which was also boosted by the translation in 2000 of Mark Epstein's book *Going to Pieces Without Falling Apart: A Buddhist Perspective on Wholeness.* Needless to say, many publishers have plans for new translations in the near future. The media have since started to report on this new trend with stories that portray Buddhism as a "fashionable" mode of living among the Brazilian elite. Indeed, a story in a weekend edition of a major Brazilian newspaper was titled "Buddha Is Pop" and featured a famous MTV presenter and her daughter, who have become Buddhists, on the cover.[15]

TECHNOSCAPES: THE CYBERSANGHA AS A VIRTUAL COMMUNITY

According to Appadurai, technoscapes are global networks of technology "both high and low, both mechanical and informational [that] now move at high speeds across various kinds of previously impervious boundaries."[16] In other words, advances in technology have led to the dissolution of cultural and political boundaries and the intensification of contact between cultures. So far, I have mentioned some mechanisms of contact such as the printed press, books, movies, TV, the Japanese diaspora, and travels. However, these mechanisms of contact overlap with a recent medium that has had a tremendous influence in the dissemination and shaping of Buddhism: the Internet. The main feature of the Internet is the possibility of creating virtual communities—that is, people may interact despite the distance that separates them in the physical world. The Internet is significant as a means of spreading a foreign religion because people who live away from the main cities, in towns where there are no Buddhist temples and/or centers, can readily meet and acquire information through cyberspace.

The number of web sites and e-mail discussion lists on Buddhism in Brazil has increased rapidly, but it is impossible to state the current number of web sites, for new ones constantly appear.[17] They follow two basic formats: either they are built and maintained by Buddhist centers, temples, and monasteries or they are personal sites. In both cases they are mainly informational sites designed to familiarize visitors with the history of the Buddhist school, its main doctrines, and terms. They also supply links to and addresses of other centers throughout the country, and in the case of Buddhist centers, there is usually an activities calendar. These personal sites range from modest ones that contain personal experiences and opinions on Buddhism to those that are highly informative and comprehensive. The connection with global Buddhism is clear in the latter ones. For instance, two of these sites were created as mirrors to two well-known international sites. Dharmanet and Accessoaoinsight (Accesstoinsight) are Brazilian sites that carry the same name as international ones but convey information in Portuguese provided by their Brazilian web masters.[18] Despite the fact that these sites are not direct translations of their foreign doubles, their creators do translate information on Buddhism mainly from English. As a result, many terms may carry "accumulated cultural baggage," that is, meanings attached to them at the time they were translated to English, French, or German. This is an important factor in understanding global flows of Buddhism into the country, as it illustrates how foreign ideas undergo many cultural translations in their itinerary around the globe.

While web sites "pop up" on a regular basis, e-mail discussion lists are more stable. There are currently six lists in Brazil; four of them are dedicated to different schools (Theravada, Zen, Jōdo Shinshū, and Tibetan Buddhism), one is transectarian (Buddhismo-L), and one is on discussions of *sūtras* and their translations.[19] An average of ten to twenty messages are posted daily on each list. Buddhismo-L, founded in 1998, carries the most messages, as nonsectarianism is one of the main characteristics of Buddhism in Brazil. Discussions in all lists range from novices' doubts about behavior and doctrine, Catholicism and Buddhism, new books on Buddhism, vegetarianism, interfaith discussions, reincarnation or rebirth, *kōan*,[20] Afro-Brazilian religions and Buddhism, Buddhism and psychoanalysis, Buddhism and philosophy, and Western intellectuals who wrote on Buddhism (such as Jung, Heidegger, Einstein, Watts, Wittgenstein, and Capra). There are also announcements of retreats in Brazil and overseas, translations of *sūtras*, poems, and biographies of important Buddhist masters, and links to Buddhist web sites (many of them in English). As it is with many web sites, some of these mailing lists carry the same name as their international counterparts, using the English spelling of the terms (for instance, Buddha-L, Theravada-L, and Vajrayāna-L). These mailing lists create virtual communities that meet in cyberspace to discuss and learn about Buddhism. Many of the members of these lists live a long way from metropolises or in countries that do not have Buddhist centers, and they have posted messages saying how invaluable the lists were in enabling them not only to learn more about Buddhism, but to feel the support of the cyber community, or "cybersangha."[21] One member, who lives in El Salvador, praised the cybersangha with the following words:

> I live in El Salvador, that is, far from any dojos [training halls], far from a Buddhist master and farther away from a Zen master (which I feel is my path). So this list has been my *sangha* for the past three years. Zen Chung Tao list is a source of inspiration and teachings for me. But it is not only an exchange of ideas, we shouldn't forget that behind the ideas on the monitor there is always a practitioner made of flesh, bones and spirit, who is searching for the Middle Way like us. [Because I] sit at home alone, I feel the need to know what other practitioners have been through, and what made them choose this path. Where have I found this? In this list!!! It is in this list that I found sites and people, *dharma* brothers and sisters, and even an "elder practitioner" who has been guiding me in the Way.[22]

Often families and friends of practitioners living away from urban centers find it difficult to understand their choice of religion. In this case, the lists also work as a forum for sharing their difficulties and exchanging ideas on how to deal with the opposition of their devout Catholic families to their choice of religion. The e-mail below illustrates this point.

> Ah . . . my problems are similar to yours. . . . [Having a Buddhist] Master far away. . . Sangha far away. . . . In my city, I think I am the only Buddhist. . . . I am still a beginner. . . . My mother is Catholic, and is always saying that when my father passed away he asked her to make sure none of the kids left the religion. . . . All my relatives are Catholic (some more than others), but they know I am practicing Buddhism.[23]

Once they log on to these lists and start to ask questions on Buddhism, they are usually directed to web sites such as www.dharmanet.com.br, where they can read *sūtras*, play mantras and *sūtras* on MP3, and learn more about the teachings and history of the different schools of Buddhism. It is noteworthy that the old Zen paradox of the impossibility of revealing one's true Buddha-nature or conveying enlightenment through words and yet using this medium to spread the dharma is also illustrated on the Zen list. According to the *Lankāvatāra-sūtra,* philosophical and discriminatory thought is inadequate to attain enlightenment since it encompasses duality.[24] The famous analogy of the finger that points to the moon is frequently used to mean that the finger (language) just points, but is not the moon (the ultimate truth). This hindrance was always a source of contention when books were the main vehicle of Buddhist teachings in the West and has naturally flowed to e-mail lists, where there is also no mind-to-mind exchange between master and disciple. As one member of the Zen list wrote,

> I remember once somebody in the list suggested that everybody shut up and meditate, and I thought: without the exchange of words the list does not exist! I don't advocate any of the extremes: one has to use words to convey the limits of words, they are useful just for that.[25]

These Internet-savvy Buddhists are upper middle-class and middle-class Brazilians who are usually well versed in the English language, which is not the case with Brazilians in general. Indeed, the ability to speak a second language fluently, translate foreign sites into Portuguese, discuss foreign ideas, philosophy, psychoanalysis, and the other issues raised on the e-mail lists, as well as travel overseas for retreats conducted in languages other than Portuguese clearly place adherents in the upper echelons of Brazilian society. Given the enormous class divide that exists in Brazil, it is not surprising that adherents and sympathizers of Buddhism all come from the upper and upper middle classes. This was clear in the survey I conducted in Brazilian Zen centers and temples and has shaped the way Buddhism is appropriated and creolized in the country.

For instance, for some months in 2001 one of the hit discussions was around the "Tibet Game" (www.tibetgame.com), an interactive game created by an American web designer, photographer, and video maker who lived in Tibet. A plethora of information on Tibetan life and beliefs and the current state of Buddhism there was conveyed in English through the game. With the help of videos showing Lhasa and parts of rural Tibet, and through virtual interaction with the characters onscreen, Brazilian players of the game were able to vicariously experience the country: they haggled in the market for prayer flags, prayer wheels, cow dung patties, and painted mandalas to be subsequently donated to monasteries and Tibetan peasants. The game includes walks in the streets and in the mountains, historical accounts of the Chinese invasion and of religion, and the frequent encounters with "bad" Chinese undercover police who disguise themselves as monks asking for a picture of the Dalai Lama. In contrast to the conventional game format—with its emphasis on accumulation and destruction—in the Tibet Game one starts with a sum of money and wins only when one has donated all of it (after buying the items described above). The game teaches that nirvāna is a realm of no money but lots of merit. I believe this is a very good example of a technoscape since the media plays a major role in constructing an imaginary of Tibet. To be sure, the technoscape is not the only "scape" involved in this process; all the other scapes (mediascape, finanscape, ethnoscape) overlap here to create this historically situated imagined world.

While Appadurai's notion of scapes aids the understanding of many contemporary situations, the framework also has its limits. He has argued that since the center-periphery model cannot explain the global cultural economy, transnational flows move around in a chaotic and unpredictable pattern. He employs chaos theory to conceptualize the dynamics of global cultural interactions, substituting a theory of global systems for uncertainty.[26] In light of the global flows of Buddhism in and out of Brazil, I contend that even if there is no single center that is the source of all global flows, there are still multiple centers and multiple peripheries. As Hannerz has argued when examining global flows in Nigeria, peripheries may act as centers to other peripheries and vice versa.[27] Indeed, I have shown throughout this book that while Japan, the United States, and Europe may be centers for Brazilian Zen, São Paulo is a center for the rest of Brazil. The south of the country, where the Japanese Zen master Moriyama rōshi lives, is a center in relation to Uruguay and Argentina, where he has a large following. Furthermore, in the Brazilian example one can see that these flows are not necessarily chaotic or unpredictable as Appadurai asserts, but are historically, politically, economically, and culturally constituted. The Japanese went to Brazil as indentured workers as a result of a confluence of historical contingencies in Japan and in Brazil. The consumption of North American cultural products in Brazil is also historically, politically, economically, and culturally constituted. As Ang and Stratton have noted, global flows do not travel in empty space, but have established historical trajectories, and therefore they are not unpredictable or chaotic.[28]

USING BUDDHISM TO WARD OFF VIOLENCE, HATRED, AND FEAR

In June 2001 the social column of the newspaper *Folha de São Paulo* featured a stylized portrait of a woman with this caption: "Bel Pedrosa, beautiful and chic, is the finance director of a bank. When she is not dealing with digits, she improves her taste for spiritual beauty: she has been a Buddhist for eleven years and is the current director of the Brazilian Committee for Free Tibet." The next entry also dealt with Buddhism; Dzongsar Khyentse Rinpoche, the lama who directed the movie *The Cup*, was visiting Brazil and declared to the delight of many Brazilians, "Buddhism is my philosophy, but soccer is my religion."[29]

As a result of its high profile in the media, Buddhism has turned into "the next cool thing" for a sector of the Brazilian population. The white, intellectual, upper middle class that consumes this media has taken the bait. I argue that "meditation" and its perceived benefits—inner peace, tranquility, and harmony—are yearned for by those living in an urban environment, where violence, crime, and stress abound. Equally important is the role of ethics and wisdom. In a country marred by corruption, social inequality, environmental destruction, pollution, fierce competition, individualism, elitism, anger, and fear, Buddhism represents an ethical way of life for the intellectual class. According to my interviewees and media reports, the world of Buddhism encompasses a diametrically opposite set of values such as nonviolence, equality, justice, compassion, love, peace, happiness, and harmony among people and nature.

Here, I will briefly delineate how such a bleak state of affairs came about in Brazilian society so that I can explain how Zen has become a marker of social distinction and a way of coping. Following rapid industrial development and an economic boom in the 1950s, 1960s, and 1970s, when there was much hype about "Brazil as an emerging power," mounting debts inherited from previous decades led to a crisis in the 1980s and the introduction of harsh economic measures. The model of development of the previous decades was premised on a gradual transition from a traditional, agrarian economy to an industrialized society. According to this model of modernization, major cities would act as large industrial centers from which the wealth created would spread out to rural areas. As it turned out, this strategy of modernization created a hybrid economy, where some regions and productive sectors accounted for "high rates of capital accumulation through the use of technology and the production of high-priced commodities, and others, [are] still relying on extractive, labor intensive production."[30] This uneven development created a very unstable society, where cities became swollen with unskilled rural migrants in search of a better quality of life, in turn leading to chronically high levels of unemployment.

Moreover, the money lent by foreign banks in the 1960s and 1970s for infrastructural development did not go to public services such as health, education, housing, or transportation, but was channeled away to finance massive energy plants and other infrastructure projects. When the oil crisis hit in 1973, 1974, and finally in 1979, Brazil, like most other developing countries, printed more currency and borrowed more money to cover debt.[31] By the mid-1980s, the economic crisis was full blown, with annual inflation rates of 233.6 percent. The International Monetary Fund (IMF) and the World Bank further deepened the crisis through loans and assistance packages that encourage countries to comply with harsh neoliberal economic reforms. These included currency devaluations, a freeze in wages, cuts in public spending, privatization of assets, and tax breaks for the productive sectors. By 1990, after four IMF packages, the annual inflation rate skyrocketed to 2,937.8 percent.[32] Because of the deep economic crisis, the 1980s and 1990s saw for the first time in Brazilian history a massive Brazilian migration to the United States, Europe, and Japan.[33]

This picture of economic crisis was even more despairing, as it coincided with a deep political crisis. In the 1980s, Brazil underwent a transition from a military dictatorship to a democratically elected government under a populist president, Collor de Mello, who won the overwhelming support of the poor. One year into his term, surrounded by accusations of corruption, drug dealings, and embezzlement, he was impeached by the Congress in the wake of mass public rallies. The next elected president, Fernando Henrique Cardoso, galvanized the hopes of many as he had a spotless record. He had been a professor of sociology at the prestigious University of São Paulo and, after being banned from the country during the military dictatorship, went on to lecture at the Sorbonne. Among his achievements in sociology was the development of dependency theory and studies on Third World poverty. However, although his economic policies and reform programs managed to contain inflation, economic output fell, giving rise to higher levels of unemployment. In the 1990s, the secondary sector greatly contracted in favor of the tertiary sector, which encompassed not only commerce and services for the urban middle and upper classes, but also the self-employed professionals, casual labor, and street commerce.

These two decades of economic and political crisis had many serious consequences. The first was a sense of chaos, followed by a general loss of faith in political, economic, and governmental institutions. Second, since spending on public services was drastically reduced, many Brazilians were left to fend for themselves — private corporations took over health, education, and transport, and people had to pay for them. As the poor could not do so, they soon became further disadvantaged. Inflation and subsequent stagflation, escalating prices, unemployment, endemic corruption, nepotism, and the information revolution all helped to widen the gap between the very rich and the very poor. Featherstone appropriately describes São Paulo, the country's largest city and one of the largest in the world, as a "global colonial city which has long undergone class polarization."[34] The world saw the high level of violence resulting from this class polarization when a picture of a policeman pointing a gun at the mouth of a street child appeared in the papers in the 1990s. The very rich shut themselves up in heavily guarded estates, in a process described as "Brazilianization," that is, "the re-emergence of fortress motifs and the spatial segregation of various social groups in global cities."[35] In the view of the Brazilian anthropologist Teresa Caldeira, São Paulo City epitomizes life in Brazil, where

> fortified enclaves are privatized, enclosed, and monitored spaces for residence, consumption, leisure and work. . . . Both symbolically and materially, these strategies operate by marking differences, imposing partitions and distances, building walls, multiplying rules of avoidance and exclusions, and restricting movement.[36]

Urban segregation clearly reflects the immense gap between social classes in Brazil. Hand in hand with soaring violence came its counterpart, fear. Together with a loss of faith in the government's ability and willingness to manage the crisis, this generated a feeling of anomie, as people no longer saw themselves as citizens and felt they had only themselves to rely on. Caetano Veloso, a well-known Brazilian composer from Bahia, neatly encapsulated this self-reliance and the consequent individualism in the words of a song: "Dumb *baianos* [people from the state of Bahia]—they never stop at traffic lights, and those who stop and wait are called foolish."[37] Brazilian sociologist José de Sousa Martins sees traffic behavior also as an illustration of the coexistence of modernity and tradition in Brazil. According to him,

> It is not unusual for modern automobiles to be driven [by middle classes and the wealthy] as if the drivers were riding a wild horse, without the least consideration for what is undoubtedly one of the components of modernity: traffic rules and regulations.[38]

Given this environment, it is not hard to see why values such as peace, nonviolence, equality, compassion, inner peace, and harmony appealed to sectors of the middle and upper middle class. Lia Diskin is a key figure in twice bringing the Dalai Lama to Brazil and a founder of Palas Athena Institute, a nongovernmental organization that offers courses on philosophy, ethics, and religion and is a publishing house as well. The reason Buddhism is drawing so many adherents is, in her view, because it is good common sense, that is, it is committed to the needs of human beings in daily life.[39]

While the lower strata of Brazilian society have moved from Catholicism to Evangelicalism, Pentecostalism, and more recently neo-Pentecostalism in search of immediate material results in the last decades, some who belong to the intellectual sectors of the middle and upper middle class have embraced Buddhism. In contrast to the lower classes, whose primary needs have to be immediately satisfied, Buddhist adherents have financial security and so can wait for the benefits of meditation and Buddhist teachings. Bourdieu has pointed out that "upwardly mobile individuals are prepared to find satisfaction in effort itself and to take the deferred gratifications from their present sacrifice at face value."[40] For him, there is a clear opposition between the tastes of necessity of the lower classes and the tastes of freedom or luxury, which derive from the possession of capital. A professor of the history of religions of the State University of São Paulo and an ordained Zen monk himself puts it more bluntly: "People who want bread don't go to meditation sessions."[41]

Therefore, adding to the qualities that made Brazilians turn to Buddhism analyzed in chapter 3 (its perceived lack of dogmatism and hierarchy, its consistency with science, and its respect for nature), adherents and sympathizers regard Buddhism as a clear method for dealing with violence, anger, fear, and suffering. Indeed, for them, Buddhism asserts the individual's responsibility for inner happiness, calls for peaceful relationships, and finally, brings in compassion as a way of living. It also has another very appealing component: it is fashionable.

THE FASHIONABLE SELF: ON HOW TO BE UNATTACHED TO WORLDLY POSSESSIONS AND STILL HOLD YOUR CULTURAL CAPITAL

Le Goff has argued that "fashion is an expression of the spirit of the time, the visible manifestation of underlying historical change. Carefully analyzed, fashion is a key to understanding the secrets of history."[42] Fashion, as part of the imaginary of a social group, points to what is seen as desired. As Featherstone has noted, there are two opposite tendencies central to the dynamic of fashion. On the one hand there is a disposition toward "emulation, equalization and imitation," and on the other hand there is a tendency toward "differentiation, individuality and distinction." For him, fashion is a "compromise between adherence and absorption into the social group and individual differentiation and distinction from other group members."[43] Accordingly, material goods should not be regarded only as utilities (having exchange and use value), but as signs of situatedness and belonging.

According to Bourdieu, the capacity to appropriate and choose elements from different fields (books, cars, magazines, houses, clothes, food, sports, entertainment, etc.) and synthesize them in a unity is given through taste, which, in turn, is the source of these meaningful, symbolic choices that will constitute the lifestyle.[44] But what exactly is this taste and lifestyle associated with Buddhism in the imaginary of Brazilians?

To find out, let us first consider a general outlook. At the end of the millennium, when the world media could talk only about topics such as the Y2K bug and millenarianism, *Folha de São Paulo*'s entertainment section ran a story purportedly following New York's media, which had coined the term "millies" to classify the new generation of the millennium.[45] In contrast to the 1980s yuppies, the millies were seen as regarding quality of life as more important than money. The reporter then interviewed Brazilian "millies." All defined quality of life as having more free time, tranquility, a healthy body and mind, and incorporating relaxation into their lifestyle. Meditation and spirituality were key factors in maintaining this desired life. The story was illustrated with a picture of a model in a Virgin Mary pose taken by the photographer Bernhard Prinz; the interior of Helmut Lang's New York City shop; furniture by the Finish designer Alvar Aalto; a sculpture of a Tibetan Buddha; and the cover of the fashion magazine *Wall Paper*. The millies interviewed were all from an upper middle-class background (video makers, people in advertising, philosophy students, architects, fashion designers, models, etc.), which corroborates the findings in my own survey. These are people with enough cultural and economic capital to emulate "tastes of luxury (or freedom)" and not the ones of necessity. The lifestyle and fashion of this group are clearly exemplified in this newspaper piece, though not all Brazilian followers of Buddhism pursue these interests.

There are many subtle distinctions within what I have referred to as "middle- and upper middle-class intellectual sectors of Brazilian society." Such differentiation is vital since their consumption and understanding of Buddhism and Zen Buddhism are distinctive. While studies on Buddhism in the West usually identify groups of non-Asian followers as a unified social sector (the white intellectual elite), differentiating this group internally according to the degree of adherence to Buddhism, they neglect to demarcate groups according to their consumption practices.[46]

CONSUMING BUDDHISM: LIBERAL PROFESSIONALS,
INTELLECTUALS, AND THE BOURGEOISIE

In my research I identified three main groups of people interested in Buddhism: liberal professionals, intellectuals, and the bourgeoisie. Although the way each group relates to Buddhism can be clearly defined, their degree of adherence varies in a continuum, as I explained in the previous chapter. In other words, regardless of which group one belongs to, one may have a superficial contact with Buddhism through the media or books, deepen one's interest by going to a Buddhist center, practice meditation, convert, or even become a monk or nun and train in Japan or another radiating center. Furthermore, the profile of the groups I describe here is an ideal-type in the Weberian sense. These categories may overlap so that an intellectual adherent may also decorate his home "Zen style," and liberal professionals may consume books on Zen and, for instance, philosophy or psychoanalysis.

Here I will briefly delineate each ideal-type and its consumption habits, as a more detailed description of each category was given in chapter 3. In general, liberal professionals are the audience targeted by Hollywood movies on Buddhism and stories on Buddhism in magazines. This sector of society is interested in cultural and educational capital, since it sees this as a path to upward mobility. Not having the cultural capital of intellectuals, it adopts a "learning mode towards culture."[47] One may see this pattern on the Buddhist e-mail discussion lists, where there is a clear distinction between liberal professionals and intellectuals. While the former ask questions on Buddhist teachings, history, and culture, the intellectuals, who have studied Buddhism for a longer time, answer these questions, relating them to Western philosophy.

E-mail lists also add to the consumption and educational capital when they teach how to cook the perfect Japanese rice gruel for Zen retreats, make *zafu* (meditation cushions), bow properly, and where to buy Buddhist "props" such as *o-juzu* (Buddhist rosary), bells, incense, and so forth. Once someone interested in Buddhism arrives at a Buddhist center there is a host of material for teaching purposes. At Busshinji, one can buy self-teaching videotapes on altar building (made by a non-Japanese-Brazilian video maker who frequents the temple), cassette tapes containing interviews given by Coen *sensei* to the radio, or borrow books on Buddhism from the small temple library. At Morro da Vargem Temple there are T-shirts, incense, ash and incense containers, organic honey (from the monastery's beehives), CDs of Buddhist music, empty *zafu*, and books. Furthermore, every time the media celebrates Buddhism as a desired lifestyle of the upper class and Brazilian and Hollywood celebrities, and every time it appears in the social column of newspapers, it sends a message to liberal professionals that Buddhism is among the markers of the upper social strata and therefore should be cultivated. Here, I reproduce a Buddhismo-L message as an example of how, by becoming fashionable, Buddhism has slowly become more accepted in Brazil.

> I remember the occasion when I was talking with Soninha [a famous MTV anchor woman] in Três Coroas [a site of a large monastery recently built by Chagdud Rinpoche followers in the Rio Grande do Sul State]. She said there was a guy who was undergoing a three-year retreat and had huge problems with his family because of the *dharma* and all. His rescue came when *Caras* magazine [equivalent to *Hello*] ran a story with Soninha at the monastery. His family saw it and thought it was beautiful and fashionable and this eased the guy's plight.[48]

In addition, not only do these liberal professionals revere, identify with, and emulate the lifestyles enjoyed by the bourgeoisie and intellectuals, but they also are cultural intermediaries for the popularization of these lifestyles for a wider audience. Good examples of this function of transmission of cultural capital are the magazine stories described earlier in this chapter. By introducing the life of Buddha and explaining Buddhist teachings, its different schools, and its practices, they make the exotic more accessible to an unfamiliar audience. The story on the millies described above clearly fulfills this function as it shows and explains the latest taste and habitus to be emulated. Featherstone has argued that this sector of society desires to "maximize and experience the range of sensations available, [which makes it] a natural consumer."[49] If according to the Western discourse on Buddhism the main pillar of Buddhism is the experience of meditation, which in turn brings sensations of inner peace and tranquility culminating in the possibility of a wondrous enlightenment, then Buddhism is a natural item of consumption for this sector. The latest style adopted from the intellectual and bourgeois sectors confers a savvy and cosmopolitan identity to this group.

The second group of consumers of Buddhism is the bourgeoisie. According to Bourdieu, this sector of society "demands of art a high degree of denial of the social world and inclines towards a hedonistic aesthetic of ease and facility."[50] This group would be inclined to buy *Casa Vogue* and decorate their homes in a minimalist, ethnic, or "Zen style," fulfilling the demand for hedonistic aestheticism. Many are businesspeople and have said that meditation appeals since it helps them become centered and keep a clear mind in face of daily stress and difficult decisions. All the people I interviewed and all the media stories portray Buddhism as an individual quest for inner peace and balance, something akin to a self-help technique/philosophy. Indeed, as the director of the Nyingma Institute (a Tibetan center in São Paulo City) put it, Buddhism is a way of "caring for oneself, finding happiness and relief from suffering."[51] The possibility that Buddhist teachings might be pursued for their application to solving problems of inequality in society at large, for example, generates surprisingly little interest. What has come to be known as "engaged Buddhism"[52] was not mentioned in any of the interviews or stories.

This group expands as some companies begin employing Buddhist meditation teachers. For instance, Nelson Chamma, a businessman in the mining industry and the husband of a famous Brazilian TV actress, began teaching Buddhism at corporations after he started his own practice at Nyingma Institute. He says his "specialty" is Buddhism and work-related issues. He adds, "Buddhist principles help us develop productivity, efficiency, concentration, cooperation, and communication among people."[53] A business consultant and lay-ordained Zen monk, follower of Tokuda *sensei* and Moriyama *rōshi*, he also teaches meditation at companies. He told me in an interview,

> Tokuda *sensei* asked me: Why don't you offer seminars for businesspeople through your consulting company? You can teach them Zen techniques and light meditation. So we now have a project of seminars addressing stress, conflicts in the office, and teaching meditation. This combines my two activities of monk and consultant.[54]

When I asked whether his work involved some form of engaged Buddhism, he told me he established "an NGO, a philanthropic institution, which disseminates Buddhism through seminars," but did not mention any present or future plan to work with the disadvantaged. When I further pressed him about it, he explained,

> Engagement is a lay activity; it doesn't have anything to do with transmission. [In my view,] Buddhism is the transmission from the Buddha to the Patriarch. If the dharma is transmitted, then there is Buddhism. Social engagement is laudable if it is motivated by compassion. But it isn't Buddhism per se.[55]

While locally engaged Buddhism is not regarded as "real" Buddhism, many may fight for a more international, fashionable, and prestigious cause. In 2002, a campaign for Free Tibet gained momentum after a Brazilian practicing Buddhism in Italy posted the following message on a Brazilian Buddhist e-mail list.

There is a *new fashion* in Europe in the struggle for Tibetan freedom. They are summoning people who sympathize with the cause to apply for Tibetan citizenship as a way of protest. More than 2800 people have acquired their "Tibetan Passport." You have an interview with the prime minister of the Tibetan government in exile, Samdhong Rinpoche. They are hoping that many of the applicants are famous people, so that this campaign has a greater impact. The site to get your passport is: www.passeport-tibetain.fr.st.[56]

To be sure, there was an attempt to tackle a Brazilian cause in 1999. A non-Japanese-Brazilian lay-ordained man practicing at Busshinji tried to establish a system of frequent visits to Carandiru, the biggest prison complex in Brazil, located in São Paulo City. His project mirrored a North American Vipassanā project he found on the Internet.[57] The venture, however, had a short life. He told me that other practitioners at Busshinji were not interested in visiting the complex and volunteering time for the project. As I showed in chapter 2, the fascination for and adoption of the causes of the metropolitan centers as a way of relating to the other has been a trait of Brazilian elites since colonial times. Indeed, Schwarz observes that "the educated people, in the colonial period, felt solidarity towards the metropolis, Western tradition and their colleagues, but not towards the local population."[58] Along similar lines, I argue that the absence of an interest in engaged Buddhism is part of the same process of elites connecting to their peers overseas and forgetting for a while that they belong to a developing country. By embracing North American and European "fashionable" social and political causes, they, too, are above their own country's problems.

Ironically, Japanese-Brazilian congregations, which practice traditional Buddhism, carry out humanitarian projects as part of their Buddhist practice. Since their arrival in the country in the late 1950s, they have established nursing homes and houses for the mentally impaired of their own community, as well as the collection and distribution of clothes and food for the homeless at the end of the year. Since they do not belong to the upper echelons of society and thus are not seeking prestige associated with European and North American Buddhism, they can afford to shift their eyes from overseas toward the country's needs.

As for intellectuals, they tend to reject ostentation and the bourgeois taste for ornament. Brazilian intellectuals often disdain followers of fashion and express interest in Buddhism mainly through the consumption of books and endless discussions of the philosophical aspects of the doctrine. Because cultural capital can be converted into social power regardless of the amount of economic capital one possesses, dominant groups seek to determine—and then consume—what are to be considered prestigious cultural goods.[59] These cultural goods are regarded as desirable because they are made scarce by these very groups. Therefore, whenever mass production or mass media make these goods accessible to the lower strata of society, possessors of high cultural capital immediately move toward establishing new and rarer tastes that will maintain the distance between social classes. This constant need for novelty, for establishing, possessing, and consuming prestigious goods, empowers intellectuals "to establish a monopoly in defining legitimate taste within the cultural realm, to distinguish, judge and hierarchize between what is tasteful and tasteless, between the pure gaze and the vulgar."[60] The intellectuals mentioned in chapter 2 provide good examples of this. Nelson Coelho's emphasis on his role as the person who introduced Zen into Brazil, while being a foreign correspondent in New York, shows the prestige and cultural capital associated with Zen (or any other exotic fresh arrival bestowed with kudos in the metropolitan centers).

This "leap-frogging social race," as Featherstone so eloquently put it, can already be seen in the expansion of Buddhism in Brazil.[61] Sensing that Buddhism has been much celebrated in the media recently, a member of a Buddhist e-mail list delegitimizes the media stories by implying that even if people are more aware of it, they do not necessarily understand it or practice it the way it should be done. He expressed his concerns in the following way:

> This morning I saw *Superinteressante* magazine and there it was! The Dalai Lama was on the cover once more. Then I thought: they are really globalizing opportunities and, as people have said in this list, many will use these Lego building blocks not to build a ladder to free all humankind, but to adorn their own prison cells. When all these Lego bits are in place in the cells there is no possibility of practice. Some teachings warn against the incessant need of the mind to keep everything in logical order, even turning diamonds into mere paperweights.[62]

Among long-standing practitioners, there is clearly an ambivalent position. While on the one hand many feel this media frenzy is helping to spread the dharma, on the other hand there is a tendency to despise the hype as "fashionable nonsense," which hinders true Buddhism from flourishing, as the list member affirmed above. In the same vein, a university professor of anthropology who started as a Zen practitioner at Busshinji in the 1980s but since then has moved into Vipassanā and now is one of the people in charge of bringing teachers from Vipassanā

Thailand and the United States to Brazil made the same point when I interviewed him.

> We live in such a confusion nowadays that people seek extraordinary, mystical experiences. Something like: "I had a wonderful sensation, I had a vision, I had a dream, or I got healed from whatever." I think meditation is good for your health, but that is not where the focus of the practice should be. For instance, the esoteric market is huge: angels, masters of I don't know what. . . . This is very much the sign of our times, [it shows] the competition and general instability we all live under. People want to grab the first thing that comes up.[63]

Here again one may see an effort to establish social distance between the intellectuals who discuss Buddhist philosophical tenets and practice meditation and the sectors of society who adopt it as a fashionable or self-help item. Although these two groups may not be distinguished by the amount of economic capital they hold, what distances them is in fact their respective cultural capital.

EQUATING ONESELF TO THE OVERSEAS UPPER CLASS

A main point in the study of urban elite Brazilian Zen is indeed this transnational class fraction, where a white, urban upper class seeks to connect with its peers overseas. This creates a feeling of belonging to a subculture group that extends beyond the national borders. According to Hannerz, "As the people of different communities and regions become more entangled with one another, what were previously more self-contained cultures turn increasingly into subcultures within the national culture."[64] By going to retreats abroad, translating *sūtras*, and publishing them independently on the Internet, Brazilian Buddhists feel that they are part of a much larger world. Likewise, the prestige Buddhism is enjoying in the developed world also confers social and cultural prestige on the Brazilian urban intellectual elite who play the role of introducing new ideas and ways of behaving into Brazil. As I mentioned before, being Buddhist in this context means belonging to the developed world and detaching oneself from the rest of the "backward" Brazilian population. The Brazilian anthropologist José Jorge Carvalho has observed, in relation to the arrival of religions in Brazil,

> Some sects have been adopted more due to a modernizing trend in our society than due to religious matters. The identity issue is crucial: to adhere

to a certain group is to adhere to what is up-to-date, it is to be able to do certain things which are currently prestigious . . . it is a way of connecting oneself to the meaning producing centers.[65]

As a result of transnational links between the Brazilian urban intellectual elite and their counterparts overseas through books, media, travel, movies, and the Internet, the diffusion of Zen Buddhism in Brazil can be seen as part of a "faculty club culture," a term coined by Berger as one of four processes of cultural globalization. According to Berger, "[the faculty club culture] is the internationalization of the Western intelligentsia, its values and ideologies carried by foundations, academic networks and non-governmental organizations."[66] Similar to "non-Japanese Zen," the "faculty club culture" is primarily an elite culture that "spreads its beliefs and values through the educational system [and] some of the media of mass communication."[67] Some examples of these values are feminism and environmentalism. Indeed, as I have shown in chapter 3, many adherents I interviewed told me that the close relationship between Buddhism and the ecological movement, as opposed to the Catholic way of approaching nature, made them adhere to Buddhism.

In the same article Berger argues that the English language is the lingua franca of globalization. As I alluded to earlier, most of the information on Zen in Brazil is carried through Portuguese translations of English material. For instance, when Coen *sensei* was the head nun of Busshinji Temple in São Paulo (1995–2000), in her weekly lectures she used to translate passages from books in English, written either by Japanese monks while they lived in America or by American scholars. At that time, there was also a *sūtra* study group, where one lay-ordained follower translated, printed, and handed out parts of books originally written in English so that they could be studied by the group. In the Zen Center of Porto Alegre, many adherents are learning English to be able to speak to Moriyama *rōshi* without the need of a translator. As I showed in chapter 3, some practitioners even choose to travel to Zen centers in the United States.

From this perspective, it would be fruitful to return to the concept of rhizome discussed earlier. Although rhizome is an apt concept to encompass flows of Buddhism in and out of Brazil, as well as the multiplicity of centers and peripheries, the above examples demonstrate that not all global flows of Buddhism are accepted and can be deployed to gain prestige, cosmopolitan capital, and superiority in the Brazilian regime of taste. I argued earlier in this chapter that global flows do not travel in empty space, but have historical trajectories. Indeed, an asymmetric geography of power can account for which global flows of Buddhism may confer social prestige in Brazil. In this context, whereas Japan functions as an acceptable source of global flows of Zen only through its diminutive monastic facet, due to Orientalist ideas and Western discourse on Zen, its value is also enhanced when Zen is mediated by American or European interpretations. However, I showed here that while other characteristics of modern and contemporary Western Buddhism such as democratization, laicization, and feminization are common, engaged Buddhism is not, although Brazil has a high degree of poverty. Because adherence to Buddhism is intended as establishing social distinction, Brazilian Buddhists focus either on inner development or foreign political causes such as Free Tibet.

FASHION, TASTE, AND LIFESTYLE IN A ZEN AMBIENCE

At last I may now unpack the imagery on the cover of *Casa Vogue* that opened this chapter. The Western discourse on Zen, informed by Romantic Orientalism and the writings of D. T. Suzuki and Alan Watts, has greatly influenced the way Brazilians see Zen Buddhism (and still do, as both authors are constantly referred to in the Buddhist discussion lists). This discourse is the origin of notions of Zen as monochromatic, refined, artistic, and not a religion but a philosophy that has its central pillar in the practice of meditation that, in turn, conveys peace and tranquility. As Zen in Brazil is regarded as a general term for the exotic, distant East, it may include ethnic ornaments from any distant culture. Hence the African rugs and guitar, together with the wooden sculptures and Indian bed, all bring a sense of exoticism, of unpolished natural materials regardless of where they come from. The painting on the wall conveys the ideas of refinement and high culture, which, as I have shown, is also emphasized by mediascapes. As noted above, non-Japanese Zen Buddhists belong to the urban upper and upper middle class and usually know how to appreciate abstract art. However, the painting is three-dimensional and all white, reinforcing the ideas of emptiness and monochrome referred to above.

There are two apparently conflicting objects: the newspapers and the bread cut in two. The ruffled, recently read newspapers have no relation to the monasticism invoked by the bread, but indicate the connections between Zen and its Brazilian audience: the well-informed, cosmopolitan, urban dwellers who are aware of novelties from overseas. The bread, one of the quintessential symbols of Christianity, unfolds an unexpected juxtaposition. Although adherents aspire to differentiate themselves from Catholicism, things associated with Zen by Brazilians do not necessarily have to do with the Japanese culture in Japan, but with the imaginary of Zen by Brazilians who make use of local "building blocks," such as Catholicism, to construct it. Because this interior decorator has most probably not lived in a monastery in Japan, the idea that readily came to his/her mind as associated with monasticism was one available to someone raised in a Catholic country such as Brazil. As Appadurai puts it, "The farther away these audiences are from the direct experience . . . the more likely they are to construct 'imagined worlds.'"[68] Contrasting with the Catholic imaginary of monasticism, if one had to choose an epitome of Zen food, it would be a bowl of white rice or rice gruel.[69]

CONCLUSION

In this chapter I have argued that the construction of a collective imaginary of Zen Buddhism occurs in and through the growing disjunctures among Appadurai's five "scapes." Collective mental images of Zen have altered throughout Brazilian and world history and were/are produced and globalized in a rhizomatic way. Accordingly, from being an obscure religion of Japanese immigrants and a philosophy and practice for a small group of intellectuals until the 1980s, Zen has become visible in mediascapes as a desired and prestigious lifestyle for a sector of the population. Mediascapes have had a fundamental role in establishing Buddhism as a trendy choice for Brazilians. Hollywood movies and celebrities, magazines, newspapers, books, writers, philosophers, and their national counterparts have all contributed to turn "Buddhism" and "Zen" into buzzwords.

In the Brazilian imaginary, "Zen" is in fact an umbrella word that encompasses most Eastern practices, from martial arts, to yoga, to Buddhism in general. Upon examining the uses of fashion, taste, lifestyle, and "habitus" as markers of social distinction in a consumer culture, I have suggested that by adhering to Buddhism, people show how cosmopolitan and savvy they are in being aware of such a different, exotic-turned-fashionable religion. Precisely because of its mysterious quality, of its nonpopular appeal, it has become fashionable. If one bears in mind the enormous gap between rich and poor and the critical Brazilian socioeconomic situation, it is clear that by becoming fashionable Buddhism has successfully been employed as a marker of social distinction from the "backward" Catholic/Evangelical lower classes, while at the same time linking the Brazilian urban elite to its emulated peers oversees. Finally, my informants and media sources alike associate Buddhism with values such as nonviolence, inner peace, compassion, equality, justice, love, happiness, and harmony. The attraction of Buddhism is partly that these values provide a powerful antidote to the stress and violence of Brazil's urban centers.

5 Doing Zen, Being Zen: Creolizing "Ethnic" and "Convert" Buddhism

In 2000, I was at Busshinji Temple for the *higan* festivities. *Higan,* literally "the other shore" (a reference to full enlightenment), occurs at the spring and autumn equinoxes. It is the time when Japanese people visit family graves and ask a priest to read Buddhist prayers for ancestors to reach "the other shore." At Busshinji Temple parishioners usually make a money donation for the names of their ancestors to be read during the ritual. On that Sunday morning there were many non-Japanese Brazilians actively participating in this rite of ancestor worship. If non-Japanese-Brazilian Zen practice were solely about meditation, one would expect to see only Japanese Brazilians in the temple for this ritual.

As it happened, I noticed that one young non-Japanese Brazilian was also making an appropriate donation for a name to be read. On closer inspection I noticed he was wearing a T-shirt depicting Nirvana, the famous rock band. I smiled and thought this was a good reminder of how Buddhism goes beyond the religious realm, just to enter it once more, this time creatively transformed by its journey into popular culture. I felt that the scene was a perfect metaphor for my study of Buddhism in Brazilian popular culture as well as in temples and how these two places are closely interconnected.

The widespread assumption that Buddhism in the West is typically fractured between "ethnic" and "convert" practices is not applicable in Brazil. "Ethnic" practices are generally defined as devotional and/or the repository of the group's cultural identity; "convert" practices are characterized by meditation and rational study of Buddhist texts. I argue that although Japanese Brazilians and non-Japanese congregations in Brazil often do have distinct and separate practices (as I have shown in chaps. 1 and 2), this does not adequately define Zen Buddhism in Brazil. There is a host of interactions, hybridizations, and creolizations that make the boundaries between the two congregations very porous. The multiple religious influences Japanese Brazilians received since arriving in Brazil in 1908, and the renewed interest in Buddhism by Japanese Brazilians and non-Japanese Brazilians alike, have made each group adopt practices that have traditionally been thought of as confined to the other. Not only do non-Japanese Brazilians use Catholic, Spiritist, New Age, or/and Afro-Brazilian syntax as matrices for new Buddhist vocabulary—in a clear process of creolization, as I have shown in chapter 3—but also (and more important), Buddhist practices that have long been called "cultural accretions" or "ethnic" in the West are incorporated into this vocabulary. On the other hand, some Japanese Brazilians whose families have long left Buddhism behind to become Catholic in order to avoid discrimination are going back to Japanese Buddhism through an interest in meditational practices, family history, and fashion.

In this context, I believe the dichotomy of "ethnic" and "non-ethnic" Buddhist congregations (used by many scholars since Prebish first formulated it); the three-category model of "elite," "missionary," and "immigrant" (proposed by Nattier); and Baumann's binary model of "traditionalist" and "modernist," which focuses on religious concepts and practices, should be afforded greater complexity when applied in the Brazilian context.[1] Through my fieldwork findings I will present a more nuanced picture of how *issei, nisei, sansei,* and *yonsei* (first, second, third, and fourth generation) Japanese Brazilians and non-Japanese Brazilians are doing and being Zen.

CATHOLIC AND/OR BUDDHIST? WHAT IS IN A RITUAL?

Nícia Tanabe, a *sansei,* organized the one-year memorial service for her deceased mother at Tenzui Zen Dōjō, Coen *sensei's* recently established temple-cum-Zen center in São Paulo City. Previously, her mother's seventh-day mass had been at a Catholic Church, but the forty-ninth-day memorial service had been officiated by Coen *sensei* at Busshinji Temple. Although Nícia and her family did not know what Buddhist tradition they belonged to, all former memorial services she remembers (those of her grandfather, grandmother, father, and mother) were held at Busshinji because, as she put it in an interview in January 2002, "my mother's sister-in-law's aunt was a nun at the temple, which made things easier." However, after having meditation sessions with Coen at her local martial arts and massage school, she decided to follow Coen to Tenzui Zen Dōjō and start learning more about Japanese Buddhism. She had already studied Tibetan Buddhism for three years and visited her lineage's Rinpoche in India, but since her mother's passing, Nícia has started a detailed inquiry into her family's history and traditions. This is how she describes her search in the same interview.

> Upon my mother's death, we realized we didn't know Buddhism. . . . For instance, we didn't know what the meaning of the altar was. My mum was the one who took care of the *butsudan* [Buddhist altar][2] and without her, we didn't know how to tend to it. Hence, someone suggested we talk to a monk at Busshinji and my sister and I made an appointment. The monk explained the meaning of having a *butsudan* at home and how to organize

it, the meaning of the *ihai* [mortuary tablets] and of the offerings, who the historical Buddha was, and so on. We, then, set another time when we would come back to show him what we had in our *butsudan*. This time he explained every little bit of what we had: *ihais* of brothers who had passed away as children, photos of my grandfather. He told us what had to be kept with us and what could be kept at Busshinji. So we kept my grandmother's, grandfather's, and my father's *ihais* and had a new one made for my mom.

At the one-year memorial service, Nícia revealed to me that her family and friends were all Catholic Japanese Brazilians. Interestingly, this included her deceased mother. The only Buddhists at the service were Coen *sensei*, her non-Japanese-Brazilian disciples who were assisting the service, and the new sympathizer Nícia.

What should we make of this? Was Nícia betraying her mother's memory by giving her a Buddhist memorial service? Were her family and friends upset? Why was Nícia so interested in Buddhism after being a Catholic herself? Those were the questions I posed to her. In her response, Nícia unraveled a world that echoed stories I had heard from other Japanese Brazilians I interviewed.

A DYNAMICALLY HYPHENATED RELIGIOUS PRACTICE

Nícia's mother was Catholic, but her grandmother and grandfather, who came from Japan, were Buddhists. Since they arrived immediately before World War II, they were prohibited from speaking Japanese, so their children went to Brazilian schools and were baptized as Catholics.[3] Nonetheless, Nícia's grandmother maintained several Japanese cultural traits, including keeping a *butsudan* in her bedroom. By contrast, Nícia's mother kept a Catholic altar in her own bedroom. When the grandmother passed away, Nícia's mother brought the *butsudan* to her own home and started tending to both altars equally. According to Nícia,

> Every day she [her mother] would bring offerings such as water, rice, flowers, candles, incense, and an occasional treat received from a visiting friend to both altars. She kept this tradition because my father was the firstborn son, so she felt the obligation to maintain the Buddhist altar. While at my grandmother's altar there was an image of the Buddha, photos and *ihai* of deceased members of the family, in her own altar she had an image of the Virgin Mary. Although my mom was Catholic, when my father passed away, she had an *ihai* made for him and put it at the fore-

front of the *butsudan*. My father was neither Buddhist nor Catholic, so my mother had my father's seventh-day mass at the Catholic Church, but had his forty-ninth-day mass and three-year mass in Busshinji.

Nícia added that her family and friends were not upset about going to the Buddhist temple for the service. In fact, they had welcomed the opportunity of getting together in the temple for lunch after the service since many lived outside of São Paulo City and had not seen each other in a long time. This would not have happened in a Catholic Church, since parishioners do not get together for a meal after a memorial mass. They were also happy because Coen spoke Portuguese to them during and after the service. Nícia pointed out that her mother's best friend, who was eighty-two years old and also came to the service, was as active a Catholic as her mother, but also had a *butsudan* at home and did all Buddhist memorial services for deceased family members.

This story mirrors those of many other Japanese-Brazilian families I interviewed. They also told me that it is common practice to have a seventh-day Catholic mass for the deceased family member (since the family has usually become Catholic) and thereafter have Buddhist memorial services held at fixed intervals (forty-nine days, first anniversary, third anniversary, and sometimes extending to seventh, thirteenth, and twenty-third anniversaries) since the late family member was a Buddhist. Furthermore, interviewees pointed out that their choice of religious sites for services was due the fact that in Catholicism, the seventh-day mass is a very important service, while the forty-ninth-day memorial service is meaningful to Buddhists as it is the moment when the mourning ends and the soul is thought to become an ancestor. On this day, the new Buddhist name (*kaimyō*) given to the departed is finally engraved on the *ihai*, which is placed in the *butsudan*.

On one particular occasion, a family member told me it was the first time the family went to Busshinji, as the deceased mother was the last Buddhist in the family. All her children were practicing Catholics while the grandchildren were nonpracticing Catholics. As I had lunch with them in the Busshinji basement after the memorial service, one of the grandchildren grimaced and exclaimed upon drinking green tea, "Ahh, this is yuck!" and immediately returned to his *guaraná* (a Brazilian soft drink). From this I gathered that going to Busshinji was not the only thing they were doing for the first time that day. Paulo Yamamoto, the son who had organized the memorial service, told me his mother had a connection with the Higashi Honganji as well, thus the first memorial service was there. But as with Nícia's family, his family was happy to have a priest who spoke Portuguese and explained a little about Buddhism. When I interviewed him at Busshinji in

FIGURE 21
Japanese-Brazilian family and friends sharing a meal in the basement of Busshinji after a memorial ritual.

March 2000, he asked me excitedly, "What is Zen? I don't know anything about Buddhism. I see many Brazilians interested in Buddhism. It is more a philosophy now. They read everything about it!"

INNOVATION AND CONTINUITY: JAPANESE IN JAPAN AND JAPANESE BRAZILIANS

I cannot help but muse on how beautifully these stories reveal the constant cultural negotiation Japanese immigrants and their descendents have been through since their arrival in Brazil. It is important to note, however, that a hyphenated religious practice does not mean that each category—Buddhist and Catholic—is stable, distinct, or homogeneous—in other words, essentialized. Quite the contrary, these stories show how second- and third-generation Japanese Brazilians strategically draw their religious identity from different sources at different occasions at will.[4] Indeed, these stories show that dynamic interactions between Japanese Brazilians and Brazilian society at large enabled hybridization and consequently innovation.

However, the process of innovation needs to be understood in the context of continuity. Belonging to two religions is not a privilege unique to Japanese Brazilians. Non-Japanese Brazilians may do it too—in Brazil having multiple religious affiliations is commonly accepted as part of a recognition of religious borders as fluid (as I have shown in chap. 3), even though Catholicism and Buddhism were never historically intermixed in the country. In Japan, it is a commonplace that being a Buddhist does not exclude being a Shintoist as well. Likewise, for Japanese Brazilians, being a Catholic does not exclude keeping one's cultural and religious traditions, which include Buddhism.

I believe that for the majority of the Japanese Brazilians who have converted to Catholicism, Buddhism and the Buddhist temple are still regarded as repositories of long-forgotten, old Japanese cultural traditions. Much like the *butsudan*, which holds memories not even identifiable by the family members anymore (as in Nícia's story), Buddhism itself is not regarded so much as a religion but as a niche of "forgotten" memories and traditions. In a diasporic community, cultural objects are frequently divorced from their original cultural meaning, acquiring other significant connotations. In this case, *butsudan* and Buddhism are regarded as a connection to Japan and family roots. At times such as a death in the family, those connections may appear fragile, occasioning a need to revisit them.

Continuity is also evident in the lack of knowledge among these families about which school of Buddhism they belong to. Undoubtedly, it indicates that connections with Buddhism have been severed in the past due to a lack of a dense Buddhist environment and the strong pressure to learn Brazilian ways in order to ascend socioeconomically. But one should not forget that in Japan, too, many families do not know which Buddhist school they belong to. During my fieldwork there, whenever I was asked what I was researching, conversation would steer toward religious affiliation. Notwithstanding their active participation in the calendrical cycle of Buddhist events such as *o-bon* (return of the souls of deceased forebears to the *ie*, the household), *higan* (spring and autumn equinoxes), and *hatsumōde* (New Year shrine or temple visit), many were not able to tell me their religious affiliation. Some became so curious they went on to find out so that they could tell me.

The lack of knowledge of one's religious affiliation needs to be understood in the context of the development of Buddhism in Japan from 1635 to 1871. During this period, the Japanese government required all households to register with the nearest Buddhist temple. That was done not to promote Buddhism as the only religion of Japan, but as a way of social control and of ensuring that no family was Christian or belonged to Nichiren Fuju fuseha (a Nichiren sect banned in 1699). Registration required disclosing the identity, genealogy, residence, occupation, property, and tax obligation of each family member. Such registration had to be renewed at the same temple every year, and failure to do so was considered a crime. Not only did Buddhist temples prohibit families from changing temple affiliation, moving to a different location, or even having a new occupation, but the temples also acquired the monopoly of funeral and ancestor rites. Indeed, even Shintō priests "had to die as Buddhists."[5] Families were also obliged to have a *butsu-dan* at home to worship ancestors. During Tokugawa Japan (1603–1868) this system, known as *danka seido* (household/parishioner system), was paramount in enforcing the rigid class distinctions that characterized the period. Clearly, the *danka* system was not one that implied faith by the household or individual family members; it was a reciprocal relationship that involved financial support in exchange for mortuary rites.[6]

Although this system was formally abolished in 1871, *danka seido* remains strong "largely because its relationship to the whole ancestral and Japanese socio-religious systems is so deeply rooted that it still continues to be the economic mainstay of Buddhism in the present."[7] Therefore, those who are bereaved seek out Buddhism. The religion is also drawn upon whenever ancestor worship rites need to be performed. By fulfilling this vital social and religious role, Buddhism continues to be meaningful in maintaining household unity and continuity.

Nonetheless, because the engine that drives the socioreligious role of Buddhism is not based on belief or faith but on a contingent and pragmatic need, many Buddhist temples situated in rural areas saw their *danka* (congregation) quickly disappear when the phenomena of industrialization and consequent urbanization took place in Japan after World War II. The revision of the civil code in postwar Japan aggravated this situation, generating a shift from a stem family system (*ie*), which supported temples, to a conjugal or nuclear family pattern. That does not mean urban nuclear families have foregone Buddhist rituals for their dead, but they have ceased to feel the need to worship extended household ancestors or be connected to the rural temple where ancestors were worshiped.[8] As a result of moving to a new setting, urban nuclear families had to find a new Buddhist temple to resort to in time of death. How was that choice made? According to Reader, people "may be attracted to a particular temple because of its geographical convenience, because its priest has a good reputation or for some personal factor such as liking its architecture or Buddhist images."[9]

Continuity is clear here since this is what has occurred in the case of Nícia and members of other families I interviewed. Nícia's family had an original connection with the Higashi Honganji sect in rural Brazil, where her family first settled. When Nícia's family moved to São Paulo City and her mother became a Catholic, she lost that association. Nonetheless, the family had found in Busshinji a temple to perform funerary rites. When Coen *sensei* lost her position at Busshinji and established her own temple, Nícia decided to follow her for three reasons: because she liked Coen *sensei*'s preaching, because Coen spoke Portuguese, and finally because Coen was giving her *zazen* instruction at her local martial arts and massage school. Likewise, many other Japanese Brazilians having a family member's memorial service at Busshinji told me they opted for the temple because Coen *sensei*'s preaching was in Portuguese and she explained things very clearly and deeply.

Indeed, stories like Nícia's are very common. For instance, another Japanese Brazilian told me that although his wife was an Evangelical and he himself adhered to no religion, when his wife passed away, he decided to have a forty-ninth-day memorial service at Busshinji after holding a Christian funeral and seventh-day mass. Even though his parents were affiliated with the Higashi Honganji temple and had their memorial services there, after reading an interview with Coen *sensei* in a Japanese-Brazilian newspaper, he chose Busshinji as the right place for the memorial.

A Japanese-Brazilian monk at Busshinji described as common the fact that many parishioners from Jōdo Shinshū come to the Sōtō temple for memorials and vice versa. He did not see any problem in that since

> many people don't differentiate between Jōdo Shinshū and Sōtō. For them, if it is Buddhism, it is OK. I know when a family does not belong to Sōtō-shū because each school has its own kind of *ihai*, and they bring theirs for the service. I have even seen families that belong to the Seichō-no-ie come to Busshinji for memorials. The interesting fact is that the Seichō-no-ie *ihai* is not even a *hotoke* [a Buddha], but a *kami* [deity of Shintō tradition]. But we don't think of this as a problem. It is fine, really, if the family wants a service, we do it.[10]

When I asked him, in the same interview, what made people decide at which temple to hold services, he said,

> People call, ask for the price first, and then ask about the hours available for the service. If the price or the time set is not suitable, they may hold their memorial service in another temple. Once I heard a Nishi Hongwanji priest say that in the future we shouldn't distinguish Japanese Buddhism in Brazil by schools. We should just call it Buddhism. Maybe he said so

because parishioners already do that informally. Even if each school has different characteristics, Buddhism as a popular movement does not have these differences. On the other hand, of course, there are parishioners that are very orthodox. Once I went to a town in the countryside that didn't have a Sōtō mission. An old man told me he had done the funerary rite for a family member with the Nishi Hongwanji. But now because I was there he was doing it all over again with the Sōtō since he followed Sōtōshū. He said that for the ancestor it was important that *some* ritual was performed, better some kind of ritual than nothing at all, isn't it?[11]

The primary importance of rites dealing with death and commemorating ancestors, as Reader has observed in Japan, is that "they should be done, not that they have to be done by a priest of a particular sect."[12] More recently, it seems they do not even have to be celebrated by a real priest. The latest technological addition to the Japanese pantheon of robots is the "robopriest," a robot that "is programmed to deliver word-perfect prayers according to the rites of seven different Buddhist sects, Shintō and two Christian faiths."[13]

Along the same line, Reader has pointed out that in 1985 76 percent of Japanese people described themselves as Buddhist, "almost always as a consequence of household belonging and affiliation and because of the occurrence of a death in the family, *consulting priests and often finding out to which sect their families are affiliated because of this situation.*"[14] In other words, Buddhism in this milieu is regarded as a religion one encounters when a family member dies. That explains why my Japanese friends, in spite of actively participating in the Buddhist calendrical festivals, could not place their temple in the range of Buddhist schools on offer. They were just too young for death to have occurred in the immediate family. They did participate in Buddhist festivals because in Japan occasions such as *o-bon, higan,* and *hatsumōde* are social and cultural events, a time for family gathering, relaxation, and sociability. Indeed, both *o-bon* and *hatsumōde* are national holidays.

To consider how this relates to Zen in Brazil, I return to Nícia's story. Like her counterparts in Japan, she got in contact with the world of Japanese Buddhism only when her mother died. She then asked a monk at Busshinji to examine her ancestors' *ihai* to discover what her family's affiliation was and how to proceed with the funerary rites. All this was so foreign to her that afterward, when I interviewed her, she could not remember which school of Buddhism her family was affiliated with anymore. By looking at a picture of her family grave in the Brazilian countryside that she showed me during the interview, I read for her the school characters—"Higashi Honganji"—written on the long wooden tablet (*tōba*). This time she made sure she wrote down the school's name.

CREOLIZING ZEN: "CAN I PUT THIS JIZŌ TOGETHER WITH THE VIRGIN MARY IN THE ALTAR?"

The process of creolization, on the other hand, is very much alive among the Japanese Brazilians. The first obvious sign of it is the ubiquitous creolization between Buddhist and Catholic practices.[15] For instance, according to a non-Japanese-Brazilian monk at Busshinji, 90 percent of deceased Japanese-Brazilian people are buried in Catholic cemeteries and only 10 percent are cremated according to Buddhist custom. This can be explained by the fact that cremation is not the normal mode of body disposal in Brazil, and there is only one crematorium in São Paulo City. Prior to its construction, the Japanese had to adopt Brazilian burial customs. When they were buried in Catholic cemeteries, however, crosses were not placed on the graves.

Equally revealing, as noted earlier, is the fact that all of my informants gave their deceased family members, be they Buddhist, Catholic, or nonreligious, a seventh-day Catholic mass and a forty-ninth-day memorial service, where an *ihai* and a Buddhist name were given to the deceased. For my Japanese-Brazilian informants there was no doubt about the "division of labor" between the Catholic Church and the Buddhist temple concerning how to deal with death. Each religion had its mortuary rites that had to be performed.

When in my interviews I asked why they would have a forty-ninth-day memorial service at a Buddhist temple if they themselves were not Buddhists, there were different answers. Some told me that a Buddhist service would please the deceased (when he/she was a Buddhist), older family members, and friends of the deceased. Conversely, a Catholic mass on the seventh day would please the younger generations who had adopted Catholicism (even if they were not active practitioners). In this case, family members and friends could choose which ritual to attend. Others said that even if the deceased family member was not Buddhist, friends had recommended that they hold a forty-ninth-day Buddhist service, since it was the most important mortuary rite and a traditional custom. Only a few told me they had a new interest in Buddhism and wanted to use their family tradition to learn more about it. As the many memorial services I took part in revealed—and this is expected from a religion that is sought mostly at a time of death—there is very little knowledge of proper behavior on such an occasion. For instance, during the service the priest had to take time to explain the school's history, the life of the historical Buddha, the images in the altar, and how to offer incense at the altar.

Another illustration of creolization is the placing, alluded to earlier, of typical Buddhist offerings such as rice, water, flowers, incense, and even treats given by friends at both the *butsudan* and the Catholic altar alike. Doubtless, the original Japanese Buddhist act of making daily food offerings at the *butsudan* "to the ancestors before the family eats as befits [the ancestor's] position as the senior members of the house"[16] worked as a matrix, a grammar, onto which a new Catholic vocabulary (dealing with a Catholic altar) could be superimposed. The meaning of such gestures was altered when the same offerings were placed before the Virgin Mary. When I inquired about a possible newly ascribed meaning, Nícia told me that making offerings was a sign of respect and if the Buddhist altar received all these offerings it would look bad for her mother if she did not take care of her own Catholic altar in the same fashion. More than an object of a particular religion, many Japanese Brazilians who had a *butsudan* at home told me it represented respect and gratitude for the ancestors. In this way, offerings are able to transcend the realm of Buddhism and be present in other settings as well.

An account of Japanese-Brazilian religious practices before World War II given by the Brazilian anthropologist Egon Schaden already revealed strong creolization between Buddhist and Catholic practices. According to Schaden,

> Even before the War there were images of Catholic saints and crosses juxtaposed with Buddhist images in the *butsudan*. There were people who would chant Christian and Buddhist prayers. When a person passed away, flowers, candles, and Japanese incense were set next to the corpse, a Catholic rosary would be put together with a *jyuzu* (Buddhist rosary), and later candles, flowers, incense and food were set on the grave. Sometimes a cross was erected by the *bochiyo*, the Buddhist mortuary pole or stone. Finally, there are people who celebrate the 7th day Catholic mass and on the 49th day after the passing celebrate the traditional *shiju-kunti*.[17]

Interestingly, Robert Smith also found a similar pattern of creolization between Christianity and Buddhism in Japan, although on a much smaller scale. For instance, Smith describes Christians having *ihai* and Buddhist rites made for Buddhist deceased family members, and one Buddhist father who put pictures of his two late Catholic nun daughters in the *butsudan*, as he felt it would be inappropriate to have *ihai* made for them since they were not Buddhists, but he could not abandon them either. As Smith notes, "not even conversion to another religion necessarily interferes with the maintenance of the relationship between the living and the dead through the idiom of ancestor worship."[18] Here, once more creolization takes place by ancestor worship supplying the idiom for a new religious lexicon to be superimposed. In Japan, taking "proper care" of the deceased—that is, giving them their daily offering of food and reporting family news to them—seems to be emphasized. In Brazil my informants revealed an attitude of respect and gratitude, but this was not necessarily translated into daily care of the *butsudan* and *ihai*. While I would not state that this is the norm for Japanese Brazilians, it was a common practice among people I interviewed.

A Japanese-Brazilian Buddhist monk at Busshinji revealed a similar overlapping of meanings, this time in the way Catholic and Buddhist images found their place on a Catholic altar. His family itself is an embodiment of a hyphenated religious affiliation. While his mother is a devout Catholic, his father's family belonged to the Sōtōshū sect in Japan. In his case, negotiations between his Buddhist practice and his mother's Catholic belief took much more effort on his part. He reminisces,

> My mom is so pious that my name is Francisco Aparecido! She worships the patron saint of Brazil [Our Lady of Aparecida]. So religion is a very serious business for her. We do have *ihai* at home, but it took ages for her to accept them. She has softened a bit now. For instance, the other day I told her, "We have Jizō, that image that protects children, at the temple for sale." She told me, "Oh, well, it is OK. You can buy it and bring it back. I'll take care of it." But she asked, "Can I put this Jizō together with the Virgin Mary in the altar?" and I said, "There is no problem, you do whatever you want to do with it." She was really worried about how to take care of the Jizō![19]

Not only are images of different traditions placed on the *butsudan*, but its placement in the home has changed, too. While in Japan it usually has a room for itself, or at least is not placed where the members of the family sleep, in Brazil it is invariably placed in the master bedroom. One possible explanation for this change was given by a Japanese-Brazilian Jōdoshū monk, Eduardo Sasaki. For him the change happened due to the strong Catholic environment immigrants lived in. Buddhist objects were better not shown for fear of racism. As I mentioned in chapter 1, Buddhist and Shintō priests were forbidden to travel to Brazil with immigrants until World War II for fear this could be taken as evidence of intent to resist assimilation.

FIGURE 22
Butsudan with image of Nossa Senhora Aparecida (the patron saint of Brazil) and the pope (courtesy Eduardo Sasaki).

Continuity and innovation between Japanese and Brazilian practices is also evident in the issue of who is responsible for looking after the *butsudan*. Traditionally in Japan, the *chōnan* (the eldest son), as the head of the *ie* (the household), would keep the altar and tend to it. In contemporary Japan, however, because of the aforementioned phenomena of urbanization and nuclear families, housewives take care of the *butsudan*, as their husbands work long hours outside of the house. In Brazil, I have seen mixed patterns—mostly, the eldest son inherits the *butsudan*, but a woman being responsible for the altar is not uncommon. In fact, that is what took place in Nícia's case: her grandmother, then mother, and subsequently herself being responsible for it. Nícia told me,

> When the monk at Busshinji told me that according to tradition the eldest son should keep the *butsudan*, my sister and I called my brother to ask if he wanted to keep it. After consulting with his family he said he didn't want

to keep it because he was not Buddhist and neither was his family. So I said I wanted to keep it particularly because of the studies I've been doing. You see, I am learning the Buddhist teachings and practicing meditation.

One Japanese Brazilian, who practices *zazen* under Coen *sensei*, told me that although he is the *chōnan* and hence the one who should keep the *butsudan*, he was denied this right because he had converted to Zen Buddhism while his family belonged to Sekai Kyūseikyō (Church of World Messianity, a Japanese NRM). The altar, therefore, was inherited by his eldest sister when their mother died. He confided that he would have liked to have kept it, but he had fallen from grace when he took up Zen. His mother clearly opposed his religious adherence "because she wanted me to follow the family religion, especially since I was the only man in the house, the heir, the one who should keep family tradition."[20]

Others do not have a *butsudan* to be passed down and are not aware that the eldest son should be responsible for such a thing. One afternoon, when I was at Busshinji, two teenage Japanese-Brazilian girls came in. They wanted to buy a *butsudan* at the temple to give to their mother as a birthday present. They thought it would be a good gift since their mother was becoming interested in Buddhism and had no altar at home. They also mentioned it would be a good way to help their mother research the Japanese family tradition that lately she had been interested in. A Japanese-Brazilian female volunteer at the temple spent some time with the girls explaining which objects should be placed in the altar and how to care for it. Contrary to what happens in Japan, where the *butsudan* should either be passed down in the family or be bought at the time of death, here the youngest in the family were buying something for a female member of their immediate family who was still alive, so that she could recollect family history and exercise her interest in Buddhism. I believe the fact that Buddhism is fashionable in Brazil can help us understand new social meanings ascribed to Buddhism. The *butsudan* continued to symbolize ancestor worship but also became a Buddhist altar (as you would have in other non-Japanese Buddhist traditions) and rather a "cool" object to have at home. As I showed in chapter 4, fashion and Buddhism have walked hand in hand in Brazil since the mid-1990s.

Japanese Brazilians are not alone in creolizing their altars; non-Japanese Brazilians add Buddhist elements to their mainly Catholic understanding of what an altar should be. In February 2003, the uses of the *butsudan* were the topic of discussion on the e-mail list Buddhismo-L. The discussion started when someone posted a message asking how to put together a *butsudan*. Whereas a non-Japanese-Brazilian Jōdo Shinshū monk criticized the mixing of images of different religions on the same altar, all other contributors to the e-mail list explicitly endorsed this mixing. One message stated,

> I am Buddhist, my wife is Spiritist, and my mother is devoted to Saint Anthony. I have a piece of furniture at home (originally, a little table for the phone) where I placed a wood carved image of the Buddha, a picture of Chico Xavier and an image of Saint Anthony.[21]

In this way, although the "altar" is still called a *butsudan*, its uses are very different from the traditional Japanese one. None of the messages mentioned placing pictures or food for ancestors. However, such a juxtaposition of images does not mean that followers are oblivious to the particularities of each religion, or that the mixing is aleatory. As Brazilian anthropologist Carlos Rodrigues Brandão argued, religions retain partial power in Brazil; each assists the follower in different aspects of life.[22] Another message posted illustrates this point.

> In my room I have an "altar" with an image of the Buddha and another of Saint Francis of Assisi. They are there neither to assert that "Buddha was a Franciscan," nor that "Saint Francis was like the Buddha or a bodhisattva." They are there because of what each one, in its own individuality, represents to me. I don't see the need for synthesis (although I don't criticize people who think it is useful). Saint Francis among the birds honoring his God through its creation . . . Buddha sitting down, "observing" emptiness. Just that.[23]

JAPANESE BRAZILIANS CONVERTING TO BUDDHISM: FAMILY HISTORY AND SPIRITUALITY

> Hello!
> I was surfing on one of the Buddhist websites and realized that because of phonetics the word *dharma* becomes *daruma* in Japanese. Can anyone tell me if they are both the same for Buddhism? I remember when I was a child my grandparents had a bunch of *daruma*s at home. They were big-eyed, red, bearded dolls that they would paint one eye when they made a wish and they would only paint the other eye when the wish came true.[24]

This message illustrates how some Japanese Brazilians, who have had a little contact with Buddhism through family tradition—in this case the folk practice of appealing to Bodhidharma, the patriarch of Zen Buddhism, for good luck—may suddenly realize that their Japanese heritage was influenced by this religion. For many, as I will show in this section, turning to Buddhism through an interest in spirituality means also going back to family history.

An important event that helps us unravel creolization by Japanese Brazilians of the so-called "devotional" or "ethnic Buddhism" practices of ancestor worship and mortuary rites and the "convert" or "Western" interest in Buddhism (mainly centered on meditation) is conversion to Buddhism. First of all, as explained earlier, traditional Japanese affiliation with a temple (hence a Buddhist sect) was by household (*ie*). Affiliation was not a matter of personal choice and individual faith. This is still the case in Japan today, notwithstanding the small Zen boom that took place in the 1980s that helped form *zazenkai* (sitting groups) in some temples. For Japanese-Brazilian converts, their family affiliation (when known) plays no role in their choice of sect. Instead of family adherence, Japanese Brazilians have adopted individual choice of religion. When I asked a *nisei* who practiced *zazen* at Busshinji if his family, who was affiliated with Jōdo Shinshū, was upset because he chose a different school of Buddhism, he replied,

> My family does not make this distinction between sects. The distinction you are making is in the realm of the study of Buddhism. My family goes to the *o-tera* [the temple] just like the *fujinkai* women here. They go to the services, but do not differentiate between Pure Land, Zen, and so on. They think: it is Buddhism, it is *o-tera*, it is fine.[25]

Interestingly, while in the previous case I mentioned that the mother would not pass the *butsudan* on to her first son because the family was affiliated with Sekai Kyūseikyō and he had converted to Zen Buddhism, in this case the family has no problem or does not even acknowledge a difference between schools of Buddhism. The different reactions derive from different attitudes toward religion. As I show here, in contrast with NRMs, which require an active role of the devotee and shunning of other religious affiliations, in Japan people get in contact with Buddhism because of mortuary rites.[26] Belonging to a new religious movement involves a constant engagement by the adherent, which is not necessarily required by Japanese Buddhism.

As much as non-Japanese Brazilians seek Buddhism as an alternative to traditional Catholicism, since they feel the latter does not answer their spiritual needs anymore, Japanese Brazilians who were mostly Catholic (active or not) have also been searching for alternative spiritual practices. Both groups have wandered through many religions such as Afro-Brazilian, Spiritism, and NRMs before finding Buddhism. As I pointed out in chapter 3, this phenomenon of constant "religious transit" has been well documented in Brazilian society.

Because Tibetan Buddhism is fashionable and very much in the print media and popular culture nowadays, it is usually this form of Buddhism that seekers start with. Adding to that, since there is no ethnic Tibetan community in Brazil, all activities are conducted either in Portuguese (by Brazilians) or in English with translation to Portuguese (by Tibetan or North American masters). Hence Tibetan Buddhism is the most easily accessible Buddhist school in Brazil. It is not surprising, then, that when Nícia became interested in Buddhism, she started with Tibetan practice and even undertook a pilgrimage to India to meet her lineage's Rinpoche. As with any fashionable trend, teenagers are the ones who spot it quickly—her youngest son has told me of his readings in Tibetan Buddhist literature and of his interest in meditation. As I mentioned earlier, Nícia recently shifted to Japanese Buddhism because of a series of factors: first, her mother's death and her subsequent search for family heritage; second, her meeting Coen *sensei* at her local martial arts school; and finally her decision to quit the other martial arts school (which was affiliated with Tibetan Buddhism) because it was too far away from her home. These factors reveal that there is an understanding that Buddhism has a univocal essence if stripped of cultural accretions (as stated in modern Buddhism) and that the choice may be made over convenience of accessibility to the nearest temple/Zen center. More important, however, is that Nícia chose Japanese Buddhism because she was interested in her family heritage beyond her own interest in Buddhism itself.

A very telling case is that of Ryuichi Watanabe, whose wife's forty-ninth-day memorial service was held at Busshinji. He told me he had no religion to resort to in such painful times, and his Japanese-Brazilian golf friends tried to help by saying that he should hold a Buddhist memorial service. Soon afterward he read an interview with Coen *sensei* in a Japanese community newspaper. Because her words touched him, he decided Busshinji was the right place for the memorial. However, even if he very much appreciated the service and still holds Coen *sensei* in high regard, shortly after the memorial he started frequenting a Shambhala Buddhist center, where his son and daughter-in-law took him and where he still goes three years after his wife's death. When asked why he had chosen Tibetan over Japanese Buddhism, he said,

> To tell you the truth I was in search of a spiritual practice, not of a religion. I think because my family belonged to Japanese Buddhism, I regarded it

as an institution, something connected to the old Japanese community. In Shambhala I use the teachings in daily life. Well, I guess Shambhala meditation is identical to the Sōtōshū's. Following fashion, I am also reading the books by the Dalai Lama.[27]

Here Ryuichi reveals that for him Japanese Buddhism is regarded as a religion because it is associated with his ethnic heritage, which implies social obligations and not individual choice. On the other hand, Shambhala Buddhism offers him not only a connection to a more cosmopolitan world through fashion, but also with a spiritual practice detached from any ethnic, "old" features.

The contrast between spiritual practice and religious practice was brought forth by Nícia, too. While telling me about the *zazen* sessions at her martial arts school, she mentioned that "it was just *zazen* practice, that is, [Coen *sensei*] doesn't bring the religious aspect of Buddhism to the *zazen* sessions." This clear distinction between religion as connected to Japanese ancestor worship and *zazen* as "spiritual" practice is disputed by Moriyama *rōshi*, the resident Japanese *rōshi* of Porto Alegre Zen Center.

Usually the Japanese community members have an interest in the temple related to ancestor worship and they don't understand the connection of Zen Buddhism and *zazen* practice. That is, they don't seek the temple for religious practice.[28]

Therefore, while for Ryuichi and Nícia the religious practice is related to mortuary rites that take place in the temple and meditation is more of a spiritual practice, a philosophy to be used in daily life, for Moriyama the religious practice is meditation itself. Other Japanese Brazilians I interviewed also differentiated between religious and spiritual practice. They told me that they do have a religious practice, but seek Zen because it offers meditation. One *nisei* told me that her family belonged to the Higashi Honganji, but also frequented Seichō-no-ie. She was baptized and hence nominally a Catholic, but she also goes to Seichō-no-ie meetings. However, because of personal problems she had been having lately, she sought Zen for its meditational aspect.

These examples show that the spiritual search of Japanese Brazilians resembles very much that of their non-Japanese-Brazilian counterparts. The way they get in contact with Zen is the same also. Books play a crucial role in sparking their interest. I should add that being of Japanese descent was also given as a reason for interest in Zen. Getting to know more about "traditional" Japanese culture and the "religion of the samurai" was a frequent answer. The myth of the samurai plays a very important role in the imaginary of the Japanese Brazilians. I gathered from interviews that the samurai is regarded as a powerful figure who lived in traditional Japan and had the world under his command. Some Japanese Brazilians proudly told me their families were descendents of samurai families and not just of peasant farmers. Being a samurai descendant is used here as a form of cultural capital and therefore empowerment. As I have alluded to in chapter 1, Japanese who migrated to Brazil were indentured workers and hence possessed low status in Brazilian society. Although they have ascended to middle-class positions, they are still seen by Brazilian upper classes as having little cultural capital.

An interest in Japanese history on the one hand and an interest in philosophy on the other was what predisposed another of my interviewees, a Japanese-Brazilian Busshinji monk, to start going to the Zen temple. As his mother was a devout Catholic, he was raised a Catholic and studied in a Catholic school. Later in life he sought out Zen Buddhism after reading D. T. Suzuki and many Western books on Zen while pursuing his Ph.D. in history at the University of São Paulo. What is noteworthy in his case is how his ordination took place.

> I started going to Busshinji for meditations on Saturdays in the mid-eighties. After some time, the monks realized I was diligent in my *zazen* practice and started to ask me about my interest in Zen Buddhism. I said I wanted to study Zen. Then a monk assured me that if I wanted to deepen my knowledge of Zen, *zazen* alone would not be enough. I would have to take a stand in the temple, I would have to become a monk. Only then would I have a commitment to Zen. At that time I did not know what that meant. They obliged me. . . . They asked me to come to the temple every Saturday and Sunday. I had no idea what for, and found out it was to help in the rituals. Until then I had never been to a memorial service or any kind of Buddhist rite![29]

This is clearly a case of a *nisei* interested in the Western construct of Zen who became aware of Japanese customs because he was of Japanese heritage. However, although his path was reversed when compared to that of other Japanese Brazilians who became interested in Zen because of *zazen*, this monk made his way back and is currently leading the temple's *zazenkai* after many years of only conducting memorial services on weekends. His case is clear evidence that Japanese Brazilians may dwell in both worlds—that of meditation and that of mortuary rites.

MERIT MAKING: TRADITIONAL AND MODERNIST?

A good example of creolization between "ethnic" and "convert" practices that shows a more nuanced picture is the occasions of merit making at Busshinji Temple. The same Japanese-Brazilian monk mentioned above told me in another interview,

> [Zen] Practice should not be regarded as hegemonic. Things are not the same for everyone. For instance, the members of the women's association may not come to *zazen*, but they are volunteers and help in the kitchen. This is also a kind of practice. There are people who come to sweep the footpath. Hence, this [what constitutes "real" Buddhist practice] has to be seen in a broader way. Dōgen said that enlightenment and practice are one thing, but what is practice? Practice is to meditate, but also to get up and do other things. How are you going to eat? The person who is in the kitchen is also practicing.[30]

Conversely, the group that was training to take lay ordination in January 2002 (90 percent of whom were non-Japanese Brazilians) had another important activity besides *zazen* and *sūtra* study—they were also asked to give *dāna*. Historically, the practice of *dāna* as almsgiving to mendicant monks was a way for laypeople to acquire merit, which in due time would lead to enlightenment. Monks, on the other hand, would acquire merit through meditation, *sūtra* studying, begging (*takuhatsu*), and *samu* (physical work such as cleaning, gardening, etc.).

However, because in the West the boundaries between laity and monastic life are blurred, new roles are adopted by each group. For instance, lay-ordained Westerners perform practices such as *zazen* that are usually reserved for monastics. Shunryū Suzuki has noted that "American students are not priests and yet not completely laymen,"[31] a trend also pointed out by Seager: "American Zen is primarily a movement of laity who practice monastic disciplines."[32] However, *dāna* as a merit-making practice has not been adopted by "converts" in North American Zen and remains in the realm of "ethnic" practices associated with Japan. As I have mentioned earlier, Baumann also classifies the practice of giving *dāna* as a trait of "traditionalist" Buddhism, that is, the Buddhism of Asian immigrants and their descendents.[33]

Nevertheless, *dāna* is very much alive for the group studying to be lay ordained at Busshinji as it consists of sewing two *zafu* (sitting cushion) and one *rakusu* (small bib representing the monk's robes), making two *o-juzu* (string of beads symbolic of Buddhist faith), sweeping floors and cleaning the temple, and finally actual donation of money and cleaning products for the temple. Both *zafu* and *o-juzu* are made for the lay ordained himself/herself and as a donation to the temple. Like the Japanese Brazilians who donated money for the reconstruction of the temple in 1995 and hence who have their names inscribed on wooden boards inside the building, each member of the lay ordination study group had his/her name and the quality and quantity of *dāna* given listed on posters affixed to the tearoom windows. Manual labor in Brazil is still regarded as appropriate only for the disenfranchised classes, a consequence of the country's history of slavery. Even today, most middle- and upper middle-class families have at least one maid in the household. There- fore, kneeling down to scrub the floor is not easy for many adherents. I have seen some followers fleeing the task by leaving the temple or chatting downstairs while cleaning is carried out by others. Giving *dāna* in the form of cleaning is hence a meaningful offering for many non-Japanese-Brazilian adherents who, as profiled in chapter 3, belong to the upper (and white) strata of Brazilian society.

Undoubtedly, there is hybridization between ethnic ideas of *dāna* and merit making and Western ideas of Buddhism as meditational. Nonmeditational Japa- nese Brazilians are validated in their *dāna* practices, while candidates for lay ordi- nation are also exhorted to give *dāna*, as well as to sit. If we use Baumann's binary system of traditionalist and modernist Buddhism, we can see that what is particular about hybridization in Brazil is that it takes place between the two kinds of Bud- dhism and not only between Buddhism and other religions such as Protestantism, Judaism, or Catholicism.

NON-JAPANESE BRAZILIANS: BORN CATHOLIC, DIE BUDDHIST

While the well-known saying for the Japanese goes, "Born Shintō, die Buddhist," a similar adage can be coined for non-Japanese Brazilians, for it is not unusual for non-Japanese members of the *zazenkai* to turn to Buddhism at the time of death. In some cases, the family has distanced itself from Catholicism and has no reli- gion to resort to when death strikes. On such an occasion, the family member who frequents Zen may offer to call a Zen priest. This is the situation Pedro, an engi- neer, was in when his mother-in-law died. Because no one in his family seemed to know what to do and because there was no Catholic priest they could call, he asked Coen *sensei* to conduct the funeral. He recollects,

> My mother-in-law died suddenly. She was in the hospital and the wake was there too. Then everyone was asking if we'd have a service or not. There

was no priest and as the hospital was so close to the temple I said, "If you want, I can call the Buddhist nun." They accepted the offer and she came. But you know, I don't really believe in mass and afterwards I sort of regretted having taken Coen *sensei* there. I mentioned this to her and she said that the service was not only for the dead person, but also for the family. That made me feel a bit better.[34]

Pedro expressed his discomfort with the ritual because he associated it with the Catholic mass (even using the Catholic term). As I showed in chapter 3, many non-Japanese Brazilians are weary of institutional religion and would like Zen to have no rituals. However, they also told me that in such a situation it was better to have Coen *sensei* speak than a priest. Pedro mentioned that after the burial, there was a seventh-day mass at a Catholic church. As with other funerals and services Coen *sensei* performed for non-Japanese Brazilians, his mother-in-law received an *ihai* inscribed with her name and dates of birth and death, which is kept at Pedro's home. Very few non-Japanese Brazilians receive a *kaimyō* (Buddhist posthumous name). Coen *sensei* mentioned they were given to only two deceased practitioners, since they had intended to take lay ordination. She pointed out that most non-Japanese Brazilians do not know about the Buddhist seventh-day service and the subsequent memorial services, and that is why they are not performed for this group. She has been spreading the word about it and some are starting to ask for these subsequent rituals.

When I inquired about the families' reactions to a Buddhist ritual, most non-Japanese disciples said their families thought the ceremony was beautiful and profound. Coen *sensei* said that after death rituals, many come to thank her for her kind words. She added,

> I've been involved in inter-religious activities for so long that I feel really comfortable when I am asked to conduct Buddhist rituals for family relatives of any religious tradition. I try to make them understand that we invoke all enlightened and benevolent beings to bless and guide people in death (funerals) as in life (weddings).[35]

This strategy of calling upon "enlightened and benevolent beings" in such general terms to "guide people" proves to be efficacious since it can be easily taken on board by adherents of the several religions practiced in Brazil. Indeed, Spiritism, Afro-Brazilian religions, NRMs, and even popular Catholicism all accept the idea of other worldly guides and guardians for human beings.

It is not only funerals that are conducted for non-Japanese Brazilians; they also participate in ancestor worship rites such as *o-bon* and *higan*, which are in turn creolized by Catholic practices. At Busshinji, *o-bon* festivities take place in mid-August, as is usual in Japan. However, a similar ritual is held on November 2, when the Catholic holiday All Souls' Day (in the temple called *ireisai*—memorial service ceremony) is commemorated. At *o-bon, ireisai,* and *higan* both Japanese Brazilians and non-Japanese Brazilians come to the temple.

According to Coen *sensei,* during these occasions non-Japanese Brazilians and Japanese Brazilians alike ask and pay for names of their deceased family members to be read during the ritual. I have also seen this happen during these rituals at Busshinji. The fact that non-Japanese Brazilians and Japanese Brazilians go to the temple for ancestor worship festivities begs the question of what these non-Japanese wish for when they ask for names of their deceased family members to be read. Are they really reverencing ancestors? Many told me that they were praying for their deceased family members to be peaceful where they were. This is a perfectly understandable explanation if one remembers the Christian saying "may s/he rest in peace." Furthermore, in Catholic Sunday masses, one can also ask for the name of a deceased family member to be read in exchange for a small fee. So the ritual was not so foreign to non-Japanese Brazilians.

When, on another occasion, I asked a Japanese-Brazilian monk at Busshinji if non-Japanese Brazilians came to the temple only for *zazen,* he told me this was so for some, but that it was not the whole picture of non-Japanese Brazilians' activities.

> There are people who come here for Saturday *zazen* because there is *sūtra* reading. There are people who make a point of coming for the Kannon ceremony. They are not family [mortuary] ceremonies. For instance, at this year's All Souls' Day, all the *zazen* people came here. They came not only because of the ceremony itself, but as a temple activity. They are people who want to participate in the temple's activities.[36]

It is interesting that the monk did not mention Japanese culture classes such as martial arts, flower arrangement, and classes on the history of Japan, which are clearly devoid of religious content, but he does include temple activities that would be regarded as of concern only to the "ethnic" congregation, since they are ritualistic and deeply religious.

OF WEDDING RINGS AND *O-JUZU*

Weddings are another activity that has been carried on in Busshinji since the late 1970s. Old photos of that time show Shingū *rōshi* conducting a wedding ceremony for non-Japanese Brazilians who belonged to the *zazenkai*. Likewise, Coen *sensei* and Moriyama *rōshi* have been asked to celebrate weddings for their *zazen* groups in São Paulo and Porto Alegre, respectively. Coen *sensei* comments that

> I've celebrated about six weddings a year since 1995, when I arrived in Brazil. It is not a big number. . . . I left my wedding registry book at Busshinji. Some [of the people who get married] are practitioners, some sympathizers. We have a practice course before the ceremony so that the couple knows which tradition they are getting affiliated with. I'll be conducting my first inter-religious (Catholic-Buddhist) wedding ceremony this coming May [2002]. The bridegroom will receive lay precepts before May. The bride and her family are devout Portuguese Catholics. Don Claudio Hummes, the archbishop of São Paulo, has authorized the ceremony in a Catholic church. Thus, I'll be discussing the ceremony details with the priest shortly.[37]

All these weddings are requested by non-Japanese Brazilians. This group is accustomed to Catholic weddings, and when they move on to another religious affiliation, they take it for granted that the same rituals are conducted in the new setting. A non-Japanese-Brazilian monk at Busshinji told me that not only *zazenkai* people seek the temple for weddings: "sometimes a person can't marry at the Catholic Church because s/he is divorced and then ends up at Busshinji because they think it is a beautiful, different place."[38] The same is true for the Higashi Honganji temple in São Paulo City; a story on different religious weddings featured in *Marie Claire* magazine reported an increase in wedding ceremonies at the temple by divorced Catholics who could not marry again in the Catholic Church. A non-Japanese monk of the temple declared, "It does not matter if people come here because they think it is exotic, cheap or beautiful; what we seek is sincerity in people's heart."[39] I believe fashion also accounts for the decision to marry at a Buddhist temple. For instance, Claudia Raia and Edson Celulari, a famous couple who act in soap operas, belong to Sōka Gakkai. Their wedding ceremony at a Sōka Gakkai *kaikan* (auditorium/meeting hall) was widely publicized in the media in 1998.

Historically in Japan weddings have been a secular bond, not a religious rite

FIGURE 23
Wedding ceremony performed by Shingū *rōshi* in the late 1970s.

of passage. Buddhist wedding ceremonies were created in 1887 and had Christian weddings as a model. The Shintō wedding that now seems as traditional was created even later, dating from the 1900s.[40] In recent years the Japanese have taken an antithetical path to those Brazilians who marry in Buddhist temples: Christian-style weddings have become extremely fashionable and now account for the majority of wedding ceremonies.[41] Reader has shown that because of the postwar urbanization and nuclear family phenomena, which weakened the bonds between families and Buddhist temples, Sōtōshū Shūmuchō published and distributed several pamphlets in the 1980s that sought to strengthen the family-temple connection. One of the "Ten Articles of Faith" (Shinkō Jūkun) is an attempt to bring families back to the temple through the marriage ritual. It reads, "Let us celebrate weddings before our ancestors in the temple."[42] This movement has not reached Brazilian shores yet, since Sōtōshū weddings usually involve non-Japanese Brazilians.

Conversely, one is bound to ask how the Japanese-Brazilian community celebrates weddings. Tomoo Handa (1906–1996), a Japanese immigrant who arrived in Brazil in 1917 and became a famous painter and journalist, is the author of several books on the Japanese-Brazilian community. In a book first published in Japanese in 1970, Handa writes about the compromises made in Brazil to satisfy *issei* and *nisei* alike.

> Funerals are usually conducted in a Catholic style for young people, whilst for the older people it is done according to the Buddhist style. However, there are cases where a Catholic mass is celebrated before burial, but then family and friends go to the cemetery with a Buddhist monk, and bury the body in a Buddhist style. The same is true for weddings: the ceremony takes place in a Catholic church but upon arriving home, there is a Japanese ceremony with *san-san-kudō*,[43] before they go on to the reception. This is certainly done to appease the *issei* as well as the *nisei*. One cannot assert things without statistical numbers, but it is only natural that weddings and funerals are more and more, year after year, in the Catholic style because of the increasing number of *nisei*.[44]

Handa's prediction certainly came true, and the trend toward creolizing Buddhist and Catholic practices to satisfy *issei, nisei, sansei,* and nowadays *yonsei* is very much alive, as demonstrated in this chapter. The head monk of the Jōdo Shinshū temple of Apucarana (Paraná State) describes wedding ceremonies for Japanese Brazilians during a discussion on Buddhismo-L.

> In Brazil, the wedding rites celebrated by the Jōdo Shinshū school were adapted to our culture, incorporating Western customs. For instance, people frequently get married in Western attire: the groom wears a suit and the bride wears a wedding gown. The couple always insists on adorning the aisle between the pews with flowers and ribbons and having the famous red carpet (which actually can be of any other color). The bridesmaids are almost indispensable and the rings are more often than not part of the rites too. Of course, all this is only cultural accretion, it does not influence the rite per se, which can be celebrated in any place, circumstance, and wearing any attire.[45]

The ceremony itself resembles very much the Catholic one with exchange of vows, rings, and rosaries. In North America, Kashima has reported this kind of creolization taking place in many of the Jōdo Shinshū activities, among them weddings. He mentions new features in the American Buddhist wedding ceremony such as a wedding gown for the bride, a tuxedo for the groom, the playing of a wedding march, the exchange of rings, and the witnessing of a wedding license.[46]

FIGURE 24
Wedding ceremony performed by Coen *sensei* at Busshinji in March 2000.

Whereas these are moves toward a more Catholic or Christian wedding ceremony performed for Japanese Brazilians and Japanese Americans, weddings in
Busshinji and in the Zen center of Porto Alegre are all celebrated for non-Japanese
Brazilians. That itself entails a different approach toward weddings in that the
couple is not seeking to copy a Christian tradition. Quite the opposite, as I have
shown in chapter 3; non-Japanese Brazilians who practice Buddhism are usually
part of the intellectual elite who have left Catholicism seeking *individual* responsibility for their "spiritual growth" or enlightenment, as well as dissociation from
any institutionalized religion. They praise Zen for its "lack of ritual" and absence
of an almighty God. Thus they expect a different—and most of the time, a less
ritualistic—ceremony than exists in the Catholic Church.

In March 2000, I witnessed the wedding ceremony of a middle-aged non-
Japanese couple—she was a yoga teacher and he was a therapist. Both were dis-

ciples of Coen *sensei*. During the short ceremony, the couple and the audience were informally dressed (a short-sleeved shirt for the groom, a simple hippie-like dress for the bride). After invoking auspicious words for the couple facing the altar, Coen *sensei* turned and gave each an *o-juzu*[47] for them to exchange to seal their partnership and Buddhist faith. The couple then sipped sake three times and read vows together. As a last rite, first the couple, then their best friends, and finally Coen *sensei* signed a registry book. The ceremony was conducted in Portuguese since none of the participants were of Japanese descent. Moreover, it was performed on Saturday evening, after *zazen* practice, when the temple was not being used for funerary and memorial rites, which occur on Saturdays and Sundays during the day. As Handa previously noted, Japanese Brazilians do not get married at the Buddhist temple, since in Japan weddings are not usually celebrated in Buddhist temples; their wedding ceremonies are usually celebrated at either the Catholic Church or most usually in secular wedding centers.

ZEN BABIES

Not only funerals, memorials, and weddings are performed for and attended by non-Japanese Brazilians. Moriyama *rōshi* told me he has so far performed four "baptism" ceremonies at the request of his disciples in Porto Alegre.[48] The mother of two children "baptized" by Moriyama *rōshi* told me it had not occurred to her that there might not be such a ceremony in Zen. She had been a nonpracticing Catholic, then Spiritist, and now she had great "affinity" with Buddhism. Neither her nor her husband's family is Buddhist, but they did not oppose the ceremony. According to her, they thought it was important that they were baptized, but it did not matter in which particular religion. When I asked what the ritual meant to her, she told me the children's dharma names would be a constant reminder to them of "their role here," that is, their path in making it a better world. She also told me that their dharma names were mostly used at home and sometimes the children themselves called each other by those names. Another mother who asked Moriyama *rōshi* for a "baptism" ceremony told me that she and her husband had wanted the baby to undergo the ritual in three religions—Catholicism, Judaism, and Buddhism—because of her upbringing, her husband's background, and their religion of choice, respectively. She explained her desire for the "baptism" ritual in the following terms.

> The baptism is like a blessing, a welcoming into a spiritual path. I feel it
> as a protection. I am very much influenced by Christianity as I had a very

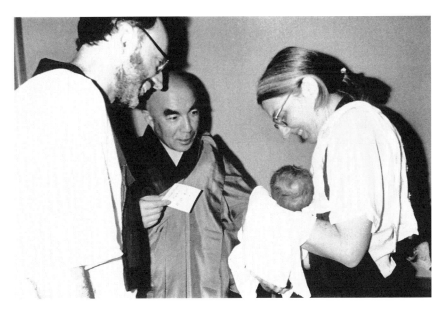

FIGURE 25
Moriyama *rōshi* "baptizing" a baby in Porto Alegre (Rio Grande do Sul State).

strong Catholic education. [After the ceremony] I felt very happy with the blessing with a sprig and some "holy water" over the baby and us and the *rōshi's* smile when the baby cried.[49]

From these stories one can see that both mothers have a creolized understanding of the "baptism" ceremony. Their desire to baptize their children, the use of this very Christian word, the idea of "baptism" as a protection, and the likening of the *rōshi's* gesture of sprinkling water to the priest's sprinkling of holy water are clear examples of a new Buddhist vocabulary superimposed on a Catholic matrix of understanding. Some of my informants who were more deeply engaged with Buddhism were aware that Buddhist "baptism" ceremonies were being created in Brazil because of strong demand, indicating an intentional, that is, conscious, creolization process.

Moriyama *rōshi* is not alone in "baptizing" his disciples' babies. Tokuda *sensei* and Christiano Daiju Bitti conduct this ceremony as well. Daiju has an interesting take in that he gives Brazilian indigenous names instead of the Japanese dharma ones. The demand for Buddhist "baptisms" is becoming so common that it was a subject of discussion for some weeks during 2002 on the Brazilian Buddhist e-mail lists. For the most part, people wanted to "baptize" their children in the Buddhist tradition as well as in the Catholic one and wanted to know which schools would have such rituals. Through this discussion, I was able to find out about creolizations performed in other Buddhist traditions. For instance, the Brazilian branch of Fo Kuang Shan has created a ceremony to address this demand. A member of the school disclosed in a message that his baby girl was six months old when she "took refuge," and the Taiwanese head nun of the order in Brazil said the girl could confirm it when she grew up. Interestingly, even if this disciple uses the Buddhist term (take refuge) instead of the Christian one (baptism), he happily describes on-the-spot creations inspired by the Catholic rituals such as the use of the godfather and godmother to chant the refuge for the baby as a "step toward the creation of a Brazilian Buddhism."[50] Creating new rituals was also carried out by the aforementioned soap opera couple who married in Sōka Gakkai. Upon the birth of their first child, they made headlines on the cover of the national weekly magazine *IstoÉ* when Claudia Raia, the proud mother, stated,

> I've been a Buddhist for thirteen years. The first thing Edson and I did when we left the maternity ward was to take our new-born baby, Enzo, to the altar and offer it to Buddha.[51]

On the other hand, as the Japanese-Brazilian community has converted to Catholicism since their arrival in Brazil, they baptize their babies in the Catholic Church. During the discussion on "baptism" on the e-mail list, a non-Japanese-Brazilian Jōdo Shinshū monk wrote that he has been trying to change this situation and have his parishioners celebrate the new baby in the temple as well. He observed,

> In Brazil, it is a common practice of the Japanese community that people baptize their children, have a first communion and even get married at the Catholic Church, but when funeral rites are involved, then they remember the Buddhist monk. Since I became the head monk of my temple in Apucarana, we have already reversed this situation. Although there is no "baptism," there is a ceremony of Thanksgiving [*hōon*] and Introduction of the newborn to the temple.[52]

Like weddings, baptism is not a ritual performed in Buddhist temples in Japan. Shinto shrines are in charge of ensuring protection for the newborn and an auspicious life. The expectation that these rituals are performed and their demand by non-Japanese Brazilians show how Buddhism is being creolized in Brazil—the adherents' Catholic syntax is used to understand the new superimposed Buddhist vocabulary. This vocabulary changes as it encounters the new syntax. The *rōshi's* sprinkling of (holy?) water with a twig clearly invokes Catholic images of baptism.

CHANGING PATTERNS OF SCHOLARSHIP:
FROM SEPARATION TO HYBRIDITY OR CREOLIZATION

Studies of Japanese Buddhism in America have tended to focus on either American converts or Japanese-American practices.[53] Similarly, studies of Buddhism in the West have focused *either* on "ethnic" groups *or* on "white," European, or Euro-American converts and their transformations and adaptations of Buddhism. In such studies, both groups are mostly essentialized, that is, their boundaries are clearly delineated as if no exchange between them existed. When both groups are analyzed, most studies emphasize insurmountable differences between them.

Numrich has analyzed two Theravada temples in the United States and established that "in such temples, under one roof and through the guidance of a shared clergy, two ethnic groups [the immigrants and the American converts] pursue largely separate and substantively distinct expressions of a common religious tradition."[54] Numrich calls this situation a phenomenon of ethnically defined "parallel congregations." Nevertheless, Numrich recognizes that "if you push these analytical categories far enough we will find that they are not 'pure.' Admittedly, each group includes a range of religious attitudes and behaviors. For instance, we will find some Asians who think a lot like American converts and some Americans who sometimes behave like Asian Buddhists (ritually speaking, that is)."[55] Since writing that, Numrich has published a comprehensive literature review article on the subject. Although he acknowledges that some scholars reject the clear division between "ethnic" and "convert" Buddhism as too simplistic, he argues for the value of the notion as a first stepping-stone for further advancement of the field.[56]

Numrich is not alone in identifying "parallel congregations" in the United States. Much earlier, Prebish noted in 1979 (and again in 1993) that there were two lines of development in American Buddhism, one practiced by the Asian-American communities and another practiced by non-Asian Americans. One has to keep in mind that the second wave of Asian immigration, which started in the mid-1960s, was still fresh when Prebish did his research and that may have accounted for the clear separation of practices between these communities.[57] More recently, Prebish has suggested some change in this picture of segregation.

Even this attempt at a rough classification is problematic: the largely Japanese American Buddhist Churches of America (BCA), for example, includes thoroughly acculturated fourth-generation Japanese Americans, as well as at least a scattering of white Americans. In fact, five out of sixty BCA ministers are white Americans. In what sense, then, can this be considered an "ethnic" or immigrant Buddhism?[58]

Along the same line, Eck has pointed out that the present dichotomy in the North American Buddhisms should not be seen as permanent. She realizes—as I have found in my fieldwork—that more and more there will be overlappings of practices between the two groups.

The impulse toward preservation among immigrant Buddhists and the impulse toward transformation among new Euro-American Buddhists may, in time, converge. It is not enough to preserve a religious or cultural heritage; that heritage must also nourish a new generation in a new environment. Many immigrant Buddhist communities are finding that the social life of the temple is not enough and that meditation classes are, in fact, attractive to young people. And Euro-American Buddhist communities are finding that meditation programs are not enough and that the social life of a gathered community is, in fact, important to young people as they come to identify themselves as part of the community.[59]

Other scholars such as Nattier have realized that trying to identify who is a Buddhist in a two-category model ("convert" and "ethnic") is inadequate at best and, at worst, erases lot of data that do not fit in the two categories. Nattier proposed a three-category typology that took the focus out of Buddhist practices and directed it to the way Buddhism was transmitted to America. Drawing on Stark and Bainbridge's typology, Nattier suggested that religions can be imported, exported, or considered baggage. Import religion is one that is "demand-driven"— that is, it is sought out actively by the recipient; in Buddhism this can be described as "elite Buddhism," since that was the strata of European and American society that imported Buddhism. Export religion, by contrast, is one that is "sold" by missionaries and could be labeled "evangelical Buddhism." As an example, Nattier mentions Sōka Gakkai International. Finally, baggage religion is that which comes with "immigrants who did not travel for religious reasons." Nattier labeled this group "ethnic Buddhism."[60] Therefore, in a way, Nattier resorts once more to the differentiation between ethnic and convert Buddhism, even if she adds one more category. Indeed, Tanaka has noted that this tripartite model is unsatisfactory and remarked that the immigrant/baggage group should more appropriately be called "furniture" Buddhism due to its century-old existence in North America.[61]

Baumann has pointed out that "the two-category dichotomy becomes blurred when faced with empirical data."[62] In contrast with the trend of identifying individuals by how they have become Buddhists ("convert" vs. "immigrant"), or taking modes of transmission as the criteria (import, export, and baggage), Baumann has suggested that one should focus on the religious concepts that practices followed. Baumann, too, identifies two types of Buddhism: traditionalist and modernist. Traditionalist "places emphasis on ritual, devotional acts of merit-making and holds specific cosmological worldviews," while modernist "emphasizes rational, scientific, and scriptural elements [of Buddhism]."[63] According to Baumann, convert Buddhists take up modernized interpretations of Buddhism, whereas immigrants usually practice traditionalist Buddhism.

Deciding the issues of how to categorize who is a Buddhist ("convert" or "ethnic"), how each particular strand arrived in the West (import, export, baggage), and the kind of Buddhism practiced (traditionalist or modernist) is essential if one wishes to understand the current traits of Buddhism in the West. However, I contend that one must also look at the dialogical relationship between these groups, as I did in the first part of this chapter, to find out empirically what is taking place at a grass-roots level. Continuity and innovation through hybridization and creolization, as well as possible future trends, can only be found in this space of encounter, dialogue, and negotiation.

In light of my ethnographic material, which shows that even Baumann's modernist and traditionalist worldviews are creolized in the nation, it seems that the Brazilian case offers new data for studies of Buddhism in the West. This is not to say that there were no conflicts and separations between the two congregations. I did find them; they were very explicit and were discussed in previous chapters. However, I believe the host of experiences in the interstices of the "big picture" so frequently depicted in studies of Buddhism in the West is significant, as it indicates new directions.

It is noteworthy, however, that more recent scholarship has complicated this picture of atomized Buddhist communities by describing hybrid practices particularly in relation to "convert" Buddhism and other religions (be they Protestant, Jewish, Catholic, or indigenous religions). In charting the identity of a Buddhist adherent, Tweed has pointed out that one should avoid the "essentialized notion of tradition, imagining the religion as static, isolated and unified."[64] He goes on to assert,

Traditions change, they have contacts and exchange with other traditions, and hybrid traditions emerge with diverse expressions claiming authenticity. . . . [R]eligious combinations are so common that, if we ignore those who affiliate with hybrid traditions, engage in creole practices, or express ambivalent identities, there would be no one left to study.[65]

In the same vein, Queen tries to encompass the identity of Buddhist adherents by coining the interpretive category "multi-layered religious identities in transition."[66] Spuler has also found hybrid practices in Australia.

Alongside changes to existing rituals, new ceremonies have also been developed in Australian Diamond Sangha groups: baby-namings, weddings, memorial services, coming-of-age (for teenagers), dojo opening and closings, and teacher installations. Aitken has also developed a ceremony to commemorate the death of an unborn child. It has not yet been performed in Australia.[67]

These examples of hybridization in the West correlate to one part of the creole phenomenon of Zen in Brazil, that is, convert non-Japanese Brazilians using a Catholic, Spiritist, New Age, or/and Afro-Brazilian syntax as a basis for new Buddhist vocabulary. But what to make of the interaction between both groups? What about non-Japanese Brazilians going devotional like their born-Buddhist counterparts? What should we make of Japanese Brazilians reading about Buddhism and sitting *zazen*?

WHAT DISTINGUISHES THE BRAZILIAN RELIGIOUS FIELD

Although more recently many scholars have criticized this division between "convert" and "ethnic" Buddhism, pointing to a convergence between them, this issue has not been the focus of full ethnographies yet. Baumann has pointed out to me that one reason for this is that this process of convergence has just started in the United States and Europe. In the same vein, Seager has noted that both strands of Buddhism are still busy establishing their communities, and thus issues of emergence of an Americanized form of Buddhism are not as pressing as those about the process of community formation. But he acknowledges that there are interactions, and "to bring out this collaboration more clearly, the history of Buddhism in America must be revisioned at least since the early twentieth century when . . . networks began to develop among Asian, Asian American and European American seekers."[68]

Undeniably, there are considerable differences between the religious field in Brazil and those of the United States or Protestant Europe, which propelled an intensified process of hybridity between the two Buddhist communities.[69] The first one is the strong Catholic influence, particularly in its popular aspect. Since Brazilians are remarkably used to devotion towards saints, performing "traditional" Buddhist devotional practices does not present difficulties for them. Second, while the predominantly Protestant environment in the United States and some European countries calls for the elimination of ritual, the Brazilian religious field abounds with it. The porosity of the Brazilian religious field also plays a part in shaping Buddhism in Brazil, as it allows the follower to regard having multiple religious affiliations as "natural." Protestantism, on the contrary, calls for adherence to one religion, in spite of the New Age movement having established a "quest culture."

In addition, there has been no new influx of Asian immigrants after the 1970s in Brazil, as there has been in the United States and Europe. The Japanese "ethnic" community is in its fourth generation, and it is very much part of mainstream Brazilian culture. This factor alone explains why, as Baumann has pointed out, it is a misnomer to call second-generation immigrant religious practices and beliefs "ethnic."[70] In this respect, Japanese Buddhism in Brazil parallels that of the Japanese immigrant population in North America, where a fifth generation has come of age. However, Japanese Brazilians are distinct from Japanese Americans in that whereas the Japanese in Brazil were historically regarded positively, this was not the case in the United States. Indeed, the admiration for the Japanese and the influence of Romantic Orientalism have led to a larger acceptance of "traditional" Buddhist practices by non-Japanese Brazilians. Therefore, although North American and European cultures are highly influential in Brazil, these prominent differences have been important in the contrasting way modern Buddhism has been shaped in Brazil.

THE NEED FOR SEPARATION AND DISTINCTION

There are additional factors that account for the lack of ethnographic data on this dialogic relation. First, there is a search for a distinctive entity that may be called Western Buddhism (and accordingly, American Buddhism, European Buddhism, etc.). The sheer volume of books and theses on the subject that have appeared in the West since the mid-1990s points to a double pursuit: on the one hand, to find what can be considered singular features of such "new" Buddhism (sometimes even called a "fourth vehicle"),[71] and on the other hand, to profile their adherents as distinct from Asian Buddhists. Upon trying to identify Western Buddhism many scholars have, whether intentionally or not, overlooked where this new form took traits from the "traditional," "devotional," "ethnic" form. One only has to think of the number of "ethnic" Buddhist monks and nuns who have taught Westerners, be it in the West itself or in Asia, to realize how interconnected they are.

Adding to that, scholars' perceptions have been shaped by their personal interest in Buddhism. As a "silent sangha"[72] Western researchers tend to look at their own kind, that is, at transformations of Buddhism by "elite" or "convert" Buddhists. Similarly, Japanese-American scholars have researched mainly Japanese-American Buddhist groups. When both of these factors—a desire to identify a distinct Western Buddhism and a personal interest in Buddhism—meet, what has been called "ethnosangha oversight" takes place.[73] This refers to the phenomenon of leaving "ethnic" Buddhism out when trying to profile Western Buddhism.

Undeniably, as Pierce argued in her study on the role of race in the development of American Buddhism (particularly the Jōdo Shinshū sect in Hawai'i), the politics of power plays an important role in determining which group and practices may claim inclusion in the category "Western Buddhism."[74] A telling example of this power politics is the nomenclature used to differentiate both groups. Some scholars have favored "immigrant" or "Asian" over "ethnic," but none have analyzed why the term "ethnic" is so problematic. When one group is able to call another "ethnic," it is establishing unequal power relations. By calling a group "ethnic," the dominant group becomes invisible, unmarked, and normalized, while the minority group becomes the exotic "Other." In this context, the dominant society, be it white European or American, is excluded from the category of "ethnic." Ethnicity as Otherness is a common assumption when scholars fail to recall that ethnicity is in fact situated and changes according to the speaker's site and time. Furthermore, as Sollors has shown, there is a religious twist to the term "ethnic." Researching the origins of the term, Sollors has found that

> the Greek word *ethnikos*, from which the English "ethnic" is derived, meant "gentile," "heathen." Going back to the noun *ethnos*, the word was used to refer not just to people in general, but also to "others." In English usage, the meaning shifted from "non-Israelite" . . . to "non-Christian." Thus the word retained its quality of defining another people contrastively, and often negatively. . . . Only in the mid-nineteenth century did the more familiar meaning of "ethnic" as "peculiar to a race or nation" re-emerge. However, the English language has retained the pagan memory of "ethnic," often secularized in the sense of ethnic as other, as non-standard, or, in America, as not fully American. . . . *The relationship between ethnicity and American identity in this respect parallels that of pagan superstition and true religion.*[75]

Given this etymology, it is easy to see why "ethnic" Buddhism comes to be considered as "not authentic" Buddhism. From this perspective, Westerners may claim that "ethnic" Buddhism has been swamped with cultural accretions over its long history in Asia, and in the process has lost its main "authentic" feature, namely meditation. Indeed, the historical belief—which originated in nineteenth-century scholarship in Europe and North America—that Buddhism was rational, agnostic, and free of ritual still plays a role in Westerners' understanding of Buddhism, as I discussed in chapter 1. In contrast, "ethnic" Buddhism is said to be composed mainly of devotional practices and rituals. In this context, Pierce has observed that

> Europeans and Americans appropriated Buddhism in such a way as to create a form of the religion which bore little or no relationship to Asian Buddhist practices, but conformed to Western understandings of what religion should be. In doing so they undermined and discredited the practice of Asian Buddhism by Asian Buddhists.[76]

Two now classical U.S. examples of the "ethnosangha oversight" phenomenon are first the debate in 1991 between *Tricycle: The Buddhist Review* editor, Helen Tworkov, and a Jōdo Shinshū priest, Ryō Iwamura, over whether Japanese Americans had made a real contribution to the establishment of American Buddhism. The second was Don Moreale's *The Complete Guide to Buddhist America*, which overlooks Buddhist temples and centers where meditation is not taught. Because meditation is not a practice commonly associated with Asian groups, they were excluded from the book. In both cases, a strong critique has been carried out by scholars in the field such as Gregory, Prebish, and Tanaka. Nonetheless, I believe it is not enough simply to advocate the inclusion of both Buddhisms as valid and authentic Buddhism. Validating "convert" and "ethnic" practices still leaves the gulf between them intact—that is, there is still the assumption that there are insurmountable differences that produce a gap between them.

Another important factor that has led to a lack of ethnographic data on negotiations and hybridizations at a grass-roots level is that earlier scholarship was shaped by a bias toward philological study. This trend had its origins in the nineteenth-century Buddhist scholarship where texts were the main source of understanding Buddhism. In this context "informants" were only an adjunct to the translation process, and superfluous once that was accomplished. As Lopez has noted, "There was little interest in the ways in which such texts were understood by the Buddhists of Asia, less interest in the ways in which such texts were put to use in the service of various ritual functions."[77] This created the current field of Buddhist studies in universities, where Buddhologists prioritize texts as a consequence of their training. Indeed, until the Tibetan diaspora of the 1960s, text was valued above direct encounter with informants. From another perspective, Buddhologists have criticized anthropologists because of the anthropologists' ignorance of classical Buddhist languages.

While sociologists and religious scholars who address Buddhism in the West have been useful in constructing typologies and attempting to chart the number of followers, Buddhism in Asia has received scholarly attention mostly from anthropologists (Tambiah, Reader, Robert Smith, Gombrich, and Obeyesekere). As a result of this contrast, the boundary between the exotic Other (Asian Buddhists) and Us (Western Buddhists) is subtly maintained. Significantly, the tasks of tracing the genealogy of Buddhist studies in Asia, of deconstructing its discourse and the Orientalist influences, have been intensively tackled by contemporary scholars.[78] However, because Buddhism in the West is such a new field, little has been done reflexively on how contemporary scholars have analyzed it. In this context, some scholars may still act as partisans and receive little criticism. They praise Western Buddhism for its faithfulness to the Buddha's teachings. Coleman has asserted as recently as 1999 that

> a new Buddhism is now emerging in the industrialized nations of the West. . . . It is also a Buddhism *unchanged* from the moment of Siddhartha Gautama's great realization under the Bodhi tree. Western Buddhists and spiritual seekers are *doing exactly what the Buddha recommended* — looking deeply to see the nature of things from their own *direct experience* — but they are doing it in ways that often contradict centuries of Asian Buddhist tradition. In contrast to the traditional forms of Asian Buddhism, men and women *practice together as equals* in this new Buddhism. . . . Ceremonies are simpler and more direct, and few people believe in their ability to produce magical effects. But most importantly, the new Buddhism makes the path of meditation and spiritual discipline available to everyone, not just to an elite group of monks.[79]

Coleman might well have considered Sharf's critique of the idea that direct experience in the form of meditation is the historical central tenet of Buddhism. Sharf has shown that the emphasis on "religious experience" is relatively recent in the West and was motivated by a desire to free one's religious practice from religious institutions.[80] When Coleman made the same assertions in his subsequent book,[81] Gregory was emphatically critical in his review.

Aside from the difficulty, if not sheer impossibility, of determining the "original" Buddhism taught by Siddhārta Gautama, this statement flies in the face of everything that is now known about early Buddhism, which began as a renunciatory, celibate movement. Indeed, it would be hard to imagine an ethos that could be more different from that of the new Buddhism Coleman seeks to describe.[82]

Thus although a critique of modern Buddhism has been proposed in the last decade, some scholars continue to disregard it when analyzing contemporary forms of Western Buddhism. By regarding this new/Western Buddhism as the repository of the "real," unchanged teachings and viewing Western cultural accretions as fundamentally a positive addition, since they are part and parcel of values of the Enlightenment (equality, democratization, laicization, engagement, and feminization), aren't some Westerners asserting their own practice as superior to the "backward," "ethnic" one? Isn't this approach an endeavor to "civilize" Buddhism? Furthermore, like Brazilians, who use modern Buddhism as a marker of social distinction, are they not deploying the same mental scheme to differentiate themselves from Asian Buddhists?

CONCLUSION

In this chapter, I have revealed several examples of converts superimposing a Buddhist vocabulary on a Brazilian religious grammar. Converts may seek the temple for the performance of weddings, "baptisms," or funerals as they would a Catholic church. The rites of passage of their previous religious matrix are expected to exist in the new religious affiliation. Such rites are, in turn, transformed (in the case of funerals) or even invented (in the case of weddings and "baptisms") when performed for these new Buddhists. Moreover, non-Japanese Brazilians also have, in a way, Buddhist ancestor practices overlapping their Catholic practice when they pay a sum for the name of a deceased relative to be read at *ireisai* or at *o-bon* rituals. In addition, merit making by giving *dāna*, a typically "ethnic" practice, also features as a way of "doing Zen and being Zen" for this group.

On the other hand, I have shown that by being innovative in the use of the *butsudan*, mortuary rites, weddings, and conversion, Japanese Brazilians also have a creolized way of "doing and being" Zen. By strategically allowing a Brazilian Catholic lexicon to be superimposed on their Japanese cultural grammar, they were able to maintain their identity in the new country. Certainly, the fact that most Japanese Brazilians are born Catholic also makes it easier for them to have a "convert" interest in Zen. Just like their non-Japanese-Brazilian counterparts, many of them have wandered through many other religious practices before finding Zen. However, unlike non-Japanese Brazilians, in seeking Zen Japanese Brazilians also endeavor to recuperate their Japanese identity, which may have been shorn off over generations. Some have an opposite attitude, which likens them to non-Japanese-Brazilian spiritual seeking: some choose to turn to Tibetan Buddhism instead of Zen because they feel the latter is too laden with institutional religiosity (as their families were once Buddhists) and has too little "spirituality."

The stories I have narrated here illuminate how the process of creolization of Buddhism takes place in Brazil. In contrast to what has been reported in other Western countries where Buddhism has arrived, in Brazil there is not a clear divide between the practices of the two groups, "convert" and "ethnic." Devotion, merit making, studies of Buddhist doctrine, and meditation can be found in both groups, even if devotion and merit making are not the main practice in "convert" Zen and studies of Buddhist doctrine and meditation are more sparingly performed among the "ethnic" congregation.

Importantly, in dissecting the roots of the commonly assumed divisions between "ethnic" and "convert," as well as the subtle self-praising of some Western scholars and Buddhists of the "New Vehicle," I have revealed that the same assumptions are present in Brazil. Although Japanese-Brazilian and non-Japanese-Brazilian practices may overlap, most non-Japanese Brazilians readily assume that contemporary Japanese Buddhism is degraded and that "real" Buddhism is the one currently practiced by Westerners. Indeed, in a strange paradox, the veneer of American/European culture functions as a layer of patina that endows Buddhist practice with authenticity. What would otherwise be recognized as simply the latest addition and creation to an old practice is in fact thought to work the other way around. As archaeologists digging for the "essential" core that brings true authentic Buddhism to light, Brazilian Buddhists praise American/European Zen as the genuine path. So powerful is this idea that they have closed their eyes to the extent of the "traditional" Buddhism in their practice. Undoubtedly, global flows of ideas radiating from metropolitan centers have an enchanting allure south of the equator.

Conclusion
Translocal Flows: The "Meditodrome"
as a Zen Style of Governing

"RECIFE CITY MAYOR MEDITATES TO GOVERN"
The mayor of Recife, João Paulo, announced the creation of a "medito-drome" near his office so that he can "continue to administrate the city with the invincible forces of nature." An adept of the Transcendental Meditation, the mayor . . . currently dedicates one hour a day *in search of inner peace*. In the morning, João Paulo spends 45 minutes meditating alone at home. In the afternoon, at 5 pm, ten members of the upper echelons of his administration join him. Endeavoring to expand this number, he announced the creation of the "meditodrome" in 2003. This is the second change promoted by him in the city hall due to his *Zen style of governing*. Right after taking office, two years ago, João Paulo moved his desk towards the east and the ocean, where the sun rises.[1]

With 1.5 million inhabitants, Recife is not a small town. However, located in the less developed and more traditional northeastern Brazil, it has not anywhere near the cosmopolitanism of the southeastern region (São Paulo and Rio de Janeiro). This *Folha de São Paulo* newspaper story reveals that the deployment of Zen as a lifestyle and an umbrella word, which encompasses all sorts of alternative spirituality (in this case Transcendental Meditation), has traveled a long way inside the country—2,660 kilometers. Furthermore, the mayor's idea of creating a "meditodrome," possibly as an answer to Rio de Janeiro's celebrated "samba-drome," is not without meaning. To be sure, like Rio, Recife is famous for its street carnival. Why not build another "sambadrome?" Clearly meditation is not as important as samba as a marker of the country's identity. Although meditation, with its perceived benefits—tranquility, improved concentration, inner peace, and harmony—is becoming increasingly significant in the lifestyles of many Brazilians. While southeastern Brazilians look up to Europe and the United States as meaning-producing centers, this mayor is probably emulating the fashion for meditation coming from the developed Brazilian southeast.

Indeed, flows of Zen develop rhizomatically assuming different forms, ramifying, connecting, disconnecting, and extending in many directions. Adding to the flows I have explored so far—from Japan, the United States, and Europe into Brazil, and from there back to these sites as well as to other countries in Latin America—this story suggests new translocal directions that took place in 2003. Indeed, the newspaper article above marked the first time I witnessed such a palpable, public, and significant imaginary of Zen outside the circuit of Rio de Janeiro-São Paulo.

RELIGION ON THE MOVE? FOCUSING ON LARGER CULTURAL FLOWS OF MODERNITY

Throughout this book I have investigated how global cultural flows arrived in Brazil, were indigenized locally, and were "exported" to other countries. Zen Buddhism provided an ideal case study for many reasons. First, its global connections are significant and highly conspicuous. Second, it is a form of Buddhism that arrived in the country as a cultural flow that was more than simply religion and covered many realms of social life. Accordingly, an imaginary of Zen has filtered through a larger population and has had different impacts on many segments of Brazilian culture. Third, it was "imported" to Brazil by both the Japanese immigrants and by cosmopolitan intellectuals. The latter group traveled, read, and translated literature produced overseas. They were at the same time "routed" and "rooted," in the words of Clifford. As local disseminators of global flows, they were a fertile sector of society for my analysis of the entanglement between the global and the local. Furthermore, from the outset, Zen in particular and Buddhism in general were perceived as carriers of modernity, as they were anointed with the prestige ascribed to them by metropolitan centers. This in turn meant that by analyzing the indigenization of Zen, I was able to explore how modernity arrived in the country and became enmeshed in tradition.

Furthermore, this study has applied recent discussions on the impact of globalization on the anthropological method. I have tracked global flows by "decentering" and "multiplying" the field of my research, recognizing that both spatially and nonspatially located sites were equally significant. Although participant observation constitutes a significant part of my fieldwork, it is by no means my only source. Here I have used supplementary sources—newspapers and magazines stories, web sites and films, e-mail lists, the Internet, and archival research—as elements of a multistranded methodology. Such a diversified approach entails a more complex understanding of the phenomenon studied while at the same time indicates that knowledge of any society is partial and situated.

In addition, through Appadurai's concept of "scapes" this study has shown the complex ways in which ideas, migrants, the media, technologies of communication, and travel have composed an imaginary of Zen in the country. The metaphor of a rhizome was helpful to demonstrate that Brazil works both as a periphery and a center for global flows. Thus global flows do not necessarily originate in Western metropolitan centers and radiate to the periphery. Peripheries can become centers, and vice-versa. By the same token, flows can spread between peripheral countries, as in the way Japan is a model for Brazilian modernity. Appadurai also suggests that globalization does not make the world more homogeneous. Hybridization and creolization play an important role in cultural negotiations and account for the diverse forms of Zen in different countries.

This book has charted the history of public perceptions of Japan, Buddhism, and Zen. These ranged from the early perceptions of nineteenth-century Brazilian intellectuals to Zen in present-day Brazil. It also looked at the way social and cultural processes by which Buddhism and Zen were adopted in Brazil. In the first two chapters, I addressed the way that flows of Zen have historically arrived in the country. Whereas in the first chapter I tracked flows of ideas carried by immigrants and missionaries, in the second chapter I followed those carried by non-Japanese-Brazilian intellectuals. In both cases Brazilian elites endeavored to "cannibalize" what they perceived as modern so that they would become modern themselves. From this perspective, modern Buddhism in particular was an ideal set of practices and beliefs to be "devoured."

Departing from the more historical approach of the previous chapters, chapter 3 took us to contemporary Brazil. By giving an overview of the Brazilian religious field, this volume demonstrated how modernity and tradition have always been articulated in the country. Furthermore, in such a plural, porous, creolized, but also class-based field, upper- and upper middle-class Brazilians have more recently chosen modern Buddhism as a way of shunning Catholicism, which is perceived as "backward." Like their North American counterparts, Brazilian adherents subscribed to values carried by global flows of religious modernity, such as pluralization and privatization of faith.

Once the religious field and followers were mapped, I focused on the role of cultural industries (particularly the media and the Internet) in creating a contemporary imaginary of Zen. I showed that following global flows of ideas coming mainly from the United States, these industries associated Buddhism in general and Zen in particular with fashion and a desirable lifestyle for cosmopolitan Brazilians. Brazilians adopted them as a sign of modernity that would work as a marker of social distinction. Finally, in the last chapter I "enter the field" in the traditional sense and leave the more ethereal and nonlocalized field of global flows of ideas. This set the stage to look closely at how Japanese Brazilians and non-Japanese Brazilians actually "do" Zen. Often, scholars researching Buddhism in Protestant countries in Europe and North America have reported a gap between immigrant (or "ethnic") and non-immigrant (or "convert") practices. While the former practice traditional Buddhism, the latter subscribe to modern practices. I did not find fixed essences, but blurred areas where both practiced traditional as well as modern Buddhism. Although the Brazilian case may differ from the European and North American ones, in their aspiration to modernity, non-Japanese Brazilians identified with this metropolitan view of separation so completely that they themselves became oblivious to their own actual "traditional" practices.

GOING BEYOND ZEN IN BRAZIL

Collectively, this book points to the broader issue of the indigenization of modernity and the multiple forms modernity takes in the world. My core aim was to analyze the complex ways in which tradition is implicated in modernity. To this end, I endeavored to see how Brazilians connect themselves with metropolitan centers. I used the notion of "quest" in my title to underscore not only ideas of journey, voyage, and pursuit, but of pilgrimage as well. These ideas are fundamental to the way Brazilians regard their connection with modernity. Indeed, if Brazilians do not perceive modernity to be thorough in Brazil, then it must either come to them through global flows of ideas, migrants, images, and media, or they have to set up a journey, or better yet, a quasi-pilgrimage to particular places of worship of modernity such as France before World War II and the United States thereafter.

This book has made a contribution to several fields of scholarship. First, it answers the calls for a decentered field and multi-sited ethnography, which have emerged recently as the process of globalization increased. By recognizing that the field is not isolated and bounded but interconnected with outside flows, I have thus given equal value to located as well as nonlocated sites of research. To this end, this book makes a contribution through its detailed ethnographic account of routed and rooted experiences. Second, this research expands our knowledge of the historical anthropology of modernity. By understanding the way in which Zen connects to aspirations toward modernity, I have illuminated the complex and unique ways in which the global and the local, as well as tradition and modernity, are articulated in Brazil.

Indeed, I did not approach Zen as an isolated religious case, but as a window into the role the discourse of modernity, globalization, and relations of hierarchy and asymmetry play on the construction of Brazilian culture and identity. From this perspective, my results support scholars who critique the idea that tradition is inexorably effaced by modernity and that modernity emanates from a core center. This book demonstrated that these binary oppositions (the West/the Rest, tradition/modernity) are not monolithic, but entangled in the interplay of the global and the local, creating, in turn, plural modernities.

Third, this book adds to the more recent trend in anthropological research of "studying up." By doing so, it complicates the place of the researcher vis-à-vis the "native"—both of us are travelers and dwellers. Moreover, like me, my "natives" are Brazilians, and some wrote books or/and were in academia. From this perspective, I believe that my being what has been called a "hybrid" or a "virtual" ethnographer,[2] that is, "one who blurs the subject/object distinction on which ethnography is conventionally founded,"[3] adds to the current anthropological debates on the place of "home" as opposed to "the field," as well as what makes an acceptable ethnographer. This book shows that this fluidity is not a hindrance, but an edge in an increasingly interconnected world. Indeed, I believe that "studying up" and "studying one's own" will become more frequent as anthropologists come to terms with how globalization forces are increasingly implicated in local sites.

Fourth, this research contributes to studies of the transplantation of religions across national boundaries. Religion can travel and dwell in complex ways, and they are not solely associated with migrant communities. By deploying Appadurai's "scapes," this book introduces a new set of tools to the body of religious studies. Indeed, this volume examines how religions travel through various media, such as newspapers, magazines, television, film, fashion, and the Internet. Furthermore, few scholarly works have so far addressed the role of the Internet in disseminating religion. By using e-mail lists as a site of research, I hope to have added to our understanding of this new development in religious studies.

Finally, this book contributes insights to the recent field of Buddhism in the West. Contrary to the scholarship suggesting that "ethnic" and "convert" practices and beliefs in Europe and North America are discrete and bounded, my fieldwork findings show that this separation is not so clear-cut in Brazil. To be sure, I have addressed conflicts between the two congregations and tracked the global flows that gave origin to them. However, my research attests to overlaps and creolizations between them. Indeed, my findings reveal what anthropologists have been saying for some time: communities are not bounded, isolated, localized, and stable, but interconnected. An anthropological approach can greatly contribute to revealing actual practices at the grass-roots level and give a more nuanced picture of Buddhism in the West. In arguing for a blurred space, I have emphasized a new thread to be followed in the current debates occurring in the studies of Buddhism in the West.

As a last point, by employing the trope of creolization to encompass the process through which global flows are localized, I have advanced the study taken up by Hannerz on how developing countries absorb and creatively transform flows of modernity. The notion of hybridity tends to be used descriptively. Creolization, by contrast, is helpful to show how cultural mixing takes place. It is a useful tool for those working both on religious studies and the anthropology of religion to understand the process of contact among cultures.

Notes

Introduction

1. Globo, with its numerous newspapers, TV channels, radio stations, and magazines, is the biggest Brazilian media network. It also exports TV programming to the United States, Europe, China, and Latin America.

2. The definition of *samsāra* provided by *The Shambhala Dictionary of Buddhism and Zen* is "literally 'journeying,' or 'the cycle of existences,' is the succession of rebirths that a being goes through until it has attained liberation and entered *nirvāna*. In the Mahāyāna tradition [which Zen belongs to], *samsāra* refers to the phenomenal world."

3. Buddhismo-L, February 3, 2003.

4. Jean and John Comaroff, "Introduction," in *Modernity and its Malcontents: Ritual and Power in Postcolonial Africa*, ed. J. and J. Comaroff (Chicago: University of Chicago Press, 1993), xiv.

5. Marshall Sahlins, "Goodbye to *Tristes Tropes*: Ethnography in the Context of Modern World History," *Journal of Modern History* 65 (1993): 21.

6. David Hess and Roberto Da Matta, *The Brazilian Puzzle: Culture on the Borderlands of the Western World* (New York: Columbia University Press, 1995).

7. The 2000 census showed that only 0.14 percent (245,871) of the population called themselves Buddhists. However, this number is debatable since many Brazilians have multiple religious affiliations, while many also regard Buddhism as a philosophy and/or way of life. Accordingly, they may continue to answer "Catholic" to the census, as I show in chap. 3.

8. These are descendants from Portuguese colonizers and European immigrants.

9. James Clifford, *Routes: Travel and Translation in the Late Twentieth Century* (Cambridge, MA: Harvard University Press, 1997), 29.

10. Akhil Gupta and James Ferguson, "Discipline and Practice: 'The Field' as the Site, Method, and Location in Anthropology," in *Anthropological Locations: Boundaries and Grounds of a Field Science,* ed. A. Gupta and J. Ferguson (Berkeley: University of California Press, 1997), 12–15.

11. Patrícia Birman, "Cultos de Possessão e Pentecostalismo no Brasil," *Religião e Sociedade* 1.2 (1985): 44–52; Carlos Rodrigues Brandão, "Ser Católico: Dimensões Brasileiras," in *Religião e Identidade Nacional*, ed. V. Sachs and S. Lamarão. (Rio de Janeiro: Graal, 1988); Maria das Dores Machado, *Carismáticos e Pentecostais: Adesão Religiosa na Esfera Familiar* (Campi-

nas: Autores Associados, 1996); Antônio Pierucci and Reginaldo Prandi, *A Realidade Social das Religiões no Brasil: Religião Sociedade e Política* (São Paulo: USP/Hucitec, 1996).

12. Leila Amaral, "Os Errantes da Nova Era e sua Religiosidade Caleidoscópica," *Caderno de Ciências Sociais* 3.4 (1993): 19–32; José Guilherme Magnani, "O Neo-esoterismo na Cidade," *Revista USP/Dossiê Magia* 31 (1996): 6–15; José Guilherme Magnani, *O Brasil da Nova Era: Coleção Descobrindo o Brasil* (São Paulo: Edusp, 2000); Luis Eduardo Soares, "Religioso Por Natureza: Cultura Alternativa e Misticismo Ecológico no Brasil," in *Sinais dos Tempos Diversidade Religiosa no Brasil,* ed. L. Landim (Rio de Janeiro: Instituto de Estudos da Religião, 1989), 121–144.

13. The Japanese term *kaikyōshi* (lit., open-teaching messenger) applies to those who are qualified to work as overseas missionaries. Though I am aware of the Christocentric implications of the terms "missionary" and "priest," I have decided to use them for *kaikyōshi* following the usual translation into English.

14. Clifford, *Routes;* Jean and John Comaroff, *Ethnography and the Historical Imagination* (Boulder, CO: Westview Press, 1992); Comaroff and Comaroff, "Introduction"; Mary Des Chene, "Locating the Past," in *Anthropological Locations,* ed. Gupta and Ferguson, 66–85; Gupta and Ferguson, "Discipline and Practice"; George Marcus, *Ethnography through Thick and Thin* (Princeton, NJ: Princeton University Press, 1998); George Marcus, "Beyond Malinowski and After *Writing Culture:* On the Future of Cultural Anthropology and the Predicament of Ethnography," *The Australian Journal of Anthropology* 13.2 (2002): 191–199; George Marcus and Michael M. Fisher, *Anthropology as Cultural Critique: An Experimental Moment in the Human Sciences* (Chicago: University of Chicago Press, 1986).

15. Marcus, *Ethnography through Thick and Thin,* 79–104.

16. Ibid., 79.

17. Clifford, *Routes,* 2.

18. Ibid., 24.

19. Arjun Appadurai, *Modernity At Large: Cultural Dimensions of Globalization* (Minneapolis: University of Minnesota Press, 1996).

20. The term was first used by Gilles Deleuze and Felix Guattari in 1987.

21. Coen is the Portuguese spelling of Koen, her Buddhist name. *Sensei* (lit., the one who was born before) is commonly used in Japan as a term of deference for teachers.

22. "Around the 1940s, the term *nikkei* began to distinguish Japanese Brazilians from both the immigrant generation and the Japanese Americans. During the 1985 Pan-American Nikkei Conference in São Paulo, *nikkei* was formally adopted as the term to describe all those of Japanese descent in the Americas"; Jeffrey Lesser, *Negotiating National Identity: Immigrants, Minorities, and the Struggle for Ethnicity in Brazil* (Durham, NC: Duke University Press, 1999), 127.

23. Buddhismo-L is a general list that started on March 15, 2000; Zen Chung Tao is a Zen list started on August 12, 1998.

24. Dharma talks are teaching sessions where typically a *sūtra* is explained in terms relevant to the congregation. Dharma itself, according to *The Shambhala Dictionary of Buddhism and Zen*, "is the central notion of Buddhism [and is] used in various meanings: 1. The cosmic law . . . the law of karmically determined rebirth; 2 the teaching of the Buddha, who recognized and formulated this 'law,' thus the teaching that expresses the universal truth; 3. Norms of behavior and ethical rules; 4. Manifestations of reality; 5. Mental content, object of thought, a reflection of a thing in the human mind; 6. Term of the so-called factors of existence" (54).

25. *Rōshi* (lit., old teacher) is the title commonly used by Zen masters.

26. See Martin Baumann, "Global Buddhism: Developmental Periods, Regional Histories, and a New Analytical Perspective," *Journal of Global Buddhism* 2 (2001): 3–5; Donald Lopez, "Introduction," in *A Modern Buddhist Bible: Essential Readings from East and West*, ed. D. Lopez (Boston: Beacon Press, 2002), vii–xli; Robert Sharf, "Buddhist Modernism and the Rhetoric of Meditative Experience," *Numen* 42 (1995): 228–283; Robert Sharf, "The Zen of Japanese Nationalism," in *Curators of the Buddha: The Study of Buddhism under Colonialism*, ed. Donald Lopez (Chicago: University of Chicago Press, 1995), 107–160.

27. Comaroff and Comaroff, "Introduction," xii.

28. Marshall Eakin, *Brazil: The Once and Future Country* (New York: St. Martin's Griffin, 1998), 188.

29. Ibid., 182.

30. Appadurai, *Modernity at Large,* 3; italics in original.

31. Ibid., 4.

32. Stuart Hall, "The West and the Rest: Discourse and Power," in *Formations of Modernity*, ed. Stuart Hall and Bram Gieben (Cambridge: Polity Press, 1992), 225–320.

33. Ibid., 313.

34. Dipesh Chakrabarty, *Provincializing Europe: Postcolonial Thought and Historical Difference* (Princeton, NJ: Princeton University Press, 2000), 7–8.

35. Naoki Sakai, "Modernity and Its Critique: The Problem of Universalism and Particularism," in *Postmodernism and Japan*, ed. Masao Miyoshi and H. D. Harootunian (Durham, NC: Duke University Press, 1989), 93–122.

36. Chakrabarty, *Provincializing Europe*, 4–7.

37. Vivian Schelling, "Introduction: Reflections on the Experience of Modernity in Latin America," in *Through the Kaleidoscope: The Experience of Modernity in Latin America*, ed. V. Schelling (London: Verso, 2000), 2.

38. Néstor García Canclini, *Hybrid Cultures: Strategies for Entering and Leaving Modernity*, trans. C. L. Chiappari and S. L. López (Minneapolis: University of Minnesota Press, 1995), 1–11, 41–65; Néstor García Canclini, "Contradictory Modernities and Globalisation in Latin America," 137–152; Ruben Oliven, "Brazil: The Modern in the Tropics," 53–71; Renato Ortiz, "Popular Culture, Modernity and Nation," 127–147; Schelling, "Introduction," 1–33; and José de Souza Martins, "The Hesitations of the Modern and the Contradictions of Modernity in Brazil," 248–274, all in *Through the Kaleidoscope*, ed. Schelling.

39. Oliven, "Brazil," 53.

40. Hall, "The West and The Rest," 280.

41. García Canclini, *Hybrid Cultures*, 47.

42. Ibid., 41–43.

43. José de Souza Martins has shown how debt slavery has spread recently in the Amazon by the most advanced modes of production. For instance, the German corporation Volkswagen employed the most sophisticated technology as well as slaves in its cattle ranch in Pará State. Alluding to the multitemporal articulation between tradition and modernity, Souza Martins asserts that "the so-called primitive accumulation of capital, on the periphery of the capitalist world, is not a moment which pre-dates capitalism, but is contemporary with actual capitalist accumulation" (Souza Martins, "The Hesitations of the Modern," 257–258). It is worth noting that the recently elected President Lula has made an antislavery drive a centerpiece of his program of reform and modernization.

44. Roberto Schwarz, *Misplaced Ideas: Essays on Brazilian Culture* (London: Verso, 1992), 15–16.

45. Néstor García Canclini, "The State of War and The State of Hybridization," in *Without Guarantees: In Honour of Stuart Hall*, ed. Paul Gilroy, Lawrence Grossberg, and Angela McRobbie (London: Verso, 2000), 38–51.

46. Ibid., 49.

47. Jürgen Habermas, "Modernity: An Incomplete Project," in *Postmodern Culture*, ed. Hal Foster (London: Pluto Press, 1987), 3–15.

48. In European colonial discourse the concept of the "cannibal" was used to differentiate Europe from its colonies. By regarding Europe as "civilized" as opposed to the "cannibals" and "savages" of the colonies, its expansion was justified as a civilizing mission; see Bill Ashcroft, Gareth Griffiths, and Helen Tiffin, *Key Concepts in Post-Colonial Studies* (London: Routledge, 1998), 29–31. Opposing this negative view of the cannibal, Oswald de Andrade (1890–1954), one of the main Brazilian modernist intellectuals, reversed the trend and gave it a strong positive quality. In his *Cannibal Manifest* of 1928, he asserted that it was necessary to "absorb the sacred enemy, transform him into a totem." A cannibal is selective and critical in choosing whom to "consume," for s/he does not devour just any enemy, but those who possess enviable attributes. Therefore, for de Andrade and other modernists, Brazilian popular tradition would not be an obstacle toward modernity, but would be an essential

condition of achieving it. Indeed, emulation of the culture of metropolitan centers does not mean a simple transplantation or imitation, but involves a process of "digestion" and re-creation giving it local qualities.

49. Lopez, ed., *A Modern Buddhist Bible*; Baumann, "Global Buddhism"; Sharf, "Buddhist Modernism."

50. Pierre Bourdieu, *Distinction: A Social Critique of the Judgement of Taste*, trans. Richard Nice (Cambridge, MA: Harvard University Press, 1984).

51. André Droogers, "Syncretism: The Problem of Definition, the Definition of the Problem," in *Dialogue and Syncretism: An Interdisciplinary Approach*, ed. Jerald D. Gort et al. (Grand Rapids, MI: William Eerdman, 1989); Charles Stewart, "Syncretism and Its Synonyms: Reflections on Cultural Mixing," *Diacritics* 29.3 (1999): 40–62; Charles Stewart and Rosalind Shaw, "Introduction: Problematizing Syncretism," in *Syncretism/Anti-syncretism: The Politics of Religious Synthesis*, ed. C. Stewart and R. Shaw (London: Routledge, 1994), 1–26.

52. Clifford, *Routes*, 7.

53. Rita Laura Segato, "Formação de Diversidade: Nação e Opções Religiosas no Contexto da Globalização," in *Globalização e Religião*, ed. Ari Pedro Oro and Carlos Alberto Steil (Petrópolis: Vozes, 1997), 236.

54. García Canclini, *Hybrid Cultures*.

55. Edward Brathwaite, cited in Ashcroft, Griffiths, and Tiffin, *Key Concepts in Post-Colonial Studies*, 58.

56. Eve Stoddard and Grant H. Cornwell, "Cosmopolitan or Mongrel? Créolité, Hybridity and 'Douglarisation' in Trinidad," *European Journal of Cultural Studies* 2.3 (1999): 337.

57. Ibid.

58. Ulf Hannerz, "The World in Creolisation," *Africa* 57.4 (1987): 551; Ulf Hannerz, *Cultural Complexity: Studies in the Social Organization of Meaning* (New York: Columbia University Press, 1992), 264–267.

59. Stoddard and Cornwell, "Cosmopolitan or Mongrel?" 340.

60. Hannerz, "The World in Creolisation"; Hannerz, *Cultural Complexity*; Nikos Papastergiadis, "Tracing Hybridity in Theory," in *Debating Cultural Hybridity: Multicultural Identities and the Politics of Anti-Racism*, ed. Pnina Werbner and Tariq Modood (London: Zed Books, 1997), 257–281; Nikos Papastergiadis, *Dialogues in the Diasporas: Essays and Conversations on Cultural Identities* (London: Rivers Oram Press, 1998); Robert J. C. Young, *Colonial Desire: Hybridity in Theory, Culture and Race* (London: Routledge, 1995).

61. Papastergiadis, "Tracing Hybridity in Theory," 258.

62. Homi Bhabha, *The Location of Culture* (London: Routledge, 1994), 218–219; italics in original.

63. Pnina Werbner, "Introduction: The Dialectics of Cultural Hybridity," in *Debating Cultural Hybridity*, ed. Werbner and Modood; Young, *Colonial Desire*.

64. Papastergiadis, "Tracing Hybridity in Theory," 258.

65. Quoted in ibid., 268.

66. Young, *Colonial Desire*.

67. Stoddard and Cornwell, "Cosmopolitan or Mongrel?" 335, 349.

68. Greg Noble and Paul Tabar, "On Being Lebanese-Australian: Hybridity, Essentialism and Strategy among Arabic-speaking Youth," in *Arab-Australians: Citizenship and Belonging*, ed. Ghassan Hage (Melbourne: Melbourne University Press, 2002), 128–144.

69. Stephen Prothero, *The White Buddhist: The Asian Odyssey of Henry Steel Olcott* (Bloomington: Indiana University Press, 1996), 187.

70. Edward Brathwaite, *The Development of Creole Society in Jamaica 1770–1820* (Oxford: Clarendon Press, 1971); Hannerz, "The World in Creolisation"; Hannerz, *Cultural Complexity*; Frank Korom, "Memory, Innovation, and Emergent Ethnicity: The Creolization of an Indo-Trinidadian Performance," *Diaspora* 3.2 (1994): 135–155; Stoddard and Cornwell, "Cosmopolitan or Mongrel?"

71. Prothero, *The White Buddhist*, 9.

72. Gupta and Ferguson, "Discipline and Practice," 37.

73. Lesser, *Negotiating National Identity*.

74. Oliven, "Brazil," 53.

75. Appadurai, *Modernity at Large*.

1. The Japanese-Brazilian Junction

1. Ian Reader, "Transformations and Changes in the Teachings of the Sōtō Zen Buddhist Sect," *Japanese Religions* 14.1 (1985): 28–48; also his "Zazenless Zen? The Position of Zazen in Institutional Zen Buddhism," *Japanese Religions* 14.3 (1986): 7–27.

2. See Stewart Lone, *The Japanese Community in Brazil, 1908–1940: Between Samurai and Carnival* (Houndmills: Palgrave, 2001), 13.

3. For a comparison between Japanese immigration to the United States and Brazil, see Robert J. Smith, "The Ethnic Japanese in Brazil," *Journal of Japanese Studies* 5.1 (1979): 53–70. Regarding Japanese immigration to Latin American countries other than Brazil, see Tomoyo Hiroishi, "La Búsquedad de la Identidade—In Search of My Identity," 56–57; Ayumi Takenaka, "Japanese Peruvians and Their Ethnic Encounters," 113–118; Kozy Amemiya, "Land, Culture, and the Power of Money: Assimilation and Resistance of Okinawan Immigrants in Bolivia," 121–130, all in *Encounters: People of Asian Descent in the Americas*, ed. Roshni Rustomji-Kerns, Rajini Srikanth, and Leny Mendoza Strobel (Lanham, MD:

Rowman & Littlefield, 1999). For more information on the Sōtō mission in Peru, see Hiro-hito Ota, "Primeiros Missionários Budistas no Peru: Cem Anos de História Desconhecida," *Caminho Zen* 8.3 (2003): 4–15.

4. See Lori Anne Pierce, "Constructing American Buddhisms: Discourses of Race and Religion in Territorial Hawai'i," Ph.D. dissertation, University of Hawai'i, 2000, 111–112, 135; also Lone, *Japanese Community in Brazil*, 14–15.

5. See Tetsuden Kashima, *Buddhism in America: The Social Organization of an Ethnic Religious Institution* (Westport, CT: Greenwood Press, 1977), 6, 13.

6. See Lesser, *Negotiating National Identity*, 109; also Takashi Maeyama, "Ancestor, Emperor and Immigrant: Religion and Group Identification of the Japanese in Rural Brazil (1908–1950)," *Journal of Interamerican Studies and World Affairs* 14.2 (1972): 162.

7. Lone, *Japanese Community in Brazil*, 19. For more on the Japanese immigration to Peru and the current state of Japanese descendants, see Takenaka, "Japanese Peruvians and their Ethnic Encounters," 113–118.

8. From 1880 to 1969, immigrants entering Brazil were divided into Portuguese (31 percent), Italian (30 percent), Spanish (14 percent), Japanese (5 percent), German (4 percent), from the Middle East (3 percent), and other (13 percent) (Lesser, *Negotiating National Identity*, 8). For a very good analysis of this whitening discourse in Brazilian society from 1865 to 1930, see Thomas Skidmore, *Black Into White: Race and Nationality in Brazilian Thought* (New York: Oxford University Press, 1974).

9. Lone, *Japanese Community in Brazil*, 29, 39; Lesser, *Negotiating National Identity*, 82.

10. Lesser, *Negotiating National Identity*, 7.

11. Ibid., 4.

12. Ibid., 7.

13. Ibid., 148–165. The construction of Japanese as the "whites of Asia" has its origins in Japan being recognized as a major power after joining an international force to suppress the Chinese Boxer Rebellion in 1901–1902. Due to its efforts in securing Western interests in China, Japan was rewarded by being invited to join the international peace conference and sign the Anglo-Japanese alliance in 1902; see Akira Iriye, "Japan's Drive to Great Power Status," in *The Emergence of Meiji Japan*, ed. Marius Jansen (Cambridge: Cambridge University Press, 1995), 320–321.

14. Lesser, *Negotiating National Identity*, 87–88.

15. Ibid., 149.

16. Ibid., 91.

17. For more on the favorable perceptions of Japanese culture and the Japanese in Brazil, see Takeyuki Tsuda, "From Ethnic Affinity to Alienation in the Global Ecumene: The Encounter between the Japanese and Japanese-Brazilian Return Migrants," *Diaspora* 10.1

(2001): 53–91. For current accounts of the globalization and localization of Japanese culture in the world, see Harumi Befu, "Globalization Theory from the Bottom Up: Japan's Contribution," *Japanese Studies* 23.1 (2003): 3–22; and Koichi Iwabuchi, *Recentering Globalization: Popular Culture and Japanese Transnationalism* (Durham, NC: Duke University Press, 2002).

18. Hirochika Nakamaki, "A Honmon Butsuryū-shū no Brasil Através de Registros do Arcebispo Nissui Ibaragui," in *O Budismo no Brasil*, ed. Frank Usarski (São Paulo: Lorosae, 2002), 85–86.

19. Sending missionaries to the Americas was a very different task from sending missionaries to Asia to assist the Japanese colonizers. While in the Americas missionaries were sent to preach only within the Japanese community, in Asia they were sent to proselytize the population at large, working as an extension of the Japanese imperialist colonizing program. For more on this, see, for instance, Nam-Lin Hur, "The Sōtō Sect and Japanese Military Imperialism in Korea," *Japanese Journal of Religious Studies* 26.1–2 (1999): 107–134.

20. See Emilio Willems, "Aspectos da Aculturação do Japonês no Estado de São Paulo," *Boletim da Faculdade de Filosofia, Ciências e Letras da USP* 82.3 (São Paulo: Universidade de São Paulo, 1948), 93, 98.

21. See Maeyama, "Ancestor, Emperor and Immigrant," 162–165; also Koichi Mori, "Vida Religiosa dos Japoneses e Seus Descendentes Residentes no Brasil e Religiões de Origem Japonesa," in *Uma Epopéia Moderna: 80 Anos da Imigração Japonesa no Brasil*, ed. Katsunori Wakisaka (São Paulo: Hucitec/Sociedade Brasileira de Cultura Japonesa, 1992), 562–563.

22. Maeyama, "Ancestor, Emperor and Immigrant," 165–166, 168.

23. Ibid., 171. This point is debated by Lone; see Lone, *Japanese Community in Brazil*, 49–51, 166–172. Unlike other scholars of Japanese immigration to Brazil, Lone argues that the Japanese arrived in Brazil to settle and were eager to assimilate into Brazilian culture. Because of the accepting attitude toward the Japanese by Brazilian society exemplified in Gilberto Freyre's 1930s celebration of racial mixture (*mestiçagem*), Lone sees the Japanese immigrants not isolated in their communities, but "more concerned with their own ambitions, wealth and leisure" than emperor worship. Lone focused his work on the small urban Japanese population, who in fact may have decided to settle in the new country for good as they were doing well in business. I believe, however, that had he analyzed the rural community he would most probably have encountered a picture more akin to other scholars' portraits.

24. Lone, *Japanese Community in Brazil*, 157.

25. Shigeru Kojima, "Um Estudo sobre os Japoneses e Seus Descendentes em Curitiba," master's thesis, Universidade Federal do Paraná, Curitiba, 1991.

26. Charles Wagley, *An Introduction to Brazil* (New York: Columbia University Press, 1963), 233. Although church and state have been separated since the institution of the republican system (1889), in practice the influence of the Catholic Church in Brazilian society

has always run deep. Nevertheless, this picture of Brazil disguises a plural religious field, as I show in chapter 3.

27. Centro de Estudos Nipo-Brasileiros, "Pesquisa da População de Descendentes de Japoneses Residentes no Brasil: 1987–1988," unpublished research, Centro de Estudos Nipo-Brasileiros, São Paulo, 1990.

28. Betina Bernardes, "Comunidade de Japoneses Formam Elite em São Paulo," *Folha de São Paulo*, October 19, 1995. The Centro de Estudos Nipo-Brasileiros conducted a census in 1988 that found there were 1.28 million Japanese migrants and their descendants resident in Brazil, 70 percent of them living in the state of São Paulo; see *Guia da Cultura Japonesa em São Paulo* (São Paulo: Aliança Cultural Brasil-Japão, 1989), 25. Later figures show the number to be 1.5 million Japanese and descendants.

29. Bernardes, "Comunidade de Japoneses."

30. Takashi Maeyama, "O Imigrante e a Religião: Estudo de uma Seita Religiosa Japonesa em São Paulo," master's thesis, Escola de Sociologia e Política, São Paulo, 1967, 84–112. Migration to São Paulo City became intense after the 1950s. The numbers of Japanese immigrants and their descendants in São Paulo grew from below 4,000 in 1939 to in excess of 62,000 some twenty years later, with around one-third of the national total concentrated in metropolitan São Paulo in the 1970s; see Mori, "Vida Religiosa dos Japoneses e Seus Descendentes," 575. This migration to the metropolis was also part of the 1950s and 1960s Brazilian economic project. The so-called "national agrarian vocation" made no sense anymore. The country was facing the upheaval of postwar industrialization and urbanization, and political power was drifting from the rural aristocracy to the industrial magnates. Due to the concentration of capital and infrastructure derived from the coffee plantations, São Paulo, with a population of 2,817,600 in 1954, emerged as the biggest Brazilian metropolis, surpassing the capital, Rio de Janeiro; see Regina Meyer, "Metrópole e Urbanismo: São Paulo Anos 50," Ph.D. dissertation, Universidade de São Paulo, 1991, 4–53.

31. The rapid process of industrialization and urbanization Japan has undergone in the past 150 years has prompted the emergence of new religions (*shin shūkyō*) from the nineteenth century into the first half of the twentieth century, and "new" new religions (*shin shinshūkyō*) after World War II, when the new constitution guaranteed freedom of religion. In endeavoring to cope with mass migrations to urban settings and a fast-changing society, such religious movements were built around the figure of a charismatic founder, were highly syncretic, and emphasized spiritual healing, millenarianism, and lay membership (as opposed to the hierarchical Buddhism and Shintoism). Examples of *shin shūkyō* are Tenrikyō, Ōmoto, and Reiyūkai, while *shin shinshūkyō* include, for instance, Mahikari, Shinnyoen, and Agonshū.

There is a significant body of scholarship on Japanese New Religious Movements in Brazil and their strong appeal to non-Japanese Brazilians. See, e.g., Robert Carpenter and Wade Roof, "The Transplanting of Seichō-no-ie from Japan to Brazil: Moving Beyond the Ethnic Enclave," *Journal of Contemporary Religion* 10.1 (1995): 41–53; Peter B. Clarke, "Japanese New Religious Movements in Brazil: From Ethnic to Universal Religions," in *New Religions: Challenge and Response*, ed. Brian Wilson and Jamie Cresswell (London: Routledge,

1999), 197–210; Maeyama, "O Imigrante e a Religião"; and Hideaki Matsuoka, "'Messianity Makes a Person Useful: Describing Differences in a Japanese Religion in Brazil,'" *Japanese Journal of Religious Studies* 28.1–2 (2001): 77–102.

32. Numbers are not accurate. While officials at Busshinji as well as Matsunaga *rōshi*, the head of the international department at Eiheiji, set the congregation at around three hundred families, a representative of Sōtōshū Shūmuchō in Tokyo told me that Busshinji had five hundred families and Zengenji had two hundred families.

33. See Ricardo Mário Gonçalves, "O Budismo Japonês no Brasil: Reflexões de um Observador Participante," in *Sinais dos Tempos: Diversidade Religiosa no Brasil*, ed. Leila Landim (Rio de Janeiro: Instituto de Estudos da Religião, 1990), 175.

34. These numbers may not be accurate, as they were given by the schools themselves. Because there are no official statistics, the schools are the only source of information on membership.

35. Bernard Faure, *Chan Insights and Oversights: An Epistemological Critique of the Chan Tradition* (Princeton, NJ: Princeton University Press, 1993), 53–88; Lopez, "Introduction," *A Modern Buddhist Bible*, vii–xii; James W. Heisig and John C. Maraldo, eds., *Rude Awakenings: Zen, the Kyoto School and the Question of Nationalism* (Honolulu: University of Hawai'i Press, 1994); and several of Sharf's writings, including "Whose Zen? Zen Nationalism Revisited," in *Rude Awakenings*, ed. Heisig and Maraldo, 40–51.

36. Sharf, "The Zen of Japanese Nationalism," 108.

37. Ibid., 124.

38. Ibid., 110.

39. Ibid., 111.

40. Suzuki, quoted in Faure, *Chan Insights and Oversights*, 57.

41. Ibid., 53.

42. Lopez, "Introduction," *A Modern Buddhist Bible*, ix. Baumann has also established a distinction between traditionalist (which places emphasis on the ritual and devotional acts of merit making) and modernist (emphasis on rational, scientific, and scriptural elements) Buddhism. However, Baumann adds a third historical development: global or postmodernist Buddhism—"a non-Buddhist, expressively non-religious understanding, highlighting individualized 'healing,' therapeutic remedy, and psychological wellbeing"; see Baumann, "Global Buddhism," 32. Since global Buddhism is a development of modernist Buddhism and part of the larger phenomenon of Buddhism in Brazil, I will disregard it, keeping the main distinction between modern and traditional Buddhism.

43. Lopez, "Introduction," *A Modern Buddhist Bible*, xxxi.

44. Ibid., xxxix.

45. Ibid., xxxvii.

46. I use "traditional" and "modern" in Lopez' and Baumann's sense, and I am not implying in any way that traditional Zen would evolve into modern Zen, or that one is superior to the other.

47. It is worth noting that such conflicting definitions have been observed in many other Western countries where Buddhism emerged and developed as a result both of immigration and religious conversion. For more on this, see Martin Baumann, "Creating a European Path to Nirvāna: Historical and Contemporary Developments of Buddhism in Europe," *Journal of Contemporary Religion* 10.1 (1995): 55–70; Baumann, "Global Buddhism"; Rick Fields, "Divided Dharma: White Buddhists, Ethnic Buddhists, and Racism," in *The Faces of Buddhism in America,* ed. Charles Prebish and Kenneth Tanaka (Berkeley: University of California Press, 1998), 196–206; Jan Nattier, "Visible and Invisible: Jan Nattier on the Politics of Representation in Buddhist America," *Tricycle: The Buddhist Review* 17 (fall 1995): 42–49; Paul Numrich, *Old Wisdom in the New World: Americanization of Two Immigrant Theravada Buddhist Temples* (Knoxville: University of Tennessee Press, 1996); Charles Prebish, "Two Buddhisms Reconsidered," *Buddhist Studies Review* 10.2 (1993): 187–206; Charles Prebish, *Luminous Passage: The Practice and Study of Buddhism in America* (Berkeley: University of California Press, 1999), 57–75.

48. See Richard Jaffe, *Neither Monk nor Layman: Clerical Marriage in Modern Japanese Buddhism* (Princeton, NJ: Princeton University Press, 2001).

49. William Bodiford, "Zen and the Art of Religious Prejudice: Efforts to Reform a Tradition of Social Discrimination," *Japanese Journal of Religious Studies* 23.1–2 (1996): 4.

50. The rotation of *kaikyōshi* among temples overseas is exemplified also by a fellow missionary sent together with Zendō Matsunaga to Brazil in 1959. Koshi Kuwahara is currently a *kaikyōshi* at Zenshūji, the *betsuin* in Los Angeles, California.

51. Personal communication, Eiheiji, October 2000.

52. Zenshūji (Los Angeles) and Sōkōji (San Francisco) are good examples of Sōtōshū temples doubling as religious and cultural sites in the United States. For more on this, see Senryō Asai and Duncan Ryūken Williams, "Japanese American Zen Temples: Cultural Identity and Economics," in *American Buddhism: Methods and Findings in Recent Scholarship,* ed. Duncan Williams and Christopher Queen (Richmond, Surrey: Curzon, 1999); Kōyū Yoshida, "Zenshū-ji Sōtō Mission in Los Angeles," *Zen Friends* (2000): 33–37; Association of Sōtō Zen Buddhists Committee Activity, *Buddha's Seed Taking Firm Root in North America's Soil,* book published for the 75th commemoration of Sōtō Zen Buddhism in North America (Los Angeles, 1997). For Jōdo Shinshū examples, see Kashima, *Buddhism in America;* Pierce, "Constructing American Buddhisms."

53. For a good critique of this book, see Shōji Yamada, "The Myth of Zen in the Art of Archery," *Japanese Journal of Religious Studies* 28.1–2 (2001): 1–30.

54. Personal communication, Nagoya, November 2000.

55. Ryōtan Tokuda, *Psicologia Budista* (Rio de Janeiro: Instituto Vitória Régia, 1997), 60.

56. Suzuki, quoted in Faure, *Chan Insights and Oversights*, 61–62.

57. Shunryū Suzuki, *Zen Mind, Beginner's Mind: Informal Talks on Zen Meditation and Practice* (New York: Weatherhill, 1980), 21.

58. Personal communication, São Paulo, October 1999; italics added.

59. David Chadwick, *Crooked Cucumber: The Life and Zen Teaching of Shunryu Suzuki* (New York: Broadway Books, 1999), 326; italics added.

60. For a good account of life in this nunnery, see Paula Arai, *Women Living in Zen: Japanese Sōtō Buddhist Nuns* (Oxford: Oxford University Press, 1999).

61. Personal communication, São Paulo, November 1998.

62. "Mass" is the common term used for funeral and memorial rites, which indicates a strong influence of Catholicism.

63. See, e.g., Kumiko Uchino, "The Status Elevation Process of Sōtō Sect Nuns in Modern Japan," *Japanese Journal of Religious Studies* 10.1–2 (1983), pp. 177–194. On 177 Uchino remarks, "In Buddhist dogma, women were regarded as impure, having a more sinful karma than men, and being unable to attain Buddhahood. . . . Even nuns, who shunned all worldly attachments, were segregated from and had heavier precepts than monks. Two hundred and fifty precepts were imposed on monks while the figure for nuns was five hundred. In addition to these precepts, there were eight laws, called the *Hakkeikai*, which were written especially for nuns and placed them under the control of monastic orders. According to the law, no matter how long a nun had been in service, she was required to obey and worship even those monks who had taken the tonsure only the day before." For contemporary discussions of feminism and Buddhism, see Rita M. Gross, *Buddhism after Patriarchy: A Feminist History, Analysis, and Reconstruction of Buddhism* (Albany, NY: SUNY Press, 1993); Noriko Kawahashi, "'Jizoku' (Priests' Wives) in Sōtō Zen Buddhism: An Ambiguous Category," *Japanese Journal of Religious Studies* 22.1–2 (1995): 161–183; Noriko Kawahashi and Masako Kuroki, eds., "Feminism and Religion in Contemporary Japan. Special Issue," *Japanese Journal of Religious Studies* 30:3–4 (2003).

64. For an account of the role of *jizoku* in Sōtō temple life, see Kawahashi, "'Jizoku' (Priests' Wives)."

65. Personal communication, Busshinji, March 2000.

66. Martin Baumann, "The Transplantation of Buddhism to Germany: Processive Modes and Strategies of Adaptation," *Method & Theory in the Study of Religion* 6.1 (1994): 35–61 (at 38). The term "recoupment" was first coined by Pye.

67. *Ishin-denshin* is a central notion of Zen. According to *The Shambhala Dictionary of Buddhism and Zen*, "[i]t comes from the Platform *sūtra* of the sixth patriarch of Ch'an (Zen) in China, Hui-neng. He points out that what is preserved in the lineage of the tradition and 'transmitted' is not book knowledge in the form of 'teachings' established in sacred

scriptures, but rather an immediate insight into the true nature of reality, to which an enlightened master can lead a student through the training in the way of Zen."

68. See, for instance, Gonçalves, "O Budismo Japonês," for Jōdo Shinshū in Brazil, and for Jōdo Shinshū in Hawai'i, George J. Tanabe, "Grafting Identity: The Hawaiian Branches of the Bodhi Tree," in *Buddhist Missionaries in the Era of Globalization*, ed. Linda Learman (Honolulu: University of Hawai'i Press, 2004), 77–100.

69. Jan Nattier, "Buddhist Studies in the Post-Colonial Age," *Journal of the American Academy of Religion* 65.2 (1997): 475.

70. Ibid.

71. Sharf, "The Zen of Japanese Nationalism," 141; see also Lopez, "Introduction," *A Modern Buddhist Bible*, xxxvii.

72. Nattier, "Buddhist Studies in the Post-Colonial Age," 475.

73. Tanabe, "Grafting Identity."

74. Personal communication, Busshinji, January 2002.

75. Eric Hobsbawm, "Introduction: Inventing Traditions," in *The Invention of Traditions*, ed. E. Hobsbawm and T. Ranger (Cambridge: Cambridge University Press, 1983), 5.

2. Non-Japanese Brazilians and the Orientalist Shaping of Zen

1. Londrina is a city in Paraná State mainly inhabited by Japanese immigrants and descendants.

2. Excerpt from an interview conducted in 2001 with a non-Japanese-Brazilian university lecturer who was ordained a Zen monk at Busshinji Temple in São Paulo City in the early 1970s.

3. Many other scholars have critiqued Said's work by pointing out that Orientalism is not monolithic, but different Western cultures have different understandings of and uses for it. For an analysis of differences between French and British Orientalist discourses, see Lisa Lowe, *Critical Terrains: French and British Orientalisms* (Ithaca, NY: Cornell University Press, 1994).

4. Schwarz, *Misplaced Ideas*, 1.

5. He rightly points out that the act of copying did not start with independence, but it was not a predicament until that time. During the colonial period (1500–1822) it was considered only natural that the colony would copy the metropolis, and even more so in the period from 1808 to 1822, when the Portuguese king João VI and his court fled to Brazil because of the imminent invasion of Portugal by Napoleon (which did not take place). During these fifteen years Brazil became the center of the Portuguese empire. However, the strong ties with the court continued after the 1822 independence, as Pedro I, the first emperor of the newly independent country, was the son of the Portuguese king himself.

6. Clientelism denotes a relationship between politicians and the electorate, where the former give benefits such as employment and tax breaks to the latter in exchange for political support, especially in the form of votes. For more on this phenomenon in Brazil, see Paul Cammack, "Clientelism and Military Government in Brazil," in *Private Patronage and Public Power: Political Clientelism in the Modern State*, ed. Christopher Clapham (Frances London: Francis Pinter, 1982).

7. Schwarz, *Misplaced Ideas*, 2.

8. Ibid., 8–9. For more on this, see Randal Johnson, "Tupy or not Tupy: Cannibalism and Nationalism in Contemporary Brazilian Culture," in *Modern Latin American Fiction: A Survey*, ed. J. King (London: Faber and Faber, 1987), 41–59.

9. For a good account on this shift from Europe to the United States as a meaning-producing center, see Serge Guilbaut, *How New York Stole the Idea of Modern Art: Abstract Expressionism, Freedom and the Cold War*, trans. A. Goldhammer (Chicago: University of Chicago Press, 1983).

10. Schwarz, *Misplaced Ideas*, 8.

11. Ibid., 2. For more on the Tropicália movement, see 140–143; see also Charles A. Perrone, *Masters of Contemporary Brazilian Song: MPB 1965–1985* (Austin: University of Texas Press, 1989).

12. Ricardo Vélez Rodriguez, "La Filosofía en Latinoamérica: Originalidad Y Método," paper presented at the Twentieth World Congress of Philosophy, University of Boston, 1998.

13. Walter Benjamin, *Illuminations* (London: Fontana Press, 1970).

14. Jacques Derrida, "Des Tours de Babel," in *Difference in Translation*, ed. J. F. Graham (Ithaca, NY: Cornell University Press, 1985), 188.

15. Gayatri Spivak, *Outside the Teaching Machine* (London: Routledge, 1993).

16. Doreen Massey, *Space, Place and Gender* (Cambridge: Polity Press, 1994), 149.

17. Schwarz, *Misplaced Ideas*, 17.

18. See Faure, *Chan Insights and Oversights*, 50–51. For more on Marinetti's 1926 lecture tour to Brazil and the dialogue between the 1920s Brazilian avant-garde movement and Futurism, see João de Castro Rocha, "Marinetti Goes to South America: Confrontos e Diálogos do Futurismo na America do Sul," Ph.D. dissertation, Stanford University, 2002. Regarding the visits by Claudel, Cendras, and Milhaud, see Nicolau Sevcenko, "Peregrinations, Visions and the City: From Canudos to Brasília, the Backlands Become the City and the City Becomes the Backlands," in *Through the Kaleidoscope*, ed. Schelling, 89–93.

19. As cited in the *Dicionário de Literatura* (Dictionary of literature, 1981), 772. My free translation of "Lá nas terras do império chinês/Num palácio de louça vermelha/Sobre um trono de azul japonês." For Orientalist fantasies of the Middle East in Brazil and Lebanese and Syrian immigration into the country, see Lesser, *Negotiating National Identity*, 41–79.

20. R. Farias Brito, O Mundo Interno: Ensaio Sobre os Dados Geraes da Philosophia do Espírito (Rio de Janeiro: Revista dos Tribunais, 1914), 105.

21. Charles Hallisey, "Roads Taken and Not Taken in the Study of Theravāda Buddhism," in Curators of the Buddha, ed. Lopez, 45.

22. Lopez, ed., Curators of the Buddha, 5, 8.

23. Farias Brito, O Mundo Interno, 122.

24. For collections of genealogies of Buddhist studies in the nineteenth century, see Lopez, ed., Curators of the Buddha.

25. For more on this Brazilian fascination with French culture, see Jeffrey D. Needell, A Tropical Belle Epoque: Elite, Culture and Society in Turn-of-the-Century Rio de Janeiro (Cambridge: Cambridge University Press, 1987).

26. Nicolau Sevcenko, Orfeu Extático na Metrópole: São Paulo, Sociedade e Cultura nos Frementes Anos 20 (São Paulo: Companhia das Letras, 1992), 236. During the nineteenth century, Europe, and particularly France, underwent a Japan craze. In the 1850s, several modern-minded artists in France discovered ukiyo-e (woodblock prints), which would arrive in the form of wrapping paper for porcelain pieces imported from Japan. These unpretentious "snapshots" from daily life in premodern Japan became part of a fad in Europe that came to be known as japonaiserie or japonisme. By the 1860s, nearly all the French artists involved in the Impressionist movement were collecting Japanese prints. Van Gogh is the best-known artist to paint in the style of the Japanese ukiyo-e. However, as I show in this section, japonaiserie involved not only painting, but also literature (with the publishing of Mme. Chrysanthème), music (Madama Butterfly), jewelry, objets d'art (lacquer, metalwork), etc.

27. Shuhei Hosokawa, "Nationalizing Chō-Chō-San: The Signification of 'Butterfly Singers' in a Japanese-Brazilian Community," Japanese Studies 19.3 (1999): 256. In the early 1920s less than 2 percent of the Japanese immigrants lived in urban areas; most of them (thirty thousand) were living in rural areas.

28. Ibid., 255–256.

29. See, for instance, Walter Benjamin, "Paris, Capital of the Nineteenth Century," in Reflections: Essays, Aphorisms, Autobiographical Writings, ed. Peter Demetz (New York: Schocken, 1978), 146–163.

30. Oliven, "Brazil," 68.

31. Takashi Maeyama, "Religion, Kinship, and the Middle Classes of the Japanese in Urban Brazil," Latin American Studies 5 (1983): 75.

32. Paulo Franchetti, "Notas Sobre a História do Haikai no Brasil," Revista de Letras, UNESP 34 (1994): 197–213.

33. Ibid. Paul-Louis Couchoud went to Japan in the beginning of the twentieth century

but learned about haiku from Basil Chamberlain's 1902 monograph *Basho and the Japanese Poetical Epigram*. Julien Vocance was a friend of Couchoud. The first verses of his *Art Poétique* were quoted later as an example of haiku by Paulo Prado, in his preface to Oswald de Andrade's *Pau-Brasil*.

34. Afrânio Peixoto's first haiku were published in his book of poems, *Trovas Populares Brasileiras*, in 1919.

35. D. T. Suzuki, *Zen and Japanese Culture* (New York: MJF Books, 1959).

36. Franchetti, "Notas Sobre a História," 2.

37. Hidezaku Masuda Goga, *O Haicai no Brasil* (São Paulo: Oriento, 1988); Franchetti, "Notas Sobre a História"; Tsuguo Koyama, "Japoneses na Amazônia: Alguns Aspectos do Processo de sua Integração Sócio-cultural," in *A Presença Japonesa no Brasil*, ed. Hiroshi Saito (São Paulo: Edusp/T. A. Queiroz, 1980), 17.

38. Franchetti, "Notas Sobre a História." For more information on haiku in Brazil, see www.kakinet.com, a Brazilian web *haiku* magazine.

39. Mike Featherstone, *Consumer Culture and Postmodernism* (London: Sage, 1991), 88-89.

40. Ibid., 92-95.

41. Ulf Hannerz, "Cosmopolitans and Locals in World Culture," in *Global Culture: Nationalism, Globalization and Modernity*, ed. Mike Featherstone (Sage, 1992), 247.

42. Ibid., 249.

43. Bruce Robbins, *Secular Vocations: Intellectuals, Professionalism, Culture* (London: Verso, 1993), 193.

44. Clifford, *Routes*.

45. Hannerz, "Cosmopolitans and Locals," 249.

46. For more on the high turnover of Japanese Brazilians in Japan, see Jeffrey Lesser, ed., *Searching for Home Abroad: Japanese Brazilians and Transnationalism* (Durham, NC: Duke University Press, 2003); Keiko Yamanaka, "'I Will Go Home, But When?' Labor Migration and Circular Diaspora formation by Japanese Brazilians in Japan," in *Japan and Global Migration: Foreign Workers and the Advent of a Multicultural Society*, ed. M. Douglass and G. Roberts (London: Routledge, 2000); and Takeyuki Tsuda, *Strangers in the Homeland: Japanese Brazilian Return Migration in Transnational Perspective* (Columbia University Press, 2003). For analyses of the Brazilian diaspora elsewhere, see Maxine Margolis, *Little Brazil: An Ethnography of Brazilian Immigrants in New York City* (Princeton, NJ: Princeton University Press, 1994); and Rossana Rocha Reis and Teresa Sales, *Cenas do Brasil Migrante* (São Paulo: Boitempo Editorial, 1999).

47. Hannerz, "Cosmopolitans and Locals", 248.

48. Bruce Robbins and Pheng Cheah, *Cosmopolitics: Thinking and Feeling Beyond the Nation* (Minneapolis: University of Minnesota Press, 1998), 1–2.

49. Bourdieu, *Distinction*, 135–137.

50. Personal communication, São Paulo, 2001.

51. Nelson Coelho, *Zen: Experiência Direta da Libertação* (Belo Horizonte: Itatiaia, 1978), 15.

52. Murilo Nunes Azevedo, *O Caminho de Cada Um: O Budismo da Terra Pura* (Rio de Janeiro: Bertrand Brasil, 1996), 20.

53. *Mondō* is a question-and-answer exchange between master and disciple to test the disciple's understanding.

54. Azevedo, *O Caminho de Cada Um*, 20–22.

55. Ricardo Mário Gonçalves, "A Trajetória de um Budista Brasileiro," in *O Budismo no Brasil*, ed. Usarski, 167–180.

56. For more on Japanese True Pure Land Buddhism (Jōdo Shinshū) in Brazil, see Regina Yoshie Matsue, "O Budismo da Terra Pura em Brasília," in *O Budismo no Brasil*, ed. Usarski, 193–219; and Gonçalves, "O Budismo Japonês no Brasil."

57. Gonçalves, "A Trajetória de um Budista Brasileiro."

58. Murilo Nunes Azevedo, "Uma Ponte para a Unidade," *Planeta* (July 1997): 22.

59. Here I am not referring to adherence to New Religious Movements of Buddhist inspiration, such as Sōka Gakkai, which demands an active role by the follower and a shunning of any other religious adherence. For more on this, see Anson Shupe, "Sōka Gakkai and the Slippery Slope from Militancy to Accommodation," in *Religion and Society in Modern Japan*, ed. Mark Mullins (Berkeley, CA: Asian Humanities Press, 1993). For an analysis of Sōka Gakkai in Brazil, see Ronan Pereira, "O Budismo Leigo da Sōka Gakkai no Brasil: Da Revolução Humana à Utopia Mundial," Ph.D. dissertation, Universidade de Campinas, 2001.

60. Reginaldo Prandi, "Religião Paga Conversão e Serviço," in *A Realidade Social das Religiões no Brasil: Religião Sociedade e Política*, ed. Antônio Pierucci and Reginaldo Prandi (São Paulo: Hucitec, 1996), 257.

61. While I lived in Kyoto in 1992–1993, I learned that the *deshi-sensei* relationship was applicable to anything one studies, from ballet and singing classes to more traditional tea ceremony classes. Many children I met were wary of starting new classes, as they would not be able to change teachers if they did not like them.

62. Gonçalves, "A Trajetória de um Budista Brasileiro," 184–185.

63. For a good story on how Claude Lévi-Strauss himself stopped short of "going native"

and bowing at a Buddhist temple, as well as a discussion of the place of the anthropologist as a "positioned subject," see Clifford, *Routes*, 74–76.

64. Azevedo, *O Caminho de Cada Um*, 13.

65. Orides Fontela was lay ordained and used her Buddhist name (Myosen Shinge) to sign some of her poems of Buddhist inspiration. See, e.g., the poem "Gatha" in Orides Fontela, *Rosácea* (São Paulo: Roswitha Kempf, 1986).

66. Personal communication, São Paulo, 2001.

67. *Ōryōki* means roughly "that which contains just enough"; it is a set of eating bowls that Zen monks and nuns receive during ordination. Their origin lies in the bowl that Buddhist monks in India used to beg for food; see *Shambhala Dictionary of Buddhism and Zen*.

68. For Brazilians, breakfast means mainly sweet foods such as jam, fruits, and coffee and milk with sugar. The idea of bacon, eggs, sausages, or beans for breakfast is preposterous for most. I clearly remember the first time I had the "typical" Japanese savory breakfast while living in Japan and how bizarre it was for me to have soup, fish, and rice in the morning.

69. Vegetarianism is closely connected with Buddhism in the West. For instance, Jan Nattier describes how her Asian-American Buddhist friends felt ill at ease at a lecture by a famous Vietnamese monk because of the "not altogether friendly stares of the mostly Caucasian (and overwhelmingly vegetarian) crowd as they tried to enjoy their hot dogs and potato chips"; see Nattier, "Buddhism Comes to Main Street." *Wilson Quarterly* 21 (1997): 72. Similarly, one of the most popular topics discussed on Brazilian Buddhist e-mail lists is whether one should be vegetarian if converted to Buddhism. The moderator of Buddha-L, a North American e-mail list, has corroborated this preoccupation in the United States as well; see Richard Hayes, "The Internet as a Window onto American Buddhism," in *American Buddhism*, ed. Williams and Queen, 174–175.

70. Bourdieu, *Distinction*, 190–193.

71. Ibid., 177.

72. Odete Lara, *Meus Passos em Busca da Paz* (Rio de Janeiro: Record, 1997).

3. The Brazilian Religious Field

1. Max Weber, *The Protestant Ethic and the Spirit of Capitalism*, trans. T. Parsons (London: Unwin Paperbacks, 1985 [1905]).

2. Peter Berger, "Secularization in Retreat," *The National Interest* 46 (1996): 3–12; Harvey G. Cox, "The Myth of the Twentieth Century: The Rise and Fall of Secularization," *Japanese Journal of Religious Studies* 27.1–2 (2000): 1–14; Paul Heelas and Linda Woodhead, "Homeless Minds Today?" In *Peter Berger and the Study of Religion*, ed. Linda Woodhead, Paul Heelas, and David Martin (London: Routledge, 2001), 43–72; Rodney Stark, "Secularization, R. I. P." *Sociology of Religion* 60.3 (1999): 249–273; Rodney Stark and William S.

Bainbridge, *The Future of Religion: Secularization, Revival and Cult Formation* (Berkeley: University of California Press, 1985).

3. Riolando Azzi, *O Catolicismo Popular no Brasil: Aspectos Históricos* (Petrópolis: Vozes, 1978); José Jorge Carvalho, "O Encontro de Velhas e Novas Religiões: Esboço de uma Teoria dos Estilos de Espiritualidade," in *Misticismo e Novas Religiões*, ed. Alberto Moreira and Renée Zicman (Petrópolis: Vozes/UFS/IFAN, 1994), 74; Christian Smith and Joshua Prokopy, *Latin American Religion in Motion* (New York: Routledge, 1999), 3.

4. Carpenter observes that while the Spanish encountered "impressive cities of the highly centralized Aztec and Incan cultures" in their colonies in the New World, the Portuguese encountered "decentralized indigenous civilizations scattered across the vast territory of Brazil." Thus the former established a centralized settlement strategy, building cathedrals and cities, while the latter's mission consisted of small plantation chapels where the priest would be subservient to the plantation owner. In addition, the late discovery of gold in the Portuguese colony (1695) led to late and small investments by the Portuguese crown, which had until then favored its colonies in India, East Asia, and Africa; see Robert Carpenter, "Religious Competition and the Spread of Alternative Spirituality in Contemporary Brazil," Ph.D. dissertation, University of California, Santa Barbara, 2001 37–40.

5. Ubiratan Machado, *Os Intelectuais e o Espiritismo: De Castro Alves a Machado de Assis* (Rio de Janeiro: Edições Antares/Instituto Nacional do Livro, 1983), 175.

6. José Jorge Carvalho, "An Enchanted Public Space: Religious Plurality and Modernity in Brazil," in *Through the Kaleidoscope*, ed. Schelling, 276.

7. According to the census figures, in 1940 Catholics made up 95.2 percent of the population; in 1950 they were 93.7 percent; in 1960, 93.1 percent; in 1970, 91.1 percent; in 1980, 89.2 percent; in 1991, 83.8 percent; and finally in 2000, 73.8 percent.

8. Reginaldo Prandi, "Religião Paga, Conversão e Serviço," in *A Realidade Social das Religiões no Brasil*, ed. Pierucci and Prandi, 261.

9. Roberto Da Matta, *O Que Faz o Brasil, Brasil?* (Rio de Janeiro: Rocca, 1994), 115–116.

10. Interview for *Veja* magazine; see Flávia Varella, "À nossa moda: Criado na França, O Espiritismo Deu Certo Apenas no Brasil, Onde a Doutrina Mística Com Pretensões Científicas é Culto da Classe Média," *Veja*, July 26, 2000.

11. Carvalho, "O Encontro de Velhas e Novas Religiões," 74.

12. Ibid. For an analysis of Kardecist Spiritism in Brazil in English, see David Hess, *Spirits and Scientists: Ideology, Spiritism and Brazilian Culture* (University Park: Pennsylvania State University Press, 1991); and Hess, *Samba in the Night: Spiritism in Brazil* (New York: Columbia University Press, 1994).

13. Whereas *jiriki* is the "'power of the mind,' that particular power that arises from the concentrated mind and that is brought about through training in zazen," *tariki* is understood as the "power of the other," referred to here as the power of the Buddha Amitābha,

who liberates all those who recite his name with devotion and have absolute trust in him" (*Shambhala Dictionary of Buddhism and Zen*).

14. From *Shambhala Dictionary of Buddhism and Zen*.

15. Buddhismo-L, July 17, 2000.

16. E-mail list Zen Chung Tao, November 10, 2000.

17. For more on Umbanda in Brazil, see Diane Brown, *Umbanda Religion and Politics in Urban Brazil* (New York: Columbia University Press, 1994); Lísias Nogueira Negrão, "Umbanda: Entre a Cruz e a Encruzilhada," *Tempo Social Revista de Sociologia* 5.1–2 (1994): 113–122; Renato Ortiz, *A Morte Branca do Feiticeiro Negro: Umbanda e Sociedade Brasileira* (São Paulo: Brasiliense, 1999).

18. Exú is a "divinity from the Yoruba pantheon who plays the role of the messenger to the other gods. Dangerous, exú can do good as well as evil; he is thus considered a trickster god"; Vivian Schelling, ed., *Through the Kaleidoscope*, 299.

19. Brown, *Umbanda Religion and Politics*, 55–77; Carmen Cinira Macedo, *A Imagem do Eterno: Religiões no Brasil* (São Paulo: Moderna, 1989), 44–46.

20. Norton Corrêa, "Para Muitos Trabalhos a Gente Precisa Invocar a Linha Oriental: Observações sobre as Representações de 'Oriente' em Religiões Afro-Brasileiras," paper read at the Twenty-Third Encontro Anual da Anpocs, Caxambu (Minas Gerais State), 1999, 5.

21. Personal communication, São Paulo, March 2000.

22. Corrêa, "Para Muitos Trabalhos," 8–9. This effort to "whiten" Umbanda has been apparent since its origin. In 1941, during the First Brazilian Congress of Umbandist Spiritism in Rio de Janeiro, all speakers denied the African origins of Umbanda, choosing instead to find them in India, Egypt, or the mythical Atlantis and Lemuria. The latter two indicate influence from Rosicrucianism and Theosophy. Carpenter, "Religious Competition," 96.

23. Personal communication, São Paulo, March 2000.

24. Carvalho, "O Encontro de Velhas e Novas Religiões," 75.

25. Ibid.

26. Weber, *The Protestant Ethic*.

27. Stark, "Secularization, R. I. P.," 252–253.

28. Respectively, Stark, "Secularization, R. I. P."; Cox, "The Myth of the Twentieth Century"; and William H. Swatos and Kevin J. Christiano, "Secularization Theory: A Course of a Concept," *Sociology of Religion* 60.3 (1999): 209–228.

29. Swatos and Christiano, "Secularization Theory," 215–219.

30. Roger Finke and Rodney Stark, *The Churching of America, 1776–1990: Winners and Losers in our Religious Economy* (New Brunswick, NJ: Rutgers University Press, 1992).

31. Not only in religious terms has secularization eluded its heralds. Jean and John Comaroff have argued for an increase of enchantment in the making of capitalism at the end of the millennium. For them, the allure of creating "wealth without production [and] value without effort" in neoliberal capitalism stimulates people to imagine the creation of wealth through magical means. In times when the gap between the rich and the poor widens, when labor is fixed and thus powerless against a more mobile capital, people resort to "fantasies of abundance without effort, of beating capitalism in its own game by drawing a winning number at the behest of unseen forces." (p. 6) In this light, the Comaroffs associate the spread of "fee-for-service" NRMs and prosperity cults with this neoliberalist spirit. For more on this, see Jean and John Comaroff, *Millennial Capitalism and the Culture of Neoliberalism* (Durham, NC: Duke University Press, 2001).

32. Peter Berger, *The Sacred Canopy: Elements of a Sociological Theory of Religion* (Garden City, NJ: Anchor Books, Doubleday & Co., Inc, 1967), 148–149.

33. Antônio Pierucci and Reginaldo Prandi, "Assim Como Não Era no Princípio: Religião e Ruptura," in *A Realidade Social das Religiões no Brasil*, ed. Pierucci and Prandi, 10.

34. Research conducted by ISER (Institute for Religious Studies) in the city of Rio de Janeiro found that from 1990 to 1992, 673 new Protestant churches were established, of which 90 percent were Pentecostal. In the same period, only one Catholic church was established; Sergio Pereira, "Society-Individual and Postmodern Condition: Understanding the Explosion of Pentecostalism in Brazil," Ph.D. dissertation, University of Notre Dame, Indiana, 2000), 16. For accounts of the expansion of Protestantism in Latin America in English, see David Martin, *Tongues of Fire: The Explosion of Protestantism in Latin America* (Oxford: Basil Blackwell, 1991); David Stoll, *Is Latin America Turning Protestant? The Politics of Evangelical Growth* (Berkeley: University of California Press, 1990).

35. Pierucci and Prandi, "Assim Como Não Era," 16–18. For a very good account in English on the decline of Liberation Theology in Brazil, see Manuel Vásquez, *The Brazilian Popular Church and the Crisis of Modernity* (Cambridge: Cambridge University Press, 1998).

36. For a short overview of this phenomenon in English, see Peter B. Clarke, "'Pop-Star' Priest and the Catholic Response to the 'Explosion' of Evangelical Protestantism in Brazil: The Beginning of the End of the 'Walkout'?" *Journal of Contemporary Religion* 14.2 (1999): 203–216.

37. José Maria Mayrink, "Fidelidade à Roma, O Apelo do Papa à CNBB," *O Estado de São Paulo*, January 24, 2003, 12.

38. Silvana Guaiume, "Igreja pode perder 9% dos fiéis Até 2010: Bispos Discutiram Pesquisa sobre Migração de Católicos na Assembléia da CNBB," *O Estado de São Paulo*, May 2, 2003, 9.

39. Prandi, "Perto da Magia, Longe da Política," in *A Realidade Social das Religiões no Brasil*, ed. Pierucci and Prandi, 94.

40. Ibid., 104–105; my italics.

41. Hess, *Spiritists and Scientists*, 2.

42. Leila Marrach Basto Albuquerque, *Seicho-no-Ie do Brasil: Agradecimento, Obediência e Salvação* (São Paulo: Fapesp/Anablume, 1999); Carpenter and Roof, "The Transplanting of Seichō-no-ie"; Matsuoka, "'Messianity Makes a Person Useful'"; José Geraldo Paiva, "Instituição Religiosa Perfeita Liberdade," in *Sinais dos Tempos: Diversidade Religiosa no Brasil*, ed. Leila Landim (Rio de Janeiro: Instituto de Estudos da Religião, 1990), 187–193; Pereira, "O Budismo Leigo da Sōka Gakkai no Brasil." Numbers of adherents are a source of contention. While the 2000 census found Seichō no ie had 27,784 followers, Pure Land had 5,465, and Sekai Kyūseikyō had 109,000 adherents (Sōka Gakkai was not researched), the religious traditions themselves have different numbers. According to them, Seichō-no-ie has 2.5 million followers, Pure Land 350,000 followers, and Sekai Kyūseikyō has 300,000 followers. Matsuoka has argued that although these numbers are inflated, there are at least one million followers of Japanese NRMs in Brazil; Matsuoka, "'Messianity Makes a Person Useful,'" 77. The disparate numbers are most probably due to the phenomenon of multiple religious affiliations discussed.

43. For an analysis of Lama Michel's trajectory, see Frank Usarski, "Seu Caloroso Coração Brasileiro e a Energia Pura de Maitreya Atuam Muito Bem Juntos: Reflexões sobre Lama Michel," in *O Budismo no Brasil*, ed. Usarski, 287–317.

44. Maile Wall, "Chagdud Tulku Rinpoche Dies at 92," *Buddhadharma* (spring 2003): 89.

45. In the years 1996–1997 I frequented the Dharma Center Shi De Choe Tsog, Lama Gangchen's healing center in São Paulo City, where Lama Segyu used to give teachings when in Brazil. I was present at such healing sessions where he employed Umbanda as well as Tibetan healing methods.

46. Robert Carpenter, "Esoteric Literature as a Microcosmic Mirror of Brazil's Religious Marketplace," in *Latin American Religion in Motion*, ed. Christian Smith and Joshua Prokopy (New York: Routledge, 1999), 243.

47. Carlos Rodriguez Brandão, "A Crise das Instituições Tradicionais Produtoras de Sentido," in *Misticismo e Novas Religiões*, ed. Alberto Moreira and Renée Zicman (Petrópolis: Vozes/UFS/IFAN, 1994), 28–29; Carpenter, "Esoteric Literature as a Microcosmic Mirror," 243–245; Pierucci and Prandi, "Assim Como Não Era"; Prandi, "Religião Paga"; Pierre Sanchis, "O Campo Religioso Contemporâneo no Brasil," in *Globalização e Religião*, ed. Ari Pedro Oro and Carlos Alberto Steil. (Petrópolis: Vozes, 1997); Soares, "Religioso Por Natureza."

48. Carlos Rodrigues Brandão, "Intervenções," in *Misticismo e Novas Religiões*, ed. Alberto Moreira and Renée Zicman (Petrópolis: Vozes/UFS/IFAN, 1994), 56. Pomba-Gira is a "feminine divinity cultivated in Umbanda. She has great sexual and magical power and is a kind of female equivalent of Exú"; Schelling, *Through the Kaleidoscope*, 300.

49. Prandi, "Religião Paga," 262–266.

50. For this survey, I distributed a one-page questionnaire while I conducted participant

observation in each of these sites. The questionnaire included questions about age, gender, ethnic background (divided into Japanese Brazilians, including which generation, and non-Japanese Brazilians), education, profession, religion of upbringing, multiple religious affiliations, reasons for adhering, and frequency of practice.

51. Thomas Tweed, "Nightstand Buddhists and Other Creatures: Sympathizers, Adherents, and the Study of Religion," in *American Buddhism*, ed. Williams and Queen, 74.

52. Maurício Moraes, "Templos Revestem Budistas de Novas Visões de Mundo," *O Estado de São Paulo*, October 27, 1998, 4–5.

53. Gisele Vitória, "O Brasil dos Budas." *IstoÉ*, March 12, 1997, 62–70.

54. Cited in Brandão, "A Crise das Instituições Tradicionais," 40–41.

55. Varella, "À nossa moda."

56. Buddhismo-L, February 8, 2002.

57. Gonçalves, "O Budismo Japonês no Brasil," 177. For more on the arrival of Japanese New Religions in Brazil and their hybridization with Afro-Brazilian religions and Catholicism, see Takashi Maeyama, "Japanese Religion in Southern Brazil: Change and Syncretism," *Latin American Studies* 6 (1983): 181–238; Koichi Mori, "O Processo de 'Amarelamento das Tradicionais Religiões Brasileiras de Possessão: Mundo Religioso de uma Okinawana,'" *Estudos Japoneses* 18 (1998): 57–76.

58. *Rakusu* is "a small rectangular piece of fabric composed of patches, which is worn on a cord around the neck. It symbolizes the patchwork robe of Shākyamuni Buddha and his disciples and is worn by monks and lay followers of *Mahāyāna* Buddhism. The *rakusu* is conferred upon one when taking the *jukai*, the initiation into Buddhism in which one takes Buddhist vows" (*Shambhala Dictionary of Buddhism and Zen*).

59. Robert Bellah, "New Religious Consciousness and the Crisis in Modernity," In *The New Religious Consciousness*, ed. Charles Glock and Robert Bellah (Berkeley: University of California Press, 1976), 341.

60. Denise Cush, "British Buddhism and the New Age," *Journal of Contemporary Religion* 11.2 (1996): 205.

61. Personal communication, São Paulo, October 1999; my italics.

62. Many books have been translated; some of the more popular titles are *The Zen Doctrine of No Mind* and *Introduction to Zen Buddhism* by D. T. Suzuki; *Zen Mind, Beginners' Mind* by Shunryū Suzuki; *The Three Pillars of Zen* by Philip Kapleau; *Nothing Special, Living Zen* by Charlotte Joko Beck; and most of the books by Thich Nhat Hanh. When I accessed the Internet site of a large Brazilian bookstore in March 2004, the word "Zen" was used in thirty-nine titles of books in Portuguese, while "Buddhism" had twenty-eight entries (http://livrariasaraiva.com.br). In addition, the list of books on Buddhism in Portuguese distributed by Busshinji Temple included sixty-four titles.

63. Hollywood movies *The Little Buddha, Seven Years in Tibet,* and *Kundun,* as well as non-Hollywood ones such as *The Cup* and *Samsara* were successful in Brazil. Although they address Tibetan Buddhism in particular, Brazilians tend to view them as generally about Buddhism, because they subscribe to the idea that Buddhism has a true, universal essence found when it is stripped of its cultural accretions. Furthermore, because of this belief in a universal essence, practitioners may frequent various Buddhist schools at once, as we will see in this chapter.

64. Personal communication, São Paulo, August 1998.

65. Personal communication, São Paulo, November 1999.

66. This Hindu-based NRM, which began in India in the early 1970s, drew on both Western and Eastern sources to form a synthesis of New Age spirituality. Bagwan Shree Rajneesh has a series of books in which he analyzes and interprets Zen doctrine. Most of them have been translated into Portuguese. Some adherents whom I interviewed had been or still are his followers. Particularly in the group headed by Moriyama *rōshi* in Porto Alegre, some adherents had a Buddhist name, which had been given at their lay ordination, and a Sannyasin name, given at their initiation in the Rajneesh movement. Some had been to Rajneesh's *ashram* in Poona, India. For a short account of the Rajneesh movement in Brazil, see Ana Cristina Abreu de Oliveira, "Rajneesh," in *Sinais dos Tempos,* ed. Landim, 205–212.

67. Soares, "Religioso Por Natureza," 121–123. Brazilian dictatorship started with a military coup in 1964 and lasted until 1989, when direct elections for the presidency were reestablished. However, in 1985 the military started yielding power by agreeing to a civilian president elected by the Congress.

68. Ibid., 122.

69. Personal communication, Morro da Vargem Temple, November 1998.

70. Personal communication, São Paulo, October 1999.

71. Shokaku Okumura, "Editor's Note," *Zen Quarterly* 10.2 (1998): 1.

72. Soares, "Religioso Por Natureza," 137; my italics.

73. Wade Clark Roof, *Spiritual Supermarket: Baby Boomers and the Remaking of American Religion* (Princeton, NJ: Princeton University Press, 1999).

74. Ibid., 47.

75. Carpenter, "Esoteric Literature as a Microcosmic Mirror," 242.

76. Hayes, "The Internet as a Window," 170.

77. Personal communication, São Paulo, October 1997.

78. Personal communication, Morro da Vargem Temple, November 1998.

79. Sharf, "Buddhist Modernism and the Rhetoric of Meditative Experience," 267.

80. Zen Chung Tao, April 6, 2003; my italics.

81. Zen Chung Tao, April 7, 2003.

82. Personal communication through e-mail, April 2003.

83. Tweed, "Nightstand Buddhists and Other Creatures," 83.

84. Vajrayāna is the "school of Buddhism that arose primarily in the northeast and northwest of India, around the middle of the first millennium. It developed out of the teachings of the Mahāyāna and reached Tibet, China, and Japan along with the Mahāyāna. . . . The teachings of the Vajrayāna formed an esoteric tradition that combined elements of yoga and of the ancient Indian nature religion with original Buddhist thought" (*Shambhala Dictionary of Buddhism and Zen*).

85. Personal communication, São Paulo, January 2002.

86. Iemanjá is a female Yoruba *orixá* (deity) identified with water, that is, the sea and rivers.

87. Tara is "an emanation of the bodhisattva Avalokiteshvara, said to arise from his tears in order to help him in his work. She embodies the feminine aspect of compassion and is a very popular deity in Tibetan Buddhism" (*Shambhala Dictionary of Buddhism and Zen*).

88. Buddhismo-L, January 23, 2001.

89. José Jorge Carvalho, "Características do Fenômeno Religioso na Sociedade Contemporânea," in *O Impacto da Modernidade Sobre a Religião*, ed. Maria Clara Bingemer (São Paulo: Loyola, 1992), 144

90. Personal communication through e-mail, January 2000.

91. Personal communication, São Paulo, October 1998.

92. Oliven, "Brazil," 70.

4. The Brazilian Imaginary of Zen

1. Clarissa Schneider, "Estilo Zen," *Casa Vogue*, 1997, 103–115.

2. Appadurai, *Modernity at Large*, 5.

3. Ibid., 31.

4. Benedict Anderson, "The New World Disorder," *New Left Review* 193 (1992): 3–13; Appadurai, *Modernity at Large*; Ulf Hannerz, *Transnational Connections, Cultures, People, Places* (London: Routledge, 1996); Jan N. Pieterse, "Globalization and Hybridization," in *Global Modernities*, ed. Mike Featherstone, Scott Lash, and Roland Robertson (London: Sage, 1995).

5. Appadurai, *Modernity At Large*, 29.

6. José Elias Croce, *Seitas e Heresias: O Engano das Falsas Religiões, Jovens e Adultos Dominical* (Rio de Janeiro: Betel, 2000).

7. Gisele Vitória and Liana Melo, "Meditação: Como usar esta Técnica Milenar para Vencer a Crise, Escapar do Stress Cotidiano, Ganhar Energia, Melhorar Sua Concentração e Tomar Decisões Difíceis," *IstoÉ*, September 9, 1998, 86–89.

8. Juliane Zaché, "Malhação Zen," *IstoÉ*, September 19, 2001, 62–63.

9. For instance, in 2004 there were 87 mentions of "Zen," 34 of "Buddhism," 228 of the "Dalai Lama," and 29 of "Buddha" throughout the paper. In 2003, there were 54 mentions of "Zen," 46 of "Buddhism," 188 of the "Dalai Lama," and 48 of "Buddha". In 2002, "Zen" had 134, "Buddhism" had 51, "Dalai Lama" had 193, and "Buddha" had 58. In 2001, "Zen" had 128, "Buddhism" had 77, "Dalai Lama" had 50, and "Buddha" had 95. In 2000 there were 116 mentions of "Zen," 43 of "Buddhism," 38 of "Dalai Lama," and 31 of "Buddha" (www.uol.com.br/cgi-bin/bibliot/arquivo.cgi?html).

10. Ricardo Kotscho, "Itamar Encarna Fase Zen de Olho no Planalto," *Folha de São Paulo*, June 3, 2001, A10; Valdo Cruz, "Topetada," *Folha de São Paulo*, June 7, 2001, A2.

11. Nancy Campos, "Onda Zen," *Elle*, June 1998, 91–94.

12. "Em Busca do Zen," *Veja*, June 17, 1998, 25.

13. This site can be seen at www.uol.com.br/bemzen.

14. Roberto Oliveira, "Fé de Pernas Cruzadas," *Revista da Folha*, July 15, 2001, 8–13.

15. "Buda É Pop," *Revista da Folha*, July 15, 2001, 8–17.

16. Appadurai, *Modernity at Large*, 34.

17. For a web directory of Brazilian Buddhist temples, monasteries and centers, Buddhist texts translated to Portuguese, virtual bookstores, and e-mail discussion list addresses, see http://cmrocha.sites.uol.com.br.

18. www.dharmanet.com.br and www.geocities.com/accessoaoinsight.

19. General: www.geocities.com/chungtao_budismo/

   Theravada-L: http://lista.cjb.net

   Dharma *sūtras*: www.egroups.com/group/dharmasutras

   Zen Chungtao: www.geocities.com/chungtao_budismo/listwin.html

   Vajrayana-L: www.dharmanet.com.br/listas/vajrayana

20. Kōan are paradoxical questions posed by a Zen teacher to a student as part of his/her training. The student will be able to answer such questions if s/he refrains from using his/her logical mind and takes a leap into the next level of comprehension, transcending conceptual thought. As a result, the student becomes aware of the limitations of thought.

21. The term was coined by Gary Ray, the editor of *CyberSangha* magazine, in 1991 as a generic term to describe the Buddhist community online. *Sangha* is the Buddhist term that meant at first the community of Buddhist monks and nuns, but with the increase of lay adherents came to include the latter as well; see Prebish, *Luminous Passage*, 203, 230.

22. Zen Chung Tao, June 10, 2003.

23. Buddhismo-L, May 13, 2001.

24. *Shambhala Dictionary of Buddhism and Zen*, 125.

25. Buddhismo-L, April 3, 2001.

26. Appadurai, *Modernity at Large*, 29, 32, 45–46.

27. Hannerz, "The World in Creolisation."

28. Ien Ang and Jon Stratton, "Asianising Australia: Notes towards a Critical Transnationalism in Cultural Studies," *Cultural Studies Journal* 10.1 (1996): 28.

29. Mônica Bergamo, "Fraternidade Vermelha, Liberdade Azul." *Folha de São Paulo*, June 4, 2001, E2.

30. Vásquez, *The Brazilian Popular Church*, 174.

31. Werner Braer, *The Brazilian Economy: Growth and Development* (New York: Praeger, 1989); Vásquez, *The Brazilian Popular Church*, 177.

32. Vásquez, *The Brazilian Popular Church*, 178.

33. For the Brazilian diaspora in the United States, see, for instance, Margolis, *Little Brazil*; and Teresa Sales, "Identidade Étnica," in *Cenas do Brasil Migrante*, ed. Rosanna Rocha Reis and Teresa Sales (São Paulo: Boitempo, 1999). Regarding the community in Japan, see Lesser, ed., *Searching for Home Abroad*; Daniel Linger, *No One Home* (Stanford University Press, 2001); Tsuda, *Strangers in the Homeland*.

34. Mike Featherstone and Scott Lash, "Globalization, Modernity and the Spatialization of Social Theory: An Introduction," in *Global Modernities*, ed. Featherstone, Lash, and Robertson, 10.

35. Ibid., 3.

36. Teresa Caldeira, *City of Walls: Crime, Segregation, and Citizenship in São Paulo* (Berkeley: University of California Press, 2000), 2–4.

37. Free translation of "Baiano burro nasce, cresce e nunca pára no sinal, e quem pára e espera o verde é que é chamado de boçal," from the song "Vamo Comer." For an account of traffic behavior and anomie in São Paulo City, see Caldeira, *City of Walls*, 315–317.

38. Souza Martins, "The Hesitations of the Modern," 261.

39. Eliane Lobato, "Um Budismo de Resultados," *IstoÉ*, May 9, 2001, 80–85.

40. Bourdieu, *Distinction*, 214.

41. Lobato, "Um Budismo de Resultados."

42. Jacques Le Goff, *The Medieval Imagination*, trans. A. Goldhammer (Chicago: University of Chicago Press, 1992), 16.

43. Featherstone, *Consumer Culture and Postmodernism*, 115.

44. Bourdieu, *Distinction*, 175.

45. Erika Palomino, "Conheça os Millies," *Folha de São Paulo*, March 21, 1998, 1–3.

46. See, for instance, Jan Nattier, "Who Is a Buddhist? Charting the Landscape of Buddhist America," in *The Faces of Buddhism in America*, ed. Charles Prebish and Kenneth Tanaka (Berkeley: University of California Press, 1998); Tweed, "Nightstand Buddhists and Other Creatures."

47. Featherstone, *Consumer Culture and Postmodernism*, 92.

48. Buddhismo-L, May 14, 2001.

49. Featherstone, *Consumer Culture and Postmodernism*, 91.

50. Bourdieu, *Distinction*, 176.

51. Lobato, "Um Budismo de Resultados," 83.

52. Engaged Buddhism is the application of Buddhist vows of compassion to the alleviation of contemporary social and humanitarian issues. See, e.g., Christopher Queen, ed., *Engaged Buddhism in the West* (Boston: Wisdom Publications, 2000).

53. Lobato, "Um Budismo de Resultados," 83.

54. Personal communication, São Paulo, January 2002.

55. Ibid.

56. Zen Chung Tao, October 16, 2002; my italics.

57. The site he referred to is www.dhamma.org/prisons.htm.

58. Schwarz, *Misplaced Ideas*, 12.

59. Featherstone, *Consumer Culture and Postmodernism*, 88.

60. Ibid., 89.

61. Ibid.

62. Buddhismo-L, August 14, 2001.

63. Personal communication, São Paulo, March 1999.

64. Hannerz, "The World in Creolisation," 549.

65. Carvalho, "O Encontro de Velhas e Novas Religiões," 77.

66. Peter Berger, "Four Faces of Global Culture," *The National Interest* 49 (1997): 23–29.

67. Ibid., 25.

68. Appadurai, *Modernity At Large*, 35.

69. Bread was introduced into Japan by Portuguese Jesuits and merchants, who arrived in the country in 1543. Accordingly, the word used for bread in Japan, "pan," derives from the Portuguese "pão." However, bread became part of the ordinary diet only in the twentieth century.

5. Doing Zen, Being Zen

1. Charles Prebish, *American Buddhism* (North Scituate: Duxbury Press, 1979); Prebish, "Two Buddhisms Reconsidered"; Nattier, "Visible and Invisible"; Nattier, "Who Is a Buddhist?"; Baumann, "Global Buddhism," 17.

2. For an account on the impact of globalization and changes in Japanese society on the *butsudan* industry, see Carla and Jerry Eades, Yuriko Nishiyama, and Hiroko Yanase, "Houses of Everlasting Bliss: Globalization and the Production of Buddhist Altars in Hikone," in *Globalization and Social Change in Contemporary Japan*, ed. Jerry S. Eades, Tom Gill, and Harumi Befu (Melbourne: Transpacific Press, 2000).

3. Because of a nationalist government in Brazil and the upcoming war, restrictions were imposed on Japanese immigrants in the late 1930s and early 1940s. These included the closing of Japanese-language newspapers and of Japanese schools and the prohibition of speaking Japanese in public or at home. For more on this, see Lesser, *Negotiating National Identity*; and Lone, *The Japanese Community in Brazil*, 137–144.

4. For more on strategic essentialism, see Gayatri Spivak, *The Post-Colonial Critic: Interviews, Strategies, Dialogues* (New York: Routledge, 1990).

5. Ian Reader, *Religion in Contemporary Japan* (Honolulu: University of Hawai'i Press, 1991), 86.

6. The *danka seido* was so significant for Japanese Buddhist sects that Williams has argued that one of the reasons Sōtō Zenshū became the largest Buddhist school in number of temples (17,548) in eighteenth-century Japan is precisely the "coercive legal and political imperative for temple registration (which was initially led by Sōtō Zen priests);" Duncan Williams, "Representations of Zen: An Institutional and Social History of Sōtō Zen Buddhism in Edo Japan," Ph.D. dissertation, Harvard University, 2000, 259. (Despite this, as Williams points out, the Jōdo Shinshū school claimed the largest number of members during the Edo period.)

7. Reader, "Zazenless Zen?" 18.

8. Kenji Ishii, "Urbanization, Depopulation, and Religion," in *Religion in Japanese Culture*, ed. Noriyoshi Tamaru and David Read (Kodansha International, 1996).

9. Reader, *Religion in Contemporary Japan*, 102.

10. Personal communication, Busshinji, January 2002. In Japan, at the time of death, the Buddhist priest conducts a posthumous ordination to allow Buddhist funeral rites for laypeople. During this ordination the deceased takes the three refuges, receives a Buddhist name, and becomes a *hotoke*, a buddha. For more on this, see William Bodiford, "Zen in the Art of Funerals: Ritual Salvation in Japanese Buddhism," *History of Religions* 32.2 (1992): 146–164.

11. Brazilian sociologist of religion Reginaldo Prandi also noted that Brazilian Catholics may seek a parish that charges the lowest fees for baptisms and memorial masses; see Prandi, "Religião Paga," 267. The lack of commitment of Japanese Brazilians toward a particular Buddhist tradition could be seen not only as a lack of awareness of differences among different Buddhist traditions, but also as being part of the Brazilian religious marketplace, where diverse religions compete for consumers, who in turn feel free to choose among them.

12. Reader, *Religion in Contemporary Japan*, 102.

13. Ben Hills, *Japan Behind the Lines* (Sydney: Hodder & Stoughton, 1996), 46–49.

14. Reader, *Religion in Contemporary Japan*, 87; my italics.

15. For an analysis of hybridization between Catholicism and Shintō NRMs in Brazil, see Maeyama, "Religion, Kinship, and the Middle Classes of the Japanese." For an account of Japanese Brazilians practicing Afro-Brazilian religions, see Mori, "O Processo de 'Amarelamento.'"

16. Robert J. Smith, *Ancestor Worship in Contemporary Japan* (Stanford, CA: Stanford University Press, 1974), 91.

17. Egon Schaden, "Imigrantes Alemães e Japoneses: Uma Visão Comparativa," in *A Presença Japonesa no Brasil*, ed. Hiroshi Saito (São Paulo: T.A. Queiroz/Edusp, 1980), 144–145.

18. Smith, *Ancestor Worship in Contemporary Japan*, p. 139.

19. Personal communication, Busshinji, October 1998.

20. Personal communication, Tenzui Zen Dōjō, January 2002.

21. Chico Xavier is the most famous Spiritist medium in Brazil. Buddhismo-L, February 5, 2003.

22. Brandão, "Ser Católico," 28.

23. Buddhismo-L, February 8, 2003.

24. E-mail sent by a Japanese Brazilian to Buddhismo-L, April 23, 2002.

25. Like the majority of the adherents, this interviewee was highly educated. When I interviewed him in February 1999 at Busshinji, he was pursuing his Ph.D. in economics and environmental sciences at the prestigious University of São Paulo.

26. The most extreme case is Sōka Gakkai's *shakubuku* (lit., break and subdue) policy, where the new devotee would be asked to aggressively proselytize to bring in new members and to burn their Buddhist altar and objects. Once this NRM became internationalized, the practice of *shakubuku* was phased out. *Shōju*, a more moderate proselytizing technique in which previous religious affiliations were not criticized, took its place.

27. Personal communication, São Paulo, November 2001.

28. Personal communication, Porto Alegre, February 1998.

29. Personal communication, Busshinji, October 1998.

30. Personal communication, Busshinji, January 2002.

31. Shunryū Suzuki, *Zen Mind, Beginner's Mind*, 133.

32. Richard H. Seager, *Buddhism in America* (New York: Columbia University Press 1999), 91.

33. Baumann, "Global Buddhism."

34. Personal communication, Busshinji, January 2002.

35. Follow-up interview through e-mail, April 2002.

36. Personal communication, Busshinji, January 2002.

37. Follow-up interview through e-mail, April 2002.

38. Personal communication, Kyoto, September 2000.

39. Leusa Araújo, "Cerimônia de Casamento," *Marie Claire*, December 1993, 86–93.

40. Jaffe, *Neither Monk nor Layman*, 169.

41. For more on the Christian wedding boom, see Michael Fisch, "The Rise of Chapel Wedding in Japan: Simulation and Performance," *Japanese Journal of Religious Studies* 28.1–2 (2001): 57–76.

42. Ian Reader, "Contemporary Zen Buddhist Tracts for the Laity: Grassroots Buddhism in Japan," in *Religions of Japan in Practice*, ed. George J. Tanabe (Princeton, NJ: Princeton University Press, 1999), 497.

43. A ritual of drinking sake performed during the wedding reception. The couple sips sake three times each (*san-san-kudō*).

44. Tomoo Handa, *O Imigrante Japonês: História da sua Vida no Brasil* (São Paulo: T.A. Queiroz, Centro de Estudos Nipo-Brasileiros, 1987), 798.

45. Buddhismo-L, August 3, 2002.

46. Kashima, *Buddhism in America* (1977), 129–131.

47. *O-juzu* is a Japanese Buddhist rosary exchanged by the couple during the Buddhist wedding ceremony as an affirmation of their commitment to the Buddhist way of life.

48. Because "baptism" is the term most commonly used by Brazilians to designate this ceremony, I decided to use it here, albeit in quotation marks to remind the reader that this is not the Catholic baptism and not a term used in Zen in Japan. For the creation of a "baptism" ceremony in Japan, see Jaffe, *Neither Monk nor Layman,* 169.

49. Interview through e-mail, September 2002.

50. Buddhismo-L, September 3, 2002.

51. Lobato, "Um Budismo de Resultados." In the case of Sōka Gakkai, the Buddha she mentions is actually a representation of Nichiren (1222–1282), as Buddhist schools in Japan worship their founders and not so much the historical Buddha. Sōka Gakkai was connected to Nichiren Shōshū (an orthodox sect of Nichiren Buddhism) until 1991, when it was excommunicated by this sect.

52. Buddhismo-L, September 3, 2002.

53. For research on American converts, see Robert Ellwood, *Zen in American Life and Letters* (Malibu: Udena Publications, University of Southern California, 1987); Addie Foye, "Buddhists in America: A Short, Biased View," *Tricycle* IV.1 (1994): 57; Franz A. Metcalf, "Why Do Americans Practice Buddhism?" Ph.D. dissertation, University of Chicago, 2000; David L. Preston, *The Social Organization of Zen: Constructing Transcultural Reality* (Cambridge: Cambridge University Press, 1988). For research on Japanese-American practices, see, for instance, Asai and Williams, "Japanese American Zen Temples"; Kashima, *Buddhism in America* (1977); Tanabe, "Grafting Identity"; Tanaka, "Issues of Ethnicity in the Buddhist Churches of America," in *American Buddhism,* ed. Williams and Queen, 3–19.

54. Numrich, *Old Wisdom in the New World,* 144.

55. Ibid., 64.

56. Paul Numrich, "Two Buddhisms Further Reconsidered," *Contemporary Buddhism* 4.1 (2003): 55–78.

57. The first wave of Asian immigration ended in 1924, when the American Congress passed the Oriental Exclusion Act. The second wave started after the legislative reforms passed in Washington in 1965.

58. Prebish, *Luminous Passage,* 58.

59. Diane Eck, cited in Prebish, *Luminous Passage,* 63.

60. Nattier, "Visible and Invisible"; Nattier, "Who Is a Buddhist?" 189–190.

61. Tanaka, "Issues of Ethnicity," 14–15.

62. Baumann, "Global Buddhism," 24.

63. Ibid., 17.

64. Tweed, "Nightstand Buddhists and Other Creatures," 72.

65. Ibid., 73.

66. Queen, "Introduction," in *American Buddhism*, ed. Williams and Queen, xvii.

67. Michelle Spuler, *Developments in Australian Buddhism: Facets of the Diamond* (London: Routledge Curzon, 2003), 48.

68. Seager, *Buddhism in America* (1999), 247.

69. I am not aware of research on the hybridization between European convert practices and Asian immigrant Buddhist practices in Catholic countries. For a good overview of references on Buddhism in Europe, see Martin Baumann's *Buddhism in Europe: an Annotated Bibliography*, http://www-user.uni-bremen.de/~mbaumann/update-3.htm.

70. Baumann, "Global Buddhism," 24.

71. James Coleman, "The New Buddhism: Some Empirical Findings," in *American Buddhism*, ed. Williams and Queen, 91–99; Numrich, *Old Wisdom in the New World*, 61; Seager, *Buddhism in America* (1999); Queen, "Introduction," xxiv. The three classical Buddhist vehicles are Theravāda, Mahāyāna, and Vajrayāna. Queen and Williams have noted that "American Buddhism points in the direction of a new, fourth vehicle, which might be styled Navayāna ("new vehicle") or Lokayāna ("world vehicle") Buddhism" (Queen, "Introduction," xxiv). According to them, its defining features are democratization (entailing both laicization and feminization), pragmatism (emphasis on ritual practice and deemphasis on beliefs), and engagement (entailing politicization and environmentalism); Queen, "Introduction," xix.

72. Prebish has coined the term "silent sangha" to designate academics who are Buddhists themselves; see Prebish, *Luminous Passage*, 173–202.

73. In an article called "Buddhist Terms Your Guru Never Taught You," in *CyberSangha* magazine, Gary Ray coins the expression "ethnosangha oversight" to describe "the exclusion of ethnic Buddhist groups (nonwhites in this case) when referring to Western Buddhism."

74. Pierce, "Constructing American Buddhisms."

75. Werner Sollors, *Beyond Ethnicity: Consent and Descent in American Culture* (Oxford: Oxford University Press, 1986), 219–220; my italics.

76. Pierce, "Constructing American Buddhisms," 7.

77. Lopez, ed., *Curators of the Buddha*, 7.

78. See ibid.; also Donald Lopez, *Prisoners of Shangri-La: Tibetan Buddhism in the West* (Chicago: University of Chicago Press, 1998).

79. Coleman, "The New Buddhism," 91–92; my italics.

80. Sharf, "Buddhist Modernism and the Rhetoric of Meditative Experience," 229.

81. Coleman, "The New Buddhism."

82. Peter Gregory, "Review of the New Buddhism: The Western Transformation of an Ancient Tradition," *Tricycle* X.3 (2001): 108.

Conclusion

1. Fabio Guibu, "Prefeito de Recife Medita para Governar," *Folha de São Paulo,* December 29, 2002, C3; my italics.

2. Kath Weston, "The Virtual Anthropologist," in *Anthropological Locations: Boundaries and Grounds of a Field Science,* ed. Akhil Gupta and James Ferguson (Berkeley: University of California Press, 1997).

3. Akhil Gupta and James Ferguson, "Discipline and Practice," in *Anthropological Locations,* ed. Gupta and Ferguson, 33.

Bibliography

Abreu de Oliveira, Ana Cristina. "Rajneesh." In *Sinais dos Tempos: Diversidade Religiosa no Brasil*, ed. L. Landim. Rio de Janeiro: Instituto de Estudos da Religião, 1991, 205–212.

Albuquerque, Leila Marrach Basto. *Seicho-no-Ie do Brasil: Agradecimento, Obediência e Salvação*. São Paulo: Fapesp/Anablume, 1999.

Amaral, Leila. "Os Errantes da Nova Era e sua Religiosidade Caleidoscópica." *Caderno de Ciências Sociais* 3.4 (1993): 19–32.

Amemiya, Kozy. "Land, Culture, and the Power of Money: Assimilation and Resistance of Okinawan Immigrants in Bolivia." In *Encounters: People of Asian Descent in the Americas*, ed. Roshni Rustomji-Kerns, Rajini Srikanth, and Leny Mendoza Strobel. Lanham, MD: Rowman & Littlefield, 1999, 121–130.

Anderson, Benedict. "The New World Disorder." *New Left Review* 193 (1992): 3–13.

Ang, Ien. *On Not Speaking Chinese: Living Between Asia and the West*. London: Routledge, 2001.

Ang, Ien, and Jon Stratton. "Asianising Australia: Notes towards a Critical Transnationalism in Cultural Studies." *Cultural Studies Journal* 10.1 (1996): 16–36.

Anjos, Augusto dos. *Toda Poesia*. Rio de Janeiro: Paz e Terra, 1976.

Appadurai, Arjun. *Modernity At Large: Cultural Dimensions of Globalization*. Minneapolis: University of Minnesota Press, 1996.

Arai, Paula. *Women Living in Zen: Japanese Sōtō Buddhist Nuns*. Oxford: Oxford University Press, 1999.

Araújo, Leusa. "Cerimônia de Casamento." *Marie Claire*, December 1993, 86–93.

Asai, Senryō, and Duncan Ryūken Williams. "Japanese American Zen Temples: Cultural Identity and Economics." In *American Buddhism: Methods and Findings in Recent Scholarship*, ed. Duncan Williams and Christopher Queen. Richmond, Surrey: Curzon, 1999, 20–35.

Ashcroft, Bill, Gareth Griffiths, and Helen Tiffin. *Key Concepts in Post-Colonial Studies*. London: Routledge, 1998.

Assmann, Hugo. *A Igreja Eletrônica e seu Impacto na América Latina*. Petrópolis: Vozes, 1986.

Association of Sōtō Zen Buddhists Committee Activity. *Buddha's Seed Taking Firm Root in North America's Soil*. Book published for the 75th commemorations of Sōtō Zen Buddhism in North America, Los Angeles, 1997.

Azevedo, Murilo Nunes. *O Caminho de Cada Um: O Budismo da Terra Pura*. Rio de Janeiro: Bertrand Brasil, 1996.

———. "Uma Ponte para a Unidade." *Planeta*, July 1997, 18–22.

Azzi, Riolando. *O Catolicismo Popular no Brasil: Aspectos Históricos*. Petrópolis: Vozes, 1978.

Batchelor, Stephen. *The Awakening of the West: The Encounter of Buddhism and Western Culture.* Berkeley, CA: Parallax Press, 1994.

Baumann, Martin. "Creating a European Path to Nirvāna: Historical and Contemporary Developments of Buddhism in Europe." *Journal of Contemporary Religion* 10.1 (1995): 55–70.

———. "Global Buddhism: Developmental Periods, Regional Histories, and a New Analytical Perspective." *Journal of Global Buddhism* 2 (2001): 1–44.

———. "The Transplantation of Buddhism to Germany: Processive Modes and Strategies of Adaptation." *Method & Theory in the Study of Religion* 6.1 (1994): 35–61.

Becker, Bertha, and Claudio Egler. *Brazil: A New Regional Power in the World Economy.* Cambridge: Cambridge University Press, 1992.

Befu, Harumi. "Globalization as Human Dispersal: From the Perspective of Japan." In *Globalization and Social Change in Contemporary Japan,* ed. J. S. Eades, T. Gill, and H. Befu. Melbourne: Transpacific Press, 2000, 17–40.

———. "Globalization Theory from the Bottom Up: Japan's Contribution." *Japanese Studies* 23.1 (2003): 3–22.

Bellah, Robert. "New Religious Consciousness and the Crisis in Modernity." In *The New Religious Consciousness,* ed. Charles Glock and Robert Bellah. Berkeley: University of California Press, 1976, 333–352.

Benjamin, Walter. *Illuminations.* London: Fontana Press, 1970.

———. "Paris, Capital of the Nineteenth Century." In *Reflections: Essays, Aphorisms, Autobiographical Writings,* ed. Peter Demetz. New York: Schocken, 1978, 146–163.

Bergamo, Mônica. "Fraternidade Vermelha, Liberdade Azul." *Folha de São Paulo,* June 4, 2001, E2.

Berger, Peter. "Four Faces of Global Culture." *The National Interest* 49 (1997): 23–29.

———. *The Sacred Canopy: Elements of a Sociological Theory of Religion.* Garden City, NY: Anchor Books, Doubleday & Co., Inc, 1967.

———. "Secularization in Retreat." *The National Interest* 46 (1996): 3–12.

Berger, Peter, Brigitte Berger, and Hansfried Kellner. *The Homeless Mind: Modernization and Consciousness.* New York: Vintage Books, 1974.

Bernardes, Betina. "Brasil Já Possui Quinta Geração." *Folha de São Paulo.* October 19, 1995, E2.

———. "Comunidade de Japoneses Formam Elite em São Paulo." *Folha de São Paulo,* October 19, 1995, E10.

Bhabha, Homi. *The Location of Culture.* London: Routledge, 1994.

Birman, Patrícia. "Cultos de Possessão e Pentecostalismo no Brasil: Passagens." *Religião e Sociedade* 1.2 (1985): 44–52.

Bodiford, William. "Zen and the Art of Religious Prejudice: Efforts to Reform a Tradition of Social Discrimination." *Japanese Journal of Religious Studies* 23.1–2 (1996): 1–27.

———. "Zen in the Art of Funerals: Ritual Salvation in Japanese Buddhism." *History of Religions* 32.2 (1992): 146–164.

Bourdieu, Pierre. *Distinction: A Social Critique of the Judgement of Taste,* trans. Richard Nice. Cambridge, MA: Harvard University Press, 1984.

———. "Genesis and Structure of the Religious Field." *Comparative Social Research* 13 (1991): 1–44.

——. "The Logic of the Fields." In *An Invitation to Reflexive Sociology*, ed. Pierre Bourdieu and Loic Wacquant. Chicago: University of Chicago Press, 1992.

——. "Utopia of Endless Exploitation: The Essence of Neoliberalism." *Le Monde Diplomatique*, December 1998, 94–115.

Braer, Werner. *The Brazilian Economy: Growth and Development*. New York: Praeger, 1989.

Brandão, Carlos Rodrigues. "A Crise das Instituições Tradicionais Produtoras de Sentido." In *Misticismo e Novas Religiões*, ed. Alberto Moreira and Renée. Zicman. Petrópolis: Vozes/UFS/IFAN, 1994, 25–41.

——. "Intervenções." In *Misticismo e Novas Religiões*, ed. Alberto Moreira and Renée Zicman. Petrópolis: Vozes/UFS/IFAN, 1994, 53–58.

——. "Ser Católico: Dimensões Brasileiras." In *Religião e Identidade Nacional*, ed. Viola Sachs and Sergio Lamerão. Rio de Janeiro: Graal, 1988.

Brathwaite, Edward. *The Development of Creole Society in Jamaica 1770–1820*. Oxford: Clarendon Press, 1971.

Brown, Diane. *Umbanda Religion and Politics in Urban Brazil*. New York: Columbia University Press, 1994.

"Buda É Pop." *Revista da Folha*, July 15, 2001, 8–17.

Caldeira, Teresa. *City of Walls: Crime, Segregation, and Citizenship in São Paulo*. Berkeley: University of California Press, 2000.

Cammack, Paul. "Clientelism and Military Government in Brazil." In *Private Patronage and Public Power: Political Clientelism in the Modern State*, ed. Christopher Clapham. London: Frances Pinter, 1982, 53–75.

Campos, Nancy. "Onda Zen." *Elle*, June 1998, 91–94.

Carpenter, Robert. "Esoteric Literature as a Microcosmic Mirror of Brazil's Religious Marketplace." In *Latin American Religion in Motion*, ed. Christian Smith and Joshua Prokopy. New York: Routledge, 1999, 235–260.

——. "Religious Competition and the Spread of Alternative Spirituality in Contemporary Brazil." Ph.D. dissertation, University of California, Santa Barbara, 2001.

Carpenter, Robert, and Wade Roof. "The Transplanting of Seichō-no-ie from Japan to Brazil: Moving Beyond the Ethnic Enclave." *Journal of Contemporary Religion* 10.1 (1995): 41–53.

Carvalho, José Jorge. "Características do Fenômeno Religioso na Sociedade Contemporânea." In *O Impacto da Modernidade Sobre a Religião*, ed. Maria Clara Bingemer. São Paulo: Loyola, 1992, 133–195.

——. "An Enchanted Public Space: Religious Plurality and Modernity in Brazil." In *Through the Kaleidoscope: The Experience of Modernity in Latin America*, ed. Vivian SchellingLondon: Verso, 2000, 275–296.

——. "O Encontro de Velhas e Novas Religiões: Esboço de uma Teoria dos Estilos de Espiritualidade." In *Misticismo e Novas Religiões*, ed. Alberto Moreira and Renée Zicman. Petrópolis: Vozes/UFS/IFAN, 1994, 69–98.

Cavalcanti, Maria Laura Viveiros de Castro. "O Espiritismo." In *Sinais dos Tempos: Diversidade Religiosa no Brasil*, ed. Leila Landim. Rio de Janeiro: Instituto de Estudos da Religião, 1990.

Centro de Estudos Nipo-Brasileiros. "Pesquisa da População de Descendentes de

Japoneses Residentes no Brasil: 1987–1988." Unpublished research, Centro de Estudos Nipo-Brasileiros, São Paulo, 1990.

Chadwick, David. *Crooked Cucumber: The Life and Zen Teaching of Shunryu Suzuki*. New York: Broadway Books, 1999.

Chakrabarty, Dipesh. *Provincializing Europe: Postcolonial Thought and Historical Difference*. Princeton, NJ: Princeton University Press, 2000.

Clarke, Peter B. "Japanese New Religious Movements in Brazil: From Ethnic to Universal Religions." In *New Religions: Challenge and Response*, ed. Brian Wilson and Jamie Cresswell. London: Routledge, 1999, 197–210.

———. "Japanese 'Old,' 'New' and 'New, New' Religious Movements in Brazil." In *Japanese New Religions in the West*, ed. Peter Clarke and Jeffrey Sommers. Richmond, Surrey: Curzon, 1996, 149–161.

———. "'Pop-Star' Priest and the Catholic Response to the 'Explosion' of Evangelical Protestantism in Brazil: The Beginning of the End of the 'Walkout'?" *Journal of Contemporary Religion* 14.2 (1999): 203–216.

Clifford, James. *Routes: Travel and Translation in the Late Twentieth Century*. Cambridge, MA: Harvard University Press, 1997.

Coelho, Nelson. *Zen: Experiência Direta da Libertação*. Belo Horizonte, Brazil: Itatiaia, 1978.

Coleman, James. "The New Buddhism: Some Empirical Findings." In *American Buddhism: Methods and Findings in Recent Scholarship*, ed. Duncan Williams and Christopher Queen. Richmond, Surrey: Curzon, 1999, 91–99.

———. *The New Buddhism: The Western Transformation of an Ancient Tradition*. Oxford: Oxford University Press, 2001.

Comaroff, Jean, and John Comaroff. *Ethnography and the Historical Imagination*. Boulder, CO: Westview Press, 1992.

———. "Introduction." In *Modernity and its Malcontents: Ritual and Power in Postcolonial Africa*. Chicago: University of Chicago Press, 1993.

———. *Millennial Capitalism and the Culture of Neoliberalism* (Durham, NC: Duke University Press, 2001).

Corrêa, Norton. "Para Muitos Trabalhos a Gente Precisa Invocar a Linha Oriental: Observações sobre as Representações de 'Oriente' em Religiões Afro-Brasileiras." Paper read at the Twenty-Third Encontro Anual da Anpocs, Caxambu (Minas Gerais State), 1999.

Coutinho, Suzana Ramos. "Jesus on Line: Comunidades Religiosas e Conflito na Rede." *Omnes Urbes—Todas as Aldeias—Revista Virtual de Antropologia* 3 (2001): 1–11.

Cox, Harvey G. "The Myth of the Twentieth Century: The Rise and Fall of Secularization." *Japanese Journal of Religious Studies* 27.1–2 (2000): 1–13.

Croce, José Elias. *Seitas e Heresias: O Engano das Falsas Religiões, Jovens e Adultos Dominical*. Rio de Janeiro: Betel, 2000.

Cruz, Valdo. "Topetada." *Folha de São Paulo*, June 7, 2001, A2.

Cush, Denise. "British Buddhism and the New Age." *Journal of Contemporary Religion* 11.2 (1996): 195–208.

Da Matta, Roberto. *O Que Faz o Brasil, Brasil?* Rio de Janeiro: Rocco, 1994.

de Castro Rocha, João Cezar. "Marinetti Goes to South America: Confrontos e Diálogos do Futurismo na America do Sul." Ph.D. dissertation, Stanford University, 2002.

Deleuze, Gilles, and Felix Guattari. *A Thousand Plateaus: Capitalism and Schizophrenia*. Minneapolis: University of Minnesota Press, 1987.

Derrida, Jacques. "Des Tours de Babel." In *Difference in Translation*, ed. Joseph F. Graham. Ithaca, NY: Cornell University Press, 1985, 165–248.

Des Chene, Mary. "Locating the Past." In *Anthropological Locations: Boundaries and Grounds of a Field Science,* ed. Akhil Gupta and James Ferguson. Berkeley: University of California Press, 1997, 66–85.

Droogers, André. "Syncretism: The Problem of Definition, the Definition of the Problem." In *Dialogue and Syncretism: An Interdisciplinary Approach,* ed. Jerald D. Gort et al. Grand Rapids, MI: William Eerdman, 1989, 7–24.

Eades, Carla, et al. "Houses of Everlasting Bliss: Globalization and the Production of Buddhist Altars in Hikone." In *Globalization and Social Change in Contemporary Japan,* ed. Jerry S. Eades, Tom Gill, and Harumi Befu. Melbourne: Transpacific Press, 2000, 159–179.

Eakin, Marshall. *Brazil: The Once and Future Country.* New York: St Martin's Griffin, 1998.

Ellwood, Robert, ed. *Zen in American Life and Letters.* Malibu: Udena Publications, University of Southern California, 1987.

"Em Busca do Zen." *Veja,* June 17, 1998, 25.

Farias Brito, R. *O Mundo Interno: Ensaio Sobre os Dados Geraes da Philosophia do Espírito.* Rio de Janeiro: Revista dos Tribunais, 1914.

Faure, Bernard. *Chan Insights and Oversights: An Epistemological Critique of the Chan Tradition.* Princeton, NJ: Princeton University Press, 1993.
    . *Visions of Power: Imagining Medieval Japanese Buddhism,* trans. P. Brooks. Princeton, NJ: Princeton University Press, 1993.

Featherstone, Mike. *Consumer Culture and Postmodernism.* London: Sage, 1991.

Featherstone, Mike, and Scott Lash. "Globalization, Modernity and the Spatialization of Social Theory: An Introduction." In *Global Modernities,* ed. Mike Featherstone, Scott Lash, and Roland Robertson. London: Sage, 1995, 1–24.

Fields, Rick. "Divided Dharma: White Buddhists, Ethnic Buddhists, and Racism." In *The Faces of Buddhism in America,* ed. Charles Prebish and Kenneth Tanaka. Berkeley: University of California Press, 1998, 196–206.

Finke, Roger, and Rodney Stark. *The Churching of America, 1776–1990: Winners and Losers in our Religious Economy.* New Brunswick, NJ: Rutgers University Press, 1992.

Fisch, Michael. "The Rise of Chapel Wedding in Japan: Simulation and Performance." *Japanese Journal of Religious Studies* 28.1–2 (2001): 57–76.

Fontela, Orides. *Rosácea.* São Paulo: Roswitha Kempf, 1986.

Foye, Addie. "Buddhists in America: A Short, Biased View. *Tricycle* IV:1 (1994): 57.

Franchetti, Paulo. "Notas Sobre a História do Haikai no Brasil." *Revista de Letras,* UNESP 34 (1994): 197–213.

García Canclini, Néstor. "Contradictory Modernities and Globalisation in Latin America." In *Through the Kaleidoscope: The Experience of Modernity in Latin America,* ed. Vivian Schelling. London: Verso, 2000, 37–52.

——. *Hybrid Cultures: Strategies for Entering and Leaving Modernity*, trans. C. L. Chiappari and S. L. López. Minneapolis: University of Minnesota Press, 1995.

——. "The State of War and The State of Hybridization." In *Without Guarantees: In Honour of Stuart Hall*, ed. Paul Gilroy, Lawrence Grossberg, and Angela McRobbie. London: Verso, 2000, 38–51.

Gonçalves, Ricardo Mário. "O Budismo Japonês no Brasil: Reflexões de um Observador Participante." In *Sinais dos Tempos: Diversidade Religiosa no Brasil*, ed. Leila Landim. Rio de Janeiro: Instituto de Estudos da Religião, 1990, 167–180.

——. "A Religião no Japão na Época da Emigração Para o Brasil e Suas Repercussões em nosso país." In *O Japonês em São Paulo e no Brasil*. São Paulo: Centro de Estudos Nipo-Brasileiros, 1971, 58–73.

——. "A Trajetória de um Budista Brasileiro." In *O Budismo no Brasil*, ed. Frank Usarski. São Paulo: Lorosae, 2002, 171–192.

Gregory, Peter. "Describing the Elephant: Buddhism in America." *Religion and American Culture: A Journal of Interpretation* 11.2 (2001): 233–263.

——. "Review of The New Buddhism: The Western Transformation of an Ancient Tradition." *Tricycle* X.3 (2001): 108.

Gross, Rita M. *Buddhism After Patriarchy: A Feminist History, Analysis, and Reconstruction of Buddhism*. Albany: SUNY Press, 1993.

Guaiume, Silvana. "Igreja Pode Perder 9% dos Fiéis Até 2010: Bispos Discutiram Pesquisa sobre Migração de Católicos na Assembléia da CNBB." *O Estado de São Paulo*, May 2, 2003, 9.

Guia da Cultura Japonesa em São Paulo. São Paulo: Aliança Cultural Brasil-Japão, 1989.

Guibu, Fabio. "Prefeito de Recife Medita para Governar." *Folha de São Paulo*, December 29, 2002, C3.

Guilbaut, Serge. *How New York Stole the Idea of Modern Art: Abstract Expressionism, Freedom and the Cold War*, trans. A. Goldhammer. Chicago: University of Chicago Press, 1983.

Gupta, Akhil, and James Ferguson. "Discipline and Practice: 'The Field' as the Site, Method, and Location in Anthropology." In *Anthropological Locations: Boundaries and Grounds of a Field Science*, ed. Akhil Gupta and James Ferguson. Berkeley: University of California Press, 1997.

Habermas, Jürgen. "Modernity: An Incomplete Project." In *Postmodern Culture*, ed. Hal Foster. London: Pluto Press, 1987, 3–15.

Hall, Stuart. "The West and the Rest: Discourse and Power." In *Formations of Modernity*, ed. Stuart Hall and Bram Gieben. Cambridge: Polity Press, 1992, 225–320.

Hallisey, Charles. "Roads Taken and Not Taken in the Study of Theravāda Buddhism." In *Curators of the Buddha: The Study of Buddhism under Colonialism*, ed. D. Lopez. Chicago: University of Chicago Press, 1995.

Handa, Tomoo. *O Imigrante Japonês: História da sua Vida no Brasil*. São Paulo: T.A. Queiroz, Centro de Estudos Nipo-Brasileiros, 1987.

Hannerz, Ulf. "Cosmopolitans and Locals in World Culture." In *Global Culture: Nationalism, Globalization and Modernity*, ed. Mike Featherstone. London: Sage, 1992, 237–251.

——. *Cultural Complexity: Studies in the Social Organization of Meaning.* New York: Columbia University Press, 1992.

——. *Transnational Connections, Cultures, People, Places.* London: Routledge, 1996.

——. "The World in Creolisation." *Africa* 57.4 (1987): 546–559.

Hayes, Richard P. "The Internet as a Window onto American Buddhism." In *American Buddhism: Methods and Findings in Recent Scholarship*, ed. Duncan Williams and Christopher Queen. Richmond, Surrey: Curzon, 1999, 168–179.

Heelas, Paul, and Linda Woodhead. "Homeless Minds Today?" In *Peter Berger and the Study of Religion*, ed. Linda Woodhead, Paul Heelas, and David Martin. London: Routledge, 2001, 43–72.

Heisig, James W., and John C. Maraldo, eds. *Rude Awakenings: Zen, the Kyoto School and the Question of Nationalism.* Honolulu: University of Hawai'i Press, 1994.

Hess, David. "Hierarchy, Heterodoxy, and the Construction of Brazilian Religious Therapies." In *The Brazilian Puzzle: Culture on the Borderlands of the Western World*, ed. David Hess and Roberto da Matta. New York: Columbia University Press, 1995, 180–208.

——. *Samba in the Night: Spiritism in Brazil.* New York: Columbia University Press, 1994.

——. *Spiritists and Scientists: Ideology, Spiritism and Brazilian Culture.* University Park: Pennsylvania State University Press, 1991.

Hess, David, and Roberto da Matta. *The Brazilian Puzzle: Culture on the Borderlands of the Western World.* New York: Columbia University Press, 1995.

Hills, Ben. *Japan Behind the Lines.* Sydney: Hodder & Stoughton, 1996.

Hiroishi, Tomoyo. "La Búsquedad De La Identidade—In Search of My Identity." In *Encounters: People of Asian Descent in the Americas*, ed. Roshni Rustomji-Kerns, Rajini Srikanth, and Leny Mendoza Strobel. Lanham, MD: Rowman & Littlefield, 1999, 56–57.

Hobsbawm, Eric. "Introduction: Inventing Traditions." In *The Invention of Traditions*, ed. E. Hobsbawm and T. Ranger. Cambridge: Cambridge University Press, 1983.

Hosokawa, Shuhei. "Nationalizing Chō-Chō-San: The Signification of 'Butterfly Singers' in a Japanese-Brazilian Community." *Japanese Studies* 19.3 (1999): 253–268.

Hur, Nam-Lin. "The Sōtō Sect and Japanese Military Imperialism in Korea." *Japanese Journal of Religious Studies* 26.1–2 (1999): 107–134.

Ireland, Rowan. *Kingdoms Come: Religion and Politics in Brazil.* Pittsburgh, PA: University of Pittsburgh Press, 1999.

Iriye, Akira. "Japan's Drive to Great Power Status." In *The Emergence of Meiji Japan*, ed. Marius Jansen. Cambridge: Cambridge University Press, 1995, 268–369.

Ishii, Kenji. "Urbanization, Depopulation, and Religion." In *Religion in Japanese Culture*, ed. Noriyoshi Tamaru and David Read. Tokyo: Kodansha International, 1996, 156–170.

Iwabuchi, Koichi. *Recentering Globalization: Popular Culture and Japanese Transnationalism.* Durham, NC: Duke University Press, 2002.

Jaffe, Richard. *Neither Monk nor Layman: Clerical Marriage in Modern Japanese Buddhism.* Princeton, NJ: Princeton University Press, 2001.

Johnson, Randal. "Tupy or not Tupy: Cannibalism and Nationalism in Contemporary

Brazilian Culture." In *Modern Latin American Fiction: A Survey,* ed. J. King. London: Faber and Faber, 1987, 41–59.

Jungblut, Airton Luiz. "Crentes Internautas: Os Evangélicos Brasileiros na Internet." Paper read at the Eighth Jornadas sobre Alternativas Religiosas na América Latina, São Paulo, 1998.

Kashima, Tetsuden. *Buddhism in America: The Social Organization of an Ethnic Religious Institution.* Westport, CT: Greenwood Press, 1977.

Kawahashi, Noriko. "'Jizoku' (Priests' Wives) in Sōtō Zen Buddhism: An Ambiguous Category." *Japanese Journal of Religious Studies* 22.1–2 (1995): 161–183.

Kawahashi, Noriko, and Masako Kuroki, eds. "Feminism and Religion in Contemporary Japan. Special Issue." *Japanese Journal of Religious Studies* 30.3–4 (2003).

Kojima, Shigeru. "Um Estudo sobre os Japoneses e Seus Descendentes em Curitiba." Master's thesis, Universidade Federal do Paraná, 1991.

Korom, Frank. "Memory, Innovation, and Emergent Ethnicity: The Creolization of an Indo-Trinidadian Performance." *Diaspora* 3.2 (1994): 135–155.

Kotscho, Ricardo. "Itamar Encarna Fase Zen de Olho no Planalto." *Folha de São Paulo,* June 3, 2001, A10.

Koyama, Tsuguo. "Japoneses na Amazônia: Alguns Aspectos do Processo de sua Integração Sócio-cultural." In *A Presença Japonesa no Brasil,* ed. Hiroshi Saito. São Paulo: Edusp/T. A.Queiroz, 1980, 11–28.

Lara, Odete. *Meus Passos em Busca da Paz.* Rio de Janeiro: Record, 1997.

le Goff, Jacques. *The Medieval Imagination,* trans. A. Goldhammer. Chicago: The University of Chicago Press, 1992.

Lesser, Jeffrey. *Negotiating National Identity: Immigrants, Minorities, and the Struggle for Ethnicity in Brazil.* Durham, NC: Duke University Press, 1999.

———, ed. *Searching for Home Abroad: Japanese Brazilians and Transnationalism.* Durham, NC: Duke University Press, 2003.

Linger, Daniel. *No One Home: Brazilian Selves Remade in Japan.* Stanford, CA: Stanford University Press, 2001.

Lobato, Eliane. "Um Budismo de Resultados." *IstoÉ,* May 9, 2001, 80–85.

Lone, Stewart. *The Japanese Community in Brazil, 1908–1940: Between Samurai and Carnival.* Houndmills: Palgrave, 2001.

Lopes, Ana Cristina. "Histórias da Diaspora Tibetana." *Revista USP/Dossiê Magia* 31 (1996): 152–162.

Lopez, Donald, ed. *Curators of the Buddha: The Study of Buddhism under Colonialism.* Chicago: University of Chicago Press, 1995.

———. "Introduction." In *A Modern Buddhist Bible: Essential Readings from East and West,* ed. Donald Lopez. Boston: Beacon Press, 2002, vii–xli.

———. "New Age Orientalism: The Case of Tibet." *Tricycle* 11 (spring 1994): 37–57.

———. *Prisoners of Shangri-La: Tibetan Buddhism in the West.* Chicago: University of Chicago Press, 1998.

Lowe, Lisa. *Critical Terrains: French and British Orientalisms.* Ithaca, NY: Cornell University Press, 1994.

Macedo, Carmen Cinira. *A Imagem do Eterno: Religiões no Brasil.* São Paulo: Moderna, 1989.

Machado, Maria das Dores. *Carismáticos e Pentecostais: Adesão Religiosa na Esfera Familiar.* Campinas: Autores Associados, 1996.

Machado, Ubiratan. *Os Intelectuais e o Espiritismo: De Castro Alves a Machado de Assis.* Rio de Janeiro: Edições Antares, Instituto Nacional do Livro, 1983.

Maeyama, Takashi. "Ancestor, Emperor and Immigrant: Religion and Group Identification of the Japanese in Rural Brazil (1908-1950)." *Journal of Interamerican Studies and World Affairs* 14 (1972): 151-182.

———. "O Imigrante e a Religião: Estudo de uma Seita Religiosa Japonesa em São Paulo." Master's thesis, Escola de Sociologia e Política, São Paulo, 1967.

———. "Japanese Religion in Southern Brazil: Change and Syncretism." *Latin American Studies* 6 (1983): 181-238.

———. "Religion, Kinship, and the Middle Classes of the Japanese in Urban Brazil." *Latin American Studies* 5 (1983): 57-82.

Magnani, José Guilherme. *O Brasil da Nova Era.* São Paulo: Edusp, 2000.

———. "O Neo-esoterismo na Cidade." *Revista USP/Dossiê Magia* 31 (1996): 6-15.

Marcus, George. "Beyond Malinowski and After *Writing Culture*: On the Future of Cultural Anthropology and the Predicament of Ethnography." *The Australian Journal of Anthropology* 13.2 (2000): 191-199.

———. "Ethnography in/of the World System: The Emergence of Multi-Sited Ethnography." In *Ethnography through Thick and Thin*, ed. G. Marcus. Princeton, NJ: Princeton University Press, 1998, 79-104.

Marcus, George, and Michael M. Fisher. *Anthropology as Cultural Critique: An Experimental Moment in the Human Sciences.* Chicago: University of Chicago Press, 1986.

Margolis, Maxine. *Little Brazil: An Ethnography of Brazilian Immigrants in New York City.* Princeton, NJ: Princeton University Press, 1994.

Martin, David. *Tongues of Fire: The Explosion of Protestantism in Latin America.* Oxford: Basil Blackwell, 1991.

———. "Towards Eliminating the Concept of Secularisation." In *Penguin Survey of the Social Sciences*, ed. J. Gould. Baltimore, MD: Penguin, 1965, 169-182.

Massey, Doreen. *Space, Place and Gender.* Cambridge, UK: Polity Press, 1994.

Masuda Goga, Hidekazu. *O Haicai no Brasil.* São Paulo: Oriento, 1988.

Matsue, Regina Yoshie. "O Budismo da Terra Pura em Brasília." In *O Budismo no Brasil*, ed. Frank Usarski. São Paulo: Lorosae, 2002, 193-219.

Matsuoka, Hideaki. "Blemish on Our Spiritists: How Brazilians Believe in a Japanese New Religion Called the Church of World Messianity." Ph.D. dissertation, University of California, Berkeley, 2000.

———. "'Messianity Makes a Person Useful': Describing Differences in a Japanese Religion in Brazil." *Japanese Journal of Religious Studies* 28.1-2 (2001): 77-102.

Mayrink, José Maria. "Fidelidade à Roma, O Apelo do Papa à CNBB." *O Estado de São Paulo*, January 24, 2003, 12.

McAra, Sally A. "The Land of the Stupa and Sacred Puriri: Creating Buddhism in the Tararu Valley, New Zealand." Master's thesis, University of Auckland, 2000.

Metcalf, Franz A. "Why Do Americans Practice Buddhism?" Ph.D. dissertation, University of Chicago, 2000.

Meyer, Regina. "Metrópole e Urbanismo: São Paulo Anos 50." Ph.D. dissertation, Universidade de São Paulo, 1991.

Moraes, Maurício. "Templos Revestem Budistas de Novas Visões de Mundo." *O Estado de São Paulo*, October, 27, 1998, 4–5.

Mori, Koichi. "O Processo de 'Amarelamento' das Tradicionais Religiões Brasileiras de Possessão: Mundo Religioso de uma Okinawana." *Estudos Japoneses* 18 (1998): 57–76.

———. "Vida Religiosa dos Japoneses e seus Descendentes Residentes no Brasil e Religiões de Origem Japonesa." In *Uma Epopéia Moderna: 80 Anos da Imigração Japonesa no Brasil*, ed. Katsunori Wakisaka. São Paulo: Hucitec/Sociedade Brasileira de Cultura Japonesa, 1992, 559–601.

Morioka, Kiyomi. *Religion in Changing Japanese Society.* Tokyo: University of Tokyo Press, 1975.

Morreale, Don, ed. *The Complete Guide to Buddhist America.* Boston: Shambhala, 1998.

Nakamaki, Hirochika. "A Honmon Butsuryū-shū no Brasil Através de Registros do Arcebispo Nissui Ibaragui." In *O Budismo no Brasil*, ed. Frank Usarski. São Paulo: Lorosae, 2002, 75–105.

———. "Mutações Contemporâneas de Religiões Japonesas: Principalmente o Budismo no Brasil e nos Estados Unidos." *Senri Ethnological Reports* 1 (1994): 87–112.

Nattier, Jan. "Buddhism Comes to Main Street." *Wilson Quarterly* 21 (1997): 72–80.

———. "Buddhist Studies in the Post-Colonial Age." *Journal of the American Academy of Religion* 65.2 (1997): 469–485.

———. "Visible and Invisible: Jan Nattier on the Politics of Representation in Buddhist America." *Tricycle* 17 (fall 1995): 42–49.

———. "Who Is a Buddhist? Charting the Landscape of Buddhist America." In *The Faces of Buddhism in America*, ed. Charles Prebish and Kenneth Tanaka. Berkeley: University of California Press, 1998, 183–195.

Needell, Jeffrey D. *A Tropical Belle Epoque: Elite, Culture and Society in Turn-of-the-Century Rio de Janeiro.* Cambridge: Cambridge University Press, 1987.

Negrão, Lísias Nogueira. "Umbanda: Entre a Cruz e a Encruzilhada." *Tempo Social, Revista de Sociologia* 5.1–2 (1994): 113–122.

Noble, Greg, and Paul Tabar. "On Being Lebanese-Australian: Hybridity, Essentialism and Strategy among Arabic-speaking Youth. In *Arab-Australians: Citizenship and Belonging*, ed. Ghassan Hage. Melbourne: Melbourne University Press, 2002, 128–144.

Numrich, Paul. *Old Wisdom in the New World: Americanization of Two Immigrant Theravada Buddhist Temples.* Knoxville: University of Tennessee Press, 1996.

———. "Two Buddhisms Further Reconsidered." *Contemporary Buddhism* 4.1 (2003): 55–78.

Okumura, Shokaku. "Editor's Note." *Zen Quarterly* 10.2 (1998): 1.

Oliveira, Roberto. "Fé de Pernas Cruzadas." *Revista da Folha*, July 15, 2001, 8–13.

Oliven, Ruben. "Brazil: The Modern in the Tropics." In *Through the Kaleidoscope: The Experience of Modernity in Latin America*, ed. Vivian Schelling. London: Verso, 2000, 53–71.

Ortiz, Renato. *A Morte Branca do Feiticeiro Negro: Umbanda e Sociedade Brasileira.* São Paulo: Brasiliense, 1999.

———. "Popular Culture, Modernity and Nation." In *Through the Kaleidoscope: The Experience of Modernity in Latin America*, ed. Vivian Schelling. London: Verso, 2000, 127–147.

Ota, Hirohito. "Primeiros Missionários Budistas no Peru: Cem Anos de História Desconhecida." *Caminho Zen* 8.3 (2003): 4–15.

Paiva, José Geraldo. "Instituição Religiosa Perfeita Liberdade." In *Sinais dos Tempos: Diversidade Religiosa no Brasil*, ed. Leila Landim. Rio de Janeiro: Instituto de Estudos da Religião, 1990, 187–193.

Palomino, Erika. "Conheça os Millies." *Folha de São Paulo*, March 21, 1998, 1–3.

Papastergiadis, Nikos. *Dialogues in the Diasporas: Essays and Conversations on Cultural Identities*. London: Rivers Oram Press, 1998.

———. "Tracing Hybridity in Theory." In *Debating Cultural Hybridity: Multicultural Identities and the Politics of Anti-Racism*, ed. Pnina Werbner and Tariq Modood. London: Zed Books, 1997, 257–281.

Passaro, Joanne. "'You Can't Take the Subway to the Field!': 'Village' Epistemologies in the Global Village." In *Anthropological Locations: Boundaries and Grounds of a Field Science*, ed. Akhil Gupta and James Ferguson. Berkeley: University of California Press, 1997, 147–162.

Patt, David. "Who's Zoomin' Who? The Commodification of Buddhism in the American Marketplace." *Tricycle* 40 (summer 2001): 45–47, 91–98.

Pereira, Ronan. "O Budismo Leigo da Sōka Gakkai no Brasil: Da Revolução Humana à Utopia Mundial." Ph.D. dissertation, Universidade de Campinas, 2001.

———. "Religiosidade Japonesa e Brasileira: Aproximações Possíveis." Paper read at the Eleventh Encontro Nacional de Professores Universitários de Língua, Literatura e Cultura Japonesa, Universidade de Brasília, 2000.

Pereira, Sergio. "Society-Individual and Postmodern Condition: Understanding the Explosion of Pentecostalism in Brazil." Ph.D. dissertation, University of Notre Dame, Indiana, 2000.

Perrone, Charles A. *Masters of Contemporary Brazilian Song: MPB 1965–1985*. Austin: University of Texas Press, 1989.

Pierce, Lori Anne. "Constructing American Buddhisms: Discourses of Race and Religion in Territorial Hawai'i." Ph.D. dissertation, University of Hawai'i, 2000.

Pierucci, Antônio. "A Encruzilhada da Fé." *Folha de São Paulo*, May 19, 2002, 4–7.

Pierucci, Antônio, and Reginaldo Prandi. "Assim Como Não Era no Princípio: Religião e Ruptura." In *A Realidade Social das Religiões no Brasil: Religião Sociedade e Política*, ed. A. Pierucci and R. Prandi. São Paulo: USP/Hucitec, 1996.

———, eds. *A Realidade Social das Religiões no Brasil: Religião Sociedade e Política*. São Paulo: USP/Hucitec, 1996.

Pieterse, Jan N. "Globalization and Hybridization." In *Global Modernities*, ed. Mike Featherstone, Scott Lash, and Roland Robertson. London: Sage, 1995, 45–68.

Prandi, Reginaldo. "As Religiões, a Cidade e o Mundo." In *A Realidade Social das Religiões no Brasil: Religião Sociedade e Política*, ed. Antônio Pierucci and Reginaldo Prandi. São Paulo: USP/Hucitec, 1996, 23–34.

———. "Perto da Magia, Longe da Política." In *A Realidade Social das Religiões no Brasil:*

Religião Sociedade e Política, ed. Antônio Pierucci and Reginaldo Prandi. São Paulo: USP/Hucitec, 1996, 93–105.

———. "Religião Paga, Conversão e Serviço." In *A Realidade Social das Religiões no Brasil: Religião Sociedade e Política*, ed. Antônio Pierucci and Reginaldo Prandi. São Paulo: USP/Hucitec, 1996, 257–273.

Prebish, Charles. *American Buddhism*. North Scituate, MA: Duxbury Press, 1979.

———. *Luminous Passage: The Practice and Study of Buddhism in America*. Berkeley: University of California Press, 1999.

———. "Two Buddhisms Reconsidered." *Buddhist Studies Review* 10.2 (1993): 187–206.

Preston, David L. *The Social Organization of Zen: Constructing Transcultural Reality*. Cambridge: Cambridge University Press, 1988.

Prothero, Stephen. *The White Buddhist: The Asian Odyssey of Henry Steel Olcott*. Bloomington: Indiana University Press, 1996.

Pye, Michael. "The Transplantation of Religions." *Numen* 16 (1969): 234–239.

Queen, Christopher, ed. *Engaged Buddhism in the West*. Boston: Wisdom Publications, 2000.

———. "Introduction." In *American Buddhism: Methods and Findings in Recent Scholarship*, ed. Duncan Williams and Christopher Queen. Richmond, Surrey: Curzon, 1999, xiv–xxxvii.

Ray, Gary L. "Buddhist Terms Your Guru Never Taught You." *CyberSangha* (spring 1996): 13.

Reader, Ian. "Contemporary Zen Buddhist Tracts for the Laity: Grassroots Buddhism in Japan." In *Religions of Japan in Practice*, ed. George J. Tanabe. Princeton, NJ: Princeton University Press, 1999.

———. *Religion in Contemporary Japan*. Honolulu: University of Hawai'i Press, 1991.

———. "Transformations and Changes in the Teachings of the Sōtō Zen Buddhist Sect." *Japanese Religions* 14.1 (1985): 28–48.

———. "Zazenless Zen? The Position of Zazen in Institutional Zen Buddhism." *Japanese Religions* 14.3 (1986): 7–27.

Robbins, Bruce. *Secular Vocations: Intellectuals, Professionalism, Culture*. London: Verso, 1993.

Robbins, Bruce, and Pheng Cheah. *Cosmopolitics: Thinking and Feeling Beyond the Nation*. Minneapolis: University of Minnesota Press, 1998.

Rocha, Cristina. "The Appropriation of Zen Buddhism in Brazil." *Japan Studies Review* 4 (2000): 33–52.

———. "Being a Zen Buddhist Brazilian: Juggling Multiple Religious Identities in the Land of Catholicism." In *Buddhist Missionaries in the Era of Globalization*, ed. Linda Learman. Honolulu: University of Hawai'i Press, 2004, 140–161.

———. "Being Zen Buddhist in the Land of Catholicism." *Revista de Estudos da Religião* 1.1 (2001): 57–72.

———. "The Brazilian *Imaginaire* of Zen: Global Influences, Rhizomatic Forms." In *Japanese Religions In and Beyond the Japanese Diaspora*, ed. Ronan Pereira and Hideaki Matsuoka. Berkeley: Center for Japanese Studies, University of California, forthcoming.

———. "Catholicism and Zen Buddhism: A Vision of the Religious Field in Brazil." In

The End of Religion? Religion in an Age of Globalization, ed. C. Cusack and P. Oldmeadow. Sydney: University of Sydney Press, 2001, 249–265.

———. "Identity and Tea Ceremony in Brazil." *Japanese Studies* 19.3 (1999): 287–295.

———. "Se Você se Deparar com Buda, Mate Buda!: Reflexões sobre a reapropriação do Zen-Budismo no Brasil." In *O Budismo no Brasil*, ed. Frank Usarski. São Paulo: Lorosae, 2002, 221–251.

———. "Tea Ceremony in Japan and Its Appropriation in Brazil: A Metaphor of the Japanese Spirit." In *Roots and Rituals: The Construction of Ethnic Identities*, ed. John Helsloot, Ton Dekker, and Carla Wijers. Amsterdam: Het Spinhuis, 2000, 527–537.

———. "Zen Buddhism in Brazil: Japanese or Brazilian?" *Journal of Global Buddhism* 1 (2000): 31–55.

Rocha Reis, Rossana, and Teresa Sales. *Cenas do Brasil Migrante*. São Paulo: Boitempo Editorial, 1999.

Rodríguez, Ricardo Vélez. "La Filosofía en Latinoamérica: Originalidad Y Método." Paper presented at the Twentieth World Congress of Philosophy, University of Boston, 1998.

Roof, Wade Clark. *Spiritual Supermarket: Baby Boomers and the Remaking of American Religion*. Princeton, NJ: Princeton University Press, 1999.

Rustomji-Kerns, Roshni, Rajini Srikanth, and Leny Mendoza Strobel, eds. *Encounters: People of Asian Descent in the Americas*. Lanham, MD: Rowman & Littlefield, 1999.

Sahlins, Marshall. "Goodbye to *Tristes Tropes*: Ethnography in the Context of Modern World History." *Journal of Modern History* 65 (1993): 1–25.

Said, Edward. *Orientalism: Western Conceptions of the Orient*. London: Penguin Books, 1995.

Saito, Hiroshi. "Participação, Mobilidade e Identidade." In *A Presença Japonesa no Brasil*, ed. H. Saito. São Paulo: T. A. Queiroz/Edusp, 1980, 81–89.

Saito, Hiroshi, and Takashi Maeyama. *Assimilação e Integração dos Japoneses no Brasil*. São Paulo: Edusp/Vozes, 1973.

Sakai, Naoki. "Modernity and Its Critique: The Problem of Universalism and Particularism." In *Postmodernism and Japan*, ed. Masao Miyoshi and H. D. Harootunian. Durham NC: Duke University Press, 1989, 93–122.

Sales, Teresa. "Identidade Étnica entre Imigrantes Brasileiros na Região de Boston, EUA." In *Cenas do Brasil Migrante*, ed. Rossana Rocha Reis and Teresa Sales. São Paulo: Boitempo, 1999, 17–44.

Sanchis, Pierre. "O Campo Religioso Contemporâneo no Brasil." In *Globalização e Religião*, ed. Ari Pedro Oro and Carlos Alberto Steil. Petrópolis: Vozes, 1997, 103–115.

Schaden, Egon. "Imigrantes Alemães e Japoneses: Uma Visão Comparativa." In *A Presença Japonesa no Brasil*, ed. Hiroshi Saito. São Paulo: T. A. Queiroz/Edusp, 1980, 135–152.

Schelling, Vivian. "Introduction: Reflections on the Experience of Modernity in Latin America." In *Through the Kaleidoscope: The Experience of Modernity in Latin America*, ed. V. Schelling. London: Verso, 2000, 1–33.

———, ed. *Through the Kaleidoscope: The Experience of Modernity in Latin America*. London: Verso, 2000.

Schneider, Clarissa. "Estilo Zen." *Casa Vogue*, 1997, 103–115.

Schwarz, Roberto. *Misplaced Ideas: Essays on Brazilian Culture.* London: Verso, 1992.

Seager, Richard H. *Buddhism in America.* New York: Columbia University Press, 1999.

Segato, Rita Laura. "Formação de Diversidade: Nação e Opções Religiosas no Contexto da Globalização." In *Globalização e Religião*, ed. Ari Pedro Oro and Carlos Alberto Steil. Petrópolis: Vozes, 1997, 219–248.

Sevcenko, Nicolau. *Orfeu Extático na Metrópole: São Paulo, Sociedade e Cultura nos Frementes Anos 20.* São Paulo: Companhia das Letras, 1992.

———. "Peregrinations, Visions and the City: From Canudos to Brasília, the Backlands Become the City and the City Becomes the Backlands." In *Through the Kaleidoscope: The Experience of Modernity in Latin America*, ed. Vivian Schelling. London: Verso, 2000, 75–107.

Sharf, Robert. "Buddhist Modernism and the Rhetoric of Meditative Experience." *Numen* 42 (1995): 228–283."

———. Whose Zen? Zen Nationalism Revisited." In *Rude Awakenings: Zen, the Kyoto School, and the Question of Nationalism*, ed. James W. Heisig and John C. Maraldo. Honolulu: University of Hawai'i Press, 1994, 40–51.

———. "The Zen of Japanese Nationalism." In *Curators of the Buddha: The Study of Buddhism under Colonialism*, ed. Donald Lopez. Chicago: University of Chicago Press, 1995, 107–160.

Shupe, Anson. "Sōka Gakkai and the Slippery Slope from Militancy to Accommodation." In *Religion and Society in Modern Japan*, ed. Mark Mullins. Berkeley, CA: Asian Humanities Press, 1993, 231–238.

Skidmore, Thomas. *Black into White: Race and Nationality in Brazilian Thought.* New York: Oxford University Press, 1974.

Smith, Christian, and Joshua Prokopy. *Latin American Religion in Motion.* New York: Routledge, 1999.

Smith, Robert J. *Ancestor Worship in Contemporary Japan.* Stanford, CA: Stanford University Press, 1974.

———. "The Ethnic Japanese in Brazil." *The Journal of Japanese Studies* 5.1 (1979): 53–70.

Soares, Luis Eduardo. "Religioso Por Natureza: Cultura Alternativa e Misticismo Ecológico no Brasil." In *Sinais dos Tempos: Diversidade Religiosa no Brasil*, ed. Leila Landim. Rio de Janeiro: Instituto de Estudos da Religião, 1989, 121–144.

Sollors, Werner. *Beyond Ethnicity: Consent and Descent in American Culture.* Oxford: Oxford University Press, 1986.

Souza Martins, José de. "The Hesitations of the Modern and the Contradictions of Modernity in Brazil." In *Through the Kaleidoscope: The Experience of Modernity in Latin America*, ed. Vivian Schelling. London: Verso, 2000, 248–274.

Spivak, Gayatri. *Outside the Teaching Machine.* London: Routledge, 1993.

———. *The Post-Colonial Critic: Interviews, Strategies, Dialogues.* New York: Routledge, 1990.

Spuler, Michelle. *Developments in Australian Buddhism: Facets of the Diamond.* London: Routledge Curzon, 2003.

Stark, Rodney. "Secularization, R. I. P." *Sociology of Religion* 60.3 (1999): 249–273.

Stark, Rodney, and William S. Bainbridge. *The Future of Religion: Secularization, Revival and Cult Formation.* Berkeley: University of California Press, 1985.

Stewart, Charles. "Syncretism and Its Synonyms: Reflections on Cultural Mixing." *Diacritics* 29.3 (1999): 40–62.

Stewart, Charles, and Rosalind Shaw. "Introduction: Problematizing Syncretism." In *Syncretism/Anti-syncretism: The Politics of Religious Synthesis*, ed. Charles Stewart and Rosalind Shaw. London: Routledge, 1994, 1–26.

Stoddard, Eve, and Grant H. Cornwell. "Cosmopolitan or Mongrel? Créolité, Hybridity and 'Douglarisation' in Trinidad." *European Journal of Cultural Studies* 2.3 (1999): 331–353.

Stoll, David. *Is Latin America Turning Protestant? The Politics of Evangelical Growth.* Berkeley: University of California Press, 1990.

Suzuki, D. T. *Essays in Zen Buddhism.* New York: Grove Press, 1961.

———. *Zen and Japanese Culture.* New York: MJF Books, 1959.

Suzuki, Shunryū. *Zen Mind, Beginner's Mind: Informal Talks on Zen Meditation and Practice.* New York: Weatherhill, 1980.

Swatos, William H., and Kevin J. Christiano. "Secularization Theory: A Course of a Concept." *Sociology of Religion* 60.3 (1999): 209–228.

Takenaka, Ayumi. "Japanese Peruvians and Their Ethnic Encounters." In *Encounters: People of Asian Descent in the Americas*, ed. Roshni Rustomji-Kerns, Rajini Srikanth, and Leny Mendoza Strobel. Lanham, MD: Rowman & Littlefield, 1999, 113–118.

Tanabe, George J. "Grafting Identity: The Hawaiian Branches of the Bodhi Tree." In *Buddhist Missionaries in the Era of Globalization*, ed. Linda Learman. Honolulu: University of Hawai'i Press, 2004, 77–100.

Tanaka, Kenneth. "Issues of Ethnicity in the Buddhist Churches of America." In *American Buddhism: Methods and Findings in Recent Scholarship*, ed. Duncan Williams and Christopher Queen. Richmond, Surrey: Curzon, 1999, 3–19.

Tokuda, Ryōtan. *Psicologia Budista.* Rio de Janeiro: Instituto Vitória Régia, 1997.

Tsuda, Takeyuki. "From Ethnic Affinity to Alienation in the Global Ecumene: The Encounter between the Japanese and Japanese-Brazilian Return Migrants." *Diaspora* 10.1 (2001): 53–91.

———. *Strangers in the Homeland: Japanese Brazilian Return Migration in Transnational Perspective.* New York: Columbia University Press, 2003.

Tweed, Thomas. *The American Encounter with Buddhism (1844–1912): Victorian Culture and the Limits of Dissent.* Bloomington: Indiana University Press, 1992.

———. "Nightstand Buddhists and Other Creatures: Sympathizers, Adherents, and the Study of Religion." In *American Buddhism: Methods and Findings in Recent Scholarship*, ed. Duncan Williams and Christopher Queen. Richmond, Surrey: Curzon, 1999, 71–90.

Uchino, Kumiko. "The Status Elevation Process of Sōtō Sect Nuns in Modern Japan." *Japanese Journal of Religious Studies* 10.1–2 (1983): 177–194.

Usarski, Frank. "Buddhism in Brazil and Its Impact on the Larger Brazilian Society." In *Westward Dharma: Buddhism Beyond Asia*, ed. Charles Prebish and Martin Baumann. Berkeley: University of California Press, 2002, 163–176.

———. "Seu Caloroso Coração Brasileiro e a Energia Pura de Maitreya Atuam Muito Bem Juntos: Reflexões sobre Lama Michel." In *O Budismo no Brasil*, ed. F. Usarski. São Paulo: Lorasae, 2002, 287–317.

Varella, Flávia. "À Nossa Moda: Criado na França, O Espiritismo Deu Certo Apenas no Brasil, Onde a Doutrina Mística Com Pretensões Científicas é Culto da Classe Média." *Veja*, July 26, 2000.

Vásquez, Manuel. *The Brazilian Popular Church and the Crisis of Modernity.* Cambridge: Cambridge University Press, 1998.

Vitória, Gisele. "O Brasil dos Budas." *IstoÉ*, March 12, 1997, 62–70.

Vitória, Gisele, and Liana Melo. "Meditação: Como Usar esta Técnica Milenar para Vencer a Crise, Escapar do Stress Cotidiano, Ganhar Energia, Melhorar Sua Concentração e Tomar Decisões Difíceis." *IstoÉ*, September 9, 1998, 86–89.

Wagley, Charles. *An Introduction to Brazil.* New York: Columbia University Press, 1963.

Wall, Maile. "Chagdud Tulku Rinpoche Dies at 92." *Buddhadharma* (spring 2003): 89.

Weber, Max. *The Protestant Ethic and the Spirit of Capitalism.* trans. T. Parsons. London: Unwin Paperbacks, 1985 [1905].

Werbner, Pnina. "Introduction: The Dialectics of Cultural Hybridity." In *Debating Cultural Hybridity: Multicultural Identities and the Politics of Anti-Racism*, ed. Pnina Werbner and Tariq Modood. London: Zed Books, 1997, 1–26.

Weston, Kath. "The Virtual Anthropologist." In *Anthropological Locations: Boundaries and Grounds of a Field Science*, ed. Akhil Gupta and James Ferguson. Berkeley: University of California Press, 1997.

Willems, Emílio. "Aspectos da Aculturação do Japonês no Estado de São Paulo." In *Boletim da Faculdade de Filosofia, Ciências e Letras da USP* 82.3. São Paulo: Universidade de São Paulo, 1948.

Williams, Duncan. *The Other Side of Zen: A Social History of Soto Zen Buddhism in Tokugawa Japan.* Princeton, NJ: Princeton University Press, 2005.

———. "Representations of Zen: An Institutional and Social History of Sōtō Zen Buddhism in Edo Japan." Ph.D. dissertation, Harvard University, 2000.

Yamada, Shōji. "The Myth of Zen in the Art of Archery." *Japanese Journal of Religious Studies* 28.1–2 (2001): 1–30.

Yamanaka, Keiko. "'I Will Go Home, But When?' Labor Migration and Circular Diaspora Formation by Japanese Brazilians in Japan." In *Japan and Global Migration: Foreign Workers and the Advent of a Multicultural Society*, ed. M. Douglass and G. Roberts. London: Routledge, 2000.

Yoshida, Kōyū. "Zenshū-ji Sōtō Mission in Los Angeles." *Zen Friends* 11.2 (2000): 33–37.

Young, Robert J. C. *Colonial Desire: Hybridity in Theory, Culture and Race.* London: Routledge, 1995.

Zaché, Juliane. "Malhação Zen." *IstoÉ*, September 19, 2001, 62–63.

Index

About the Author

Cristina Rocha teaches at the School of Archaeology and Anthropology at the Australian National University. She received her Phd from the Centre for Cultural Research at the University of Western Sydney, Australia (2003), and her master's degree (by research) from the University of São Paulo, Brazil (1996). She was the recipient of the Japan Foundation Fellowship (2000) and the Urasenke Foundation Scholarship (1992–1993). Her writings include "The Brazilian Imaginaire of Zen: Global Influences, Rhizomatic Forms," in *Japanese Religions In and Beyond the Japanese Diaspora*, edited by Ronan Pereira and Hideo Matsuoka (Berkeley: Center for Japanese Studies, University of California, forthcoming); "Being a Zen Buddhist Brazilian: Juggling Multiple Religious Identities in the Land of Catholicism," in *Buddhist Missionaries in the Era of Globalization*, edited by Linda Learman (Honolulu: University of Hawai'i Press, 2004); "Zazen or Not Zazen: The Predicament of Sōtōshū's Kaikyōshi in Brazil," *Japanese Journal of Religious Studies* 31.1 (2004).

Production Notes for Rocha/*Zen in Brazil*

Series design by Elsa Carl, Clarence Lee Design, in Goudy Old Style and display in Hiroshige

Text composition by Tseng Information Systems, Inc.

Printing and binding by The Maple-Vail Book Manufacturing Group

Printed on 60 lb. Sebago Eggshell, 420 ppi